Shakespeare's Monarchies

ALSO BY CONSTANCE JORDAN

Renaissance Feminism: Literary Texts and Political Models

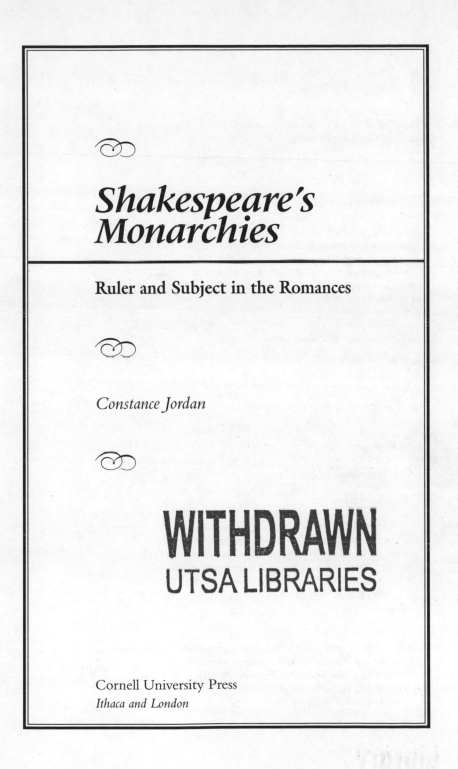

Shakespeare's Monarchies

Ruler and Subject in the Romances

Constance Jordan

Cornell University Press
Ithaca and London

Publication of this book was made possible, in part, by a grant from
Claremont Graduate University.

First published 1997 by Cornell University Press.

Printed in the United States of America.

Jordan, Contance.
    Shakespeare's monarchies : ruler and subject in the romances /
Constance Jordan.
      p. cm.
    Includes index.
    ISBN 0-8014-2828-9 (cloth : alk. paper)
    1. Shakespeare, William, 1564-1616—Tragicomedies.
2. Shakespeare, William, 1564-1616—Characters—Kings and
rulers. 3. Politics and literature—Great Britain—History—
17th century. 4. Political plays, English—History and criticism.
5. Kings and rulers in literature. 6. Monarchy in literature.
7. Tragicomedy. I. Title.
PR2981.5.J67 1997
822.3'3—dc21   97-13665

Cornell University Press strives to utilize environmentally responsible
suppliers and materials to the fullest extent possible in the publishing
of its books. Such materials include vegetable-based, low-VOC inks
and acid-free papers that are also either recycled, totally chlorine-free,
or partly composed of nonwood fibers.

Cloth printing   10 9 8 7 6 5 4 3 2 1

For Edward

Contents

Acknowledgments

THIS BOOK WAS COMPLETED WITH THE HELP OF FELLOWSHIPS GENEROUSLY
provided by the American Council of Learned Societies, the National
Endowment for the Humanities, and the Folger Library: I would like
to thank these institutions for their support. I am also indebted to the
staffs of the Folger Shakespeare Library, the Huntington Library, and
the Honnold Library of the Claremont Colleges who provided assistance at all stages of my research. My project took shape around con-
versations with numerous friends and colleagues: Leeds Barroll, A. R.
Braunmuller, Dympna Callaghan, David Cressy, Heather Dubrow,
Richard Helgerson, Margo Hendricks, Peter Holland, Karen Ordahl
Kupperman, Barbara Mowat, Alan Nelson, Louisa Newlin, Lena
Cowen Orlin, Gail Kern Paster, Annabel Patterson, David Quint, Phyllis Rackin, Mary Beth Rose, Gordon Schochet, Murray Schwartz,
Kevin Sharpe, Julie Solomon, Georgianna Ziegler, and Steven Zwicker.
I also had the benefit of comments from those who read all or por-
tions of the manuscript: Rebecca Bushnell, Frances Dolan, Lori Anne
Ferrell, Andrew Gurr, Lorna Hutson, Victoria Kahn, David Scott Kas-
tan, Russ McDonald, Susan Porter, and Peggy Muñoz Simonds. To
these friends and colleagues, I am most grateful. David Harris Sacks,
who patiently answered my many questions on matters involving
Jacobean politics, deserves my special thanks. I would like also to
acknowledge the encouragement of Bernhard Kendler of Cornell University Press, who maintained an interest in this project from its very
beginning. My thanks also to the editors of *Renaissance Drama* and
Northwestern University for permission to publish versions of an essay
that appeared first under their imprint.

Finally, although this book is dedicated to my husband as a way of thanking him in part for his support over a number of years, it was written for my colleagues and students; it is, in fact, the kind of book I thought I needed when I first began to read Shakespeare's plays. In it I specifically attempt to clarify the more or less obvious situatedness—in the intellectual traditions and historical settings of Jacobean England—of the plays we know as the romances. I have been less concerned to argue for an interpretation of any particular romance than to supply commentary that would establish and clarify what might be called the interpretative coordinates of the romances as a group of plays. Inevitably, some references, texts, and topics will appear more relevant and to the point than others. But it is my hope that in general the information, analyses, and observations this book provides will prove useful for readers who see in these plays not only images of conflict between authoritative agents and subordinated subjects as it was known to Shakespeare, but also, with suggestive differences, elements of the contested political cultures of the present day.

CONSTANCE JORDAN

Claremont, California

Shakespeare's Monarchies

CHAPTER I

Shakespeare's Romances and Jacobean Political Thought

SOUTHWARK, 1611. PLAYGOERS PATRONIZING THE GLOBE HAD A CHANCE to see two new plays by William Shakespeare, *The Winter's Tale* and *The Tempest*. Of a curiously mixed genre, the tragicomedy, they followed new productions of two earlier plays similarly composed: *Pericles*, in 1608, and *Cymbeline*, in 1610. Later generations would term them romances. Formally hybrids, their imagery and conventions draw on narratives of heroic journeys punctuated by the loss and return of children and wives, the wreck of ships at sea, the intervention of gods descending in creaking machinery or revealed in scenes of decorous choreography. They also share a common subject—the restoration of good government. The plays depict the precarious state of rulers who by their absence invite anarchy or by their presumption threaten tyranny. These rulers stand decisively apart from their subjects. They are human but also like gods in some respects. Their ambiguous status has doubtful effects. Chastened by various trials, Pericles, Cymbeline, Leontes, and Prospero submit at last to the constraints that attend mortality. Defining a monarch in 1610, James wrote: "*Vos Dij estis [ye are Gods] . . . But ye shall die like men.*" Broadly conceived, this enigma provided the terms of his monarchy and generated the principal political themes represented in Shakespeare's romances.

In practice a rule that literalizes the figurative divinity of rulers causes subjects to suffer terribly. Rulers, too, whether driven to surrender their authority and power by an impostor or moved to some form of misrule themselves, become victims of their own presumptions and fears. In the romances, the ruler's vulnerability is marked as a psychological event: Pericles, in successive and self-imposed exile, eventually sickens with a deep apathy; Cymbeline is virtually senile, a headless head of state ruled by a tyrannical wife; Leontes is stricken with an "Affection"; and Prospero contends with an abstracted bookishness, a fabulous and strange art. Their states of mind isolate them from their people; they are indices of a radical, dangerous, and specious difference between ruler and subject. Of course, these rulers make entirely human mistakes, easily described if not accounted for: the neglect of a wife, the abandonment of a child, the abuse of servants. Their errors of government, the twinned conditions of tyranny and anarchy, are of a more complex character. Their association reflects what was widely held to be the truth of absolute rule: insulated from the will of subjects, it easily degenerates into despotism, incites popular rebellion, and creates political chaos.

These plays construct many of their conflicts from *typically* political issues: they are chiefly, a subject's obedience to authority and a ruler's obligation to his people. Ancillary topics include the uses of deception to maintain order, the nature of a right as opposed to a petition for grace, and the status of agreements and promises. Treatises dedicated to matters of government had evolved terms by which to discuss the conduct of monarch and subject, but, in the first decade of the seventeenth century, these terms had nothing like a consensual formulation. Their vagueness led to a diversity of perspectives that was probably greater than what was registered by popular opinion, but this only made them more attractive to writers seeking to represent conflict. The conditions of rule under James I were in any case different than they had been under the Tudors. Social and economic forces were transforming past practices. The virtues of a mixed monarchy, generally thought to have sustained the English people in the past, were regularly disputed; the idea of sovereignty had yet to be clearly understood. Apologies for one or another view often exploited devices of rhetoric (especially analogy and metaphor) that provoked rather than settled debate. The more popular the discourse, the more likely it was to employ the language of ordinary experience.

Political thought in this period was not only evolving and, in the process, made to serve different and opposed ends, it was also pervasive in ways that are quite alien to us. I count as "political" any social relation that has as its principal coordinates the concepts of an office, its authority and power, its obligations and limitations. Few social relations escaped such definition. Whole lives were imagined in terms of an office; identities were drawn to the pattern of duties. Not that these definitions were fixed: the hierarchies taking shape from aggregates of relations were far from stable. Historians of culture as well as political thought point to their regular and systematic innovation, to shifts in wealth, status, and locale that disrupted social formations and cast theoretical models of personal and public conduct into the shade of divisive debate. But, however mobile these structures were, they retained what is essential to politics: a nuclear formation composed of a superior and a subordinate. A political relation always involves at least two agents. To one is given the authority to interpret (and sometimes make) the law, to coerce compliance by appeal to law; to the other is given the raw power of resistance and its more disturbing realizations in rebellion and revolution.

The antagonisms and dependencies of the political duo are heavily inscribed in early modern culture. They underlie the often apparently innocuous expressions of obligation and even affection that feature so largely in works of fiction. Their darker outlines are sketched in works of education, moral philosophy, and the so-called arts of government. In my reading of pro-woman argument for *Renaissance Feminism: Literary Texts and Political Models*, I discovered what, in a sense, I was least prepared for—a notion of gender shaped virtually by concepts of office, marital and uxorial, their rights and duties. These concepts fell short of constituting coherent doctrine. Their character as pure theory was often betrayed by the kinds of complaints that were supposed to justify them; to insist that an unruly wife must be put in her place is to testify that she is often elsewhere and that her husband is either indifferent or helpless. The rhetorical effect of many rigorous expositions of gender relations was often paradoxical: orthodoxy could insinuate a defense of what it meant to condemn. But whatever the intention or the effect, notions of gender were framed in the language of politics—family politics. The duties of husband and wife, parent and child, master and servant were thought to reflect the order of an ideal commonwealth, a community of persons dedicated to a common prosperity. Informing personal behavior were the disciplines enjoined of particular offices. Relations less intimate than those within the household were even more susceptible to political construction. Politics in this sense did not touch only matters of state, its mysteries, its arcana; they were part of the general social fabric.

But little in the politics that Shakespeare and his contemporaries knew was simple or unqualified. Absolutism, in the sense of a theory sustaining an institution of government in which the authority and power of the head of state were limitless, was a concept essentially alien to the English experience of monarchy. In England the useful fiction of an ancient constitution guaranteeing the liberties of the subject (who was generally understood to be a man who possessed a certain amount of property) informed arguments against the claim of any officeholder, even a monarch, that presumed he (or she) was above positive law. Absolutism also faced other and more fundamental challenges. Almost from its initial formulation, Christian doctrine had insisted that the faithful had a double allegiance. Authority was not one but two. Obviously entrenched in the structures of the state, authority emanated also from ethereal forms of a perfected Christian society. In this perspective, a secular office, whether answering to divine, natural, or positive law, had no decisive authority over subjects, however much its actual power might impose on them. Its full and often terrifying force, if dedicated to achieving godless ends, could and should be resisted—some said passively and with an acceptance of punishment, others argued with acts of rebellion and revolution. In short, embedded in all systems of government, assuming they were Christian, were a provision and a means for their undoing. A subject would know his politics by the terms of his office and of those he answered to; he would know them in a more mysterious and fearful sense through the exercise of his conscience. He was bound by a double allegiance and his security depended on keeping them compatible, but the claims of faith were to have priority. To avoid dissent, disobedience, or outright rebellion, an absolute ruler had to observe divine and natural law; he was generally expected to observe positive law. Were his subjects to challenge him, he had either to persuade them that he spoke with the voice of God in man, as James I would say, or he had to resort to deceit or coercion.

This book is about the fate of rulers and the future of subjects in Shakespeare's romances. Its subject is misrule. It looks at the conditions of a restoration to office, both of the head of the family and of the state. The romances in general display obviously tragicomic lines of plot; their rulers undergo different forms of estrangement, apparently caught in the web of their own misdoings. Removed from the seat of their authority and power, they also become alienated in mind. They think not as heads of state, but in ways that take them from their principal business. The agencies responsible for their return to a proper government are various and in some cases ambiguous. *Cymbeline, The Winter's Tale,* and *The Tempest* subscribe to a providentialist view of history to some degree, but all the plays reveal comic outcomes of princely errors that are tied to the exercise of conscience. In each, conscientious deliberation establishes the sanity of rule and the health of the state, but this deliberation is not conclusive. The motifs and tropes typical of romance—heroic passion, exile, a wandering across time and space, the temptation to embrace a specious divinity, the arduous labor of homecoming, the *nostos* terminating an odyssey—indicate the importance of process. Typically this entails privation: Pericles, Cymbeline, Leontes, and Prospero all lose kin and status for a period of time. The work of return cannot, it seems, be encompassed only by equitable judgments; it also requires patience and suffering.

The imagery of the romances suggests the supervening presence of deities whose spheres of influence are experienced in time. Gods and goddesses act to enforce the virtue—temperance—associated with deliberation, delay, and even frustration. The periodic appearances of Diana, Jupiter, Apollo, Iris, and Ceres interrupt dramatic action to articulate the principles of interpretation that give episodes form and clarity. Their pagan names and features, a consequence perhaps of the censor's prohibition against alluding to the God of Scripture or Jesus Christ, impose a sense of the numinous on these stories of rulers who have themselves appropriated the trappings of divinity. Providence manifests its power especially by preserving children who are in line to inherit rule: Marina, Imogen, Guiderius and Arviragus, Perdita, and Miranda. In keeping with the notion that God works through nature to protect dynasty, these heirs are associated with the breath of life (or airs) that guarantees the continued vitality of the state. This association is expressed literally in word play and figuratively as music, the consonance or harmony of diverse elements comprised in the body politic.

An understanding of the terms admitting a return to rule is, I argue, a basis for discovering why the romances are comedic—why, that is, they conclude with the reestablishment of a political order which is also an order sustaining generation and therefore benign in the most positive sense. These terms are fashioned in part from the popular lore of government, a knowledge diffused so widely throughout the culture that any single literary representation of it seems partial and dated. They also find correlatives in the more theoretical formulations of government in humanist and legal texts. They are not, on the whole, terms that are easily reconciled in a comprehensive system of rule. They reflect, rather, how the idea of rule was contested: the differing assumptions sustaining various concepts of authority, of the offices commanding authority, and of the resources deployed to exercise the power of those offices.

England's political culture during the early years of James I's reign exhibited what might be called a divided consciousness. Arguments for absolute rule tended to support the monarch's authority and power as without limitation in positive law. They were countered by assertions of the people's liberties and even liberty, and reflected a belief that England's origins in feudalism justified a government in which monarch and people stood in collaborative relations that imitated those between lord and vassal. While not overtly contractual, these relations were thought to depend on the performance of mutually complementary duties; they were held to have been defined in general ways by the common law, the practices growing up around the monarch's council or parliament, and the obligation of subjects to support the monarchy in return for its protection—all notions that were collected under the term "constitution." The points of difference between apologies for absolutism and their counters in constitutionalism were matters of opinion and not, as they would become by midcentury, grounds for action. Certainly there was consensus on a broad array of issues. The monarch's grace—his ability in certain cases to forgive or forgo a prerogative right that otherwise was absolute—remained virtually unquestioned; it delimited what the subject could demand by way of securing his liberties. But there was also resistance to some of the terms of absolute rule, and specifically to its claim that a secular ruler had a kind of divinity about him, a divine right that extended beyond his God-given right to rule and transformed his every word into law.

The rulers of Shakespeare's romances, because their misrule is often occasioned by some abuse of power explicable in absolutist terms, have a presumptive place as examples of absolutist rule in contemporary political debate. The questions I have asked of these plays are not intended to reveal what they reflect or contribute to that debate. Such an inquiry risks faltering on a false distinction between the status of a text as opposed to its contexts; it suggests that intertextual relations are causative rather than paradigmatic. (They can, of course, be both. James I's *The Trew Law of Free Monarchies* is a deliberate answer to his former tutor's republican treatise, George Buchanan's *De iure apud scotos*; it is also shaped to fit the terms of a republican challenge to absolute monarchy.) I have looked at the romances rather as hypothetical renderings of that debate, as projections of the possibilities it announces, as tests of the structures it theorizes. My interpretations have relied on *ideas* of government; they have been based on the assumption that no authority or power lacks conceptual formulation and, therefore, that its exercise and expression are analyzable in theoretical terms. Such ideas are not generated outside historical and material settings, but we know of their settings only secondhand and contextually, through cultural records that are themselves shaped by conceptions and a way of thinking to which they have given local and temporal references. The thinking that gives government its particular character is inseparable from government's effects. As an institution, the monarchy was represented according to different concepts which were thought to justify (more or less) its actual practices. These practices need to be understood in relation to the concepts by which they were thought to be (more or less) justified.

Shakespeare's Theater

Any historicist study of Shakespeare's plays must take account of his theater: the work of specific companies, their repertory, their buildings, and more generally, the theater as a social institution. Recent studies have described the experience of playgoing in Tudor and Stuart London as a cultural phenomenon, contrasting its functions with the generally regulated practices of court, church, and marketplace. Situated in localities immune from the oversight of municipal authorities, public theaters enjoyed a certain freedom in the kinds of plays they produced and in the conditions in which the public saw them. Their paying audiences comprised all social ranks and economic classes; their conditions of performance were chaotic by modern standards; and, owing to the incidence of plague, their productions were often staged on short notice.[1] Any individual play doubtless had multiple effects on its audiences; it must have been understood in different ways by particular parties. Twentieth-century critics have, however, agreed on one general function of the drama in this period. As plays proposed categories of conflict, their performances provided moments in which outcomes could be subjected to the innocuous trials of the imagination. No decisions that affected actual persons or society at large depended on the matter of the drama, at least none that history has registered, but the capacity to make decisions was radically indebted to its representations.[2]

---

[1]For the locales of public theater and the conditions of performance, see Andrew Gurr, *The Shakespearean Stage: 1574–1642*, 3d edition (Cambridge: Cambridge University Press, 1992); see also Steven Mullaney, *The Place of the Stage: License, Play, and Power in Renaissance England* (Chicago: University of Chicago Press, 1988). For their audiences, see Andrew Gurr, *Playgoing in Shakespeare's London* (Cambridge: Cambridge University Press, 1987); see also Ann Jennalie Cook, *The Privileged Playgoers of Shakespeare's London 1576–1642* (Princeton: Princeton University Press, 1981). On the timing and place of performances, see Leeds Barroll, *Politics, Plague, and Shakespeare's Theater: The Stuart Years* (Ithaca: Cornell University Press, 1991).

[2]On the interrogatory function of Shakespeare's drama, see especially David Riggs, *Shakespeare's Heroical Histories* (Cambridge: Harvard University Press, 1971); and Graham Bradshaw, *Misrepresentations: Shakespeare and the Materialists* (Ithaca: Cornell University Press, 1993). On political debate in the drama generally, see Joel B. Altman, *The Tudor Play of Mind: Rhetorical Inquiry and the Development of Elizabethan Drama* (Berkeley: University of California Press, 1978); and in the Stuart period particularly, see Margot Heinemann, *Puritanism and Theatre: Thomas Middleton and Opposition Drama under the Early Stuarts* (Cambridge: Cambridge University Press, 1980).

This much is intuitive. But to discover what kind of culture the experience of playgoing in Tudor and Stuart London both expressed and promoted is a project of many perspectives.

The role of the theater in shaping forms of social life must, I think, remain largely indeterminate. The suggestive heterodoxies common to many playtexts have left no clear record of their translation into forms of social practice.[3] They testify rather to the relative instability of corresponding orthodoxies, to the fact that notions of social order were highly mutable subjects of dispute. The pronouncements of such critics as Thomas Heywood—who in 1612 insisted that drama should "ayme . . . to teach the subjects obedience to their King . . . exhorting them to allegeance, dehorting them from all traytcrous and fellonious stratagems"—were clearly not taken as prescriptive.[4] Contemporary drama rather realized these subjects in fictions open to wide interpretation; its productions were not only characterized by figurative language but also charged with the particularities of time and place. Its effect was to make provisional and fluid what was usually held to be permanent and fixed. As Margot Heinemann has observed, "the drama empowers ordinary people in the audience to think and judge for themselves of matters usually considered 'mysteries of state' in which no one but the 'natural rulers'—the nobility and gentry and professional elites—should be allowed to meddle."[5] To such audiences, the theater was neither doctrinaire nor subversive but rather functioned as a place of a temporary and improvised authority. It demanded neither allegiance nor tithe (apart from the price of admission), but putting all

[3]Jean Howard remarks that "theatrical power was . . . not only used to create good subjects for absolutist monarchy, but to subject the king to the fashioning powers of the playwright"; that is, its powers were formative of distinct social characters; Jean Howard, *The Stage and Social Struggle in Early Modern England* (New York: Routledge, 1994), 11. But our knowledge of these outcomes is largely inferential. For further comment on the effects of drama on social form, see Phyllis Rackin, *Stages of History: Shakespeare's English Chronicles* (Ithaca: Cornell University Press, 1990). For objections to topical interpretation, see Richard Levin, "The Relation of External Evidence to the Allegorical and Thematic Interpretation of Shakespeare," *Shakespeare Studies* 13 (1980): 1–29.

[4]Thomas Heywood, *Apology for Actors*, quoted in Annabel Patterson, "'The Very Age and Body of the Time His Form and Pressure': Rehistoricizing Shakespeare's Theater," *New Literary History* 20, 1 (1980): 83–104, 92–93.

[5]"'Demystifying the Mystery of State': *King Lear* and the World Upside Down," *Shakespeare Survey* 44 (1992): 75–83; 76.

modes of obligation into play, gave each playgoer the freedom to fashion an image of his own government. For J. W. Lever, Jacobean drama was never apolitical: "contemporary issues constantly lurk below the surface of [its] historical or fictitious settings."[6] Andrew Gurr speculates more directly on the drama as a source of incentives to shape policy; as "analogues" to "political realities," the fictions dramatized on Tudor and Stuart stages provided occasion and material for political debate (*Playgoing*, 112–13). And Peter Thomson insists that Shakespeare, politically aware if not committed, could fashion a play to speak directly to the king. On the intention of *Measure for Measure*, he states: "Seen in the context of James's first full year on the English throne, it is nothing short of a *caveat Rex* from the nation's leading playwright to the new monarch."[7] Common to all these accounts is an interest in the dramatic reference. The playtext is assumed to speak a language of state, at least to some degree; that language must have a political character if it is to stir political thoughts and reactions.

As the record of actions of state, albeit fictional, Shakespeare's *history* plays are political in a traditional sense. They focus on the fate and fortunes of England as they were thought to have been determined by its monarchs, magistrates, and people. Projecting their subjects through the lens of an incipient nationalism, they screen issues of a private or emotional character to concentrate on matters of public moment; in Alexander Leggatt's words, they show "the ordering and enforcing, the gaining and losing of public power in the state."[8] Their representations of national interest and sentiment make use of tropes of ironic disjunction. Idealizing myths that exemplify a perfect political order at home and abroad are challenged by instances of disturbing degradation: Richard II's narcissism, Henry IV's ambition, Hal's folly, Henry V's cunning—vices that are grandly manifest in the malaise of the body politic as a whole. The histories inspire critical thought by the factor of inwardness; to reflect on the matter of these plays is to recognize

[6]J. W. Lever, *The Tragedy of State* (London: Methuen, 1971), 2.

[7]Peter Thomson, *Shakespeare's Professional Career* (Cambridge: Cambridge University Press, 1992), 169. For a useful survey of political issues in Shakespeare's plays, see Robin Headlam Wells, *Shakespeare: Politics and the State* (London: Macmillan, 1986).

[8]Alexander Leggatt, *Shakespeare's Political Drama: The History Plays and the Roman Plays* (New York: Routledge, 1988), ix.

the irony of their pieties. It is by this reflection that the subject—both the subject of the play and the playgoer—is defined not merely morally, but within the overlapping networks of society that both constrain and liberate.

The histories further engage the factor of inwardness by their representation of causality. The tension between obligations to conform to ethical convention and desires fueled by individual aspiration opens a space, especially in the later histories, for representing a kind of spirituality. These plays reveal striking amplifications of meaning conveyed by visions of history whose coordinates are prophecy on the one hand and retrospection on the other. As David Riggs states, these visions "take on a genuine significance because they are embedded in those metaphors (the garden of the state, the body politic) by which Shakespeare assimilated political obligation to 'the hatch and brood of time.' " The speeches of prophecy and retrospection that confer meaning on the plays' chronicles of events depend, Riggs continues, "on an *analogy* between the political and the natural order, each of which gravitates inexorably from disorder through a period of cleansing and expiation to a final stability" (*Heroical Histories*, 48). Here the concept of politics—as indexed in the forms and relations of the natural world—acquires its widest relevance. In a sense, everything subsumed in points of conscientious reflection has a political dimension. Providence, supposed to realize the dictates of natural and divine law, has a political character; it is ambiguous to the extent that events and outcomes compromise the obvious interests and claims of the just.

Finally, the histories are also self-reflexive. They represent not only history but also its modes of representation. In this sense they are a collective enterprise in historiography, conveying a sense of the political in their reception, by audiences and readers, as stories of origin and order. They form varying templates of English historical consciousness. Repositories of the myth of nationhood variously reworked to challenge orthodoxy, the plays give voice, as Phyllis Rackin states, to silenced subjects by providing fictions to fill "the erasures in the official historical record" (*Stages of History*, xi). The opportunity afforded by such gaps provided a challenge to say what had not been said—a challenge motivated, in part, by a suspicion that such omissions were substantive if not deliberate.

Like the histories, the *romances* speak the language of politics. True, their plots follow romance models (only *Cymbeline* is linked to chronicle history), and their form is tragicomic. Criticism has generally considered them as reflections upon the tragedies, as settled and optimistic visions of worlds renewed after the depredations occasioned by a tragic heroism.[9] Thematically, however, they project the matter of the histories on a scale both vaster and more subtle. Again, their subject is the fate of rulers, their states, and peoples. They relate stories not of England and France but of empires, unions and conjunctions of nations: Tyre and Pentapolis, Britain and Rome, Bohemia and Sicilia, Milan and Naples. These alliances are fashioned according to the model of marriage and their terms derive from that institution: respect for generation and prohibition of incest; obligations that depend on a promise; and equity for partners of unequal rank or status. But the alliances depend on the work and the words of the rulers who enter into them. The romances are at their most political precisely here—in their focus on the characters of Pericles, Cymbeline, Leontes, and Prospero. Assuming absolute rule, they portray the conditions in which its effects become pernicious.

Shakespeare's romances may, of course, be appreciated as stories in which families are brought together after long periods of trial, but they acquire a presumptive political dimension when they are also understood as romances—that is, in light of what have been recognized conventionally as their generic determinants. For it is the generic character of the romances as romance, rather than comedy or tragedy transformed to comedy (and I admit that their generic character was identified well after the plays were produced for the first time), that permits so effective a dramatization of their most important theme: the

[9]For the implications of genre, see Joan Hartwig, *Shakespeare's Tragicomic Vision* (Baton Rouge: Louisiana State University Press, 1972), and the essays collected in *Renaissance Tragicomedy: Explorations in Genre and Politics*, ed. Nancy Klein Maguire (New York: AMS Press, 1987), and in *The Politics of Tragicomedy: Shakespeare and After*, ed. Gordon McMullan and Jonathan Hope (New York: Routledge, 1992). On Shakespeare's "kinds," see Stephen Orgel, "Shakespeare and the Kinds of Drama," *Critical Inquiry* 6, 1 (1979): 107–23. For the norms of romance in relation to Shakespeare's plays, see Howard Felperin, *Shakespearean Romance* (Princeton: Princeton University Press, 1972); and Robert Uphaus, *Beyond Tragedy: Structure and Experience in Shakespeare's Romances* (Lexington: University Press of Kentucky, 1981). For reviews of criticism, see Philip Edwards, "Shakespearean Romances," *Shakespeare Survey* 11 (1958): 1–30, and F. David Hoeniger, "Shakespeare's Romances since 1958: A Retrospect," *Shakespeare Survey* 29 (1979): 1–10.

ruler's status as a mortal rather than a god or godlike creature. This theme is apparent in each of the plays, from Pericles' perception of Antiochus's Daughter as divine to Prospero's renunciation of a magic that has appeared to make him superhuman. Its origins or first instances are Homeric, exemplified by Odysseus's temptations to remain on the islands of goddesses, Circe and Kalypso, and to share their immortality rather than return home to a merely human existence. The genial feature of Shakespeare's romances is their linkage of the ruler's fate to the conditions in which he or his kin return home or to a place of origin, actions that signify both a restoration of status and an admission of generation and hence also of mortality.

In short, the plays we call romances are *generically* suited to a figured drama in which images of the family and the physical body of the monarch function as political metaphors. Such metaphors, while they do not inhibit responses to the plays as powerful vehicles for representing emotional conflict, allow us to see Shakespeare's persistent interest in matters of government and to take account of the particular expressions of this interest in the romances. Initially illustrated in the history plays (most forcefully in *Richard II*), issues of rule and self-rule are further set out in the tragic perspectives of *Macbeth* and especially *King Lear*, and finally addressed through the pervasive allusions to tyranny in the romances. To move from an acknowledgment of Richard II's tyrannical confiscation of his subjects' property, to King Lear's crazed yet profound realization of his humanity, to representations of rule and providence in *Henry VIII* and *The Two Noble Kinsman* is to recognize a thematic coherence in Shakespeare's dramatization of forms of government in the course of his career as playwright. The connections between the romances, *Henry VIII* (obviously a history play), and *Two Noble Kinsman* (very nearly a pure fantasy) are particularly clear; like the romances, Shakespeare's two last plays represent the reform of tyranny (the defeat of Wolsey in *Henry VIII*) and the hand of providence in history. Theseus's confession of helplessness before evidence of a divine will in *The Two Noble Kinsman*—"The gods my justice/Take from my hand and they themselves become/The executioners"[10]—could have been made by Pericles, Cymbeline, Leontes, or Prospero.

[10]William Shakespeare, *The Two Noble Kinsmen*, ed. Eugene M. Waith (New York: Oxford University Press, 1994), 5.4.120–22.

To focus on the politics in the romances is, however, to consider more than their generic, philosophic, and historical determinants. It is to see them as models of conflict between patterns of thought and varieties of argument. They are the fictional and sometimes symbolic record of the discontinuities in systematic relations of government rather than of their coherence.[11] They feature as elements of a vast intertext in which the place of any particular work is multirelational and overdetermined. They reflect the pressure of actual events in dense aggregates of metaphor, but these events, in any case evident only in their textual records, can be understood only in light of other texts that make these records legible. By 1603, the authority and power of the monarch and their association with divine law and divine will had received a complicated and often contradictory representation in English law and theories of government. Provoked by actual matters and moments of contention, texts representing ideas of rule often reproduced the conflicts they were attempting to resolve.

A "Free and Absolute" Monarchy

When James VI of Scotland published *The Trew Law of Free Monarchies* in 1598, his apology for that office was full of equivocation: the monarch himself was not divine, James declared, but he was the agent and representative of God. His authority and power were, however, total and irresistible; were he to have been a god, he could not have achieved a

---

[11]Cf. the positivist readings of such critics as E. M. W. Tillyard who in his brilliant and influential study, *The Elizabethan World Picture* (New York: Macmillan, 1942), tried to clarify the historicity of fictions by identifying the relatively dated ideas they were supposed to embody. Texts were juxtaposed with other texts and their composite picture was thought to convey a certain totalizing coherence. The poet was not in the picture except as an exponent of cultural consensus, and the reader, who was supposed to function aculturally, was to be not only a neo-Elizabethan (or Jacobean) but without any of the prejudices, opinions, or beliefs endemic in those periods. Criticism of historicist approaches in general is well summarized by Louis Montrose, in his essay "New Historicisms," *Redrawing the Boundaries: The Transformation of English and American Studies*, ed. Stephen Greenblatt and Giles Gunn (New York: The Modern Language Association of America, 1992), 392–418. For Shakespeare in particular, see Walter Cohen, "Political Criticism of Shakespeare" in *Shakespeare Reproduced: The Text in History and Ideology*, ed. Jean E. Howard and Marion F. O'Connor (New York: Methuen, 1987), 18–46.

greater presence. James described his ideal form of government in images of great antiquity. Chief among them was the figure from which he sought to justify his own absolute authority and power in Scotland: the king was a father to his people; hence he was to be free and absolute, to be the law in and of his kingdom. The fact that James himself lacked such standing as King of Scotland may have inspired this grandiosity. He went on to declare that his power was a "Diuine power" to create or destroy his people and to appropriate at will their persons and property for his own use—a power that rested on the presumption that all property, including the property subjects had in their own persons, was ultimately held by the king whose progenitors had won the kingdom by conquest.[12] He was not a god, except in his descriptions in Scripture (64); but as "God's lieutenant" (65), his person and his actions were imbued with the spirit of divinity. God had showed him that the "style of the God of Hosts" was his to imitate (80).[13]

In essence, James claimed, a "free and absolute monarche" is the "true patterne of Diuinitie" (63): his will is law and, most important, it can be exercised against, as well as for, the interests of the people. Whatever action he takes is overpowering even though it may offend "iustice and equitie" (68). His political subject is his "vassal" and also his "child" (73, 65). Both are under his law. A king, wrote James, is "*Dominus omnium honorum* and *Dominus directus totius Dominij,* the whole subiects being but his vassals, and from him holding all their lands as their ouer-lord who . . . chaungeth their holding . . . without aduice or authoritie of either Parliament or any other subalterin iudiciall seate." As vassals, the king's subjects have no proprietary rights at all, since there is no law, no "iudiciall seate," by which they may be claimed (73). As children, his subjects are effectively placed under the Roman *potestas patria*: a king is

[12]James VI and I, *Political Writings,* ed. Johann P. Sommerville (Cambridge: Cambridge University Press, 1994), 63. For a summary of debate on James's theory of monarchy and an analysis of its relation to I Samuel in particular, see Sommerville, "English and European Political Ideas in the Early Seventeenth Century: Revisionism and the Case of Absolutism," *Journal of British Studies* 35, 2 (1996): 168–94. For a study of absolutist theory in relation to political patriarchalism, see Gordon J. Schochet, *Patriarchalism and Political Thought* (New York: Basic Books, 1975).

[13]For a study of James's self-representations, see Jonathan Goldberg, *James I and the Politics of Literature: Jonson, Shakespeare, Donne, and their Contemporaries* (Baltimore: Johns Hopkins University Press, 1983).

"naturall Father to all his Lieges at his Coronation: And as the Father of his fatherly duty is bound to care for the nourishing, education, and vertuous gouernment of his children; euen so is the king bound to care for all his subiects" (65). Against the judgment and wishes of this father his children have no recourse: "Suppose the father were furiously following his sonnes with a drawen sword, is it lawfull for them to turne and strike againe, or make any resistance but by flight?" (77). James concluded by observing that however "monstrously vicious" a monarch, his rule is better than the anarchy that resistance to him would provoke. Better misrule by one than by many: "better it is to liue in a Common-wealth where nothing is lawfull, then where all things are lawfull to all men" (79).

These points illustrate the most important feature of *The Trew Law*—its representation of absolute rule as inherently abusive. In less extreme formulations, absolutism did not have such a terrible character. As Glenn Burgess notes, absolutism as Jean Bodin and others described it, simply "held that kings had their authority directly from God (which meant that it was not conferred on them by their people), and that subjects were never justified in resisting the commands of their rulers (although on rare occasions they might be justified in passively refusing to obey.)"[14] In this context, the monarch was supposed to be above positive law; in effect, his proclamations had the effect of law and were comparable to statutes, common laws, and custom. Proper rule was guaranteed by his piety; although insusceptible to restrictions in positive law, he had to obey divine and natural law. Were he to behave in a godless or unnatural way, however, his subjects had no recourse except prayer or martyrdom. They were obliged to suffer his misrule.

None of James's subsequent works insist so forcefully on the monarch's right to impose his will upon his subjects as does *The Trew Law*. James's later pictures of the monarch—"iustly" called a God because he exercises a "manner or resemblance of Diuine power vpon earth

[14]Glenn Burgess, *The Politics of the Ancient Constitution: An Introduction to English Political Thought, 1603–1642* (University Park: University of Pennsylvania State Press, 1992), 110–11. An important treatment of absolutism and constitutionalism as systematic political thought, with a primary emphasis on their formulations on the continent, is in Quentin Skinner, *The Foundations of Modern Political Thought* (Cambridge: Cambridge University Press, 1978), 2: 254–75.

. . . to create, or destroy, make, or vnmake at his pleasure, to giue life, or send death"—reproduce the principal features of an absolute rule without entertaining its worst risks ("Speech to parliament, 21 March 1610," *Political Writings*, 181). Certainly James recognized that the association of absolutism with tyranny was not inevitable. Classical philosophers had defined a tyrant as a ruler who put his own interests above those of his subjects (and therefore tended to abuse them), not as a ruler who was absolute and subject only to divine and natural law,[15] and James agreed with this definition. In *Basilicon Doron*, 1599, he wrote:"an vsurping Tyran . . . will . . . frame the common-weale euer to aduance his particular: building his suretie vpon his peoples miserie" (*Political Writings*, 20). An absolute monarch, by contrast, should rule in the people's interest because he is accountable to God; moreover, by his "good will, and for good example-giuing to his subiects," he will even frame all his actions according to positive law (*Trew Law*, 75).[16] But despite his concession to law and the people's interest, James never repudiated the most drastic tenet of absolutism—were a monarch's goodwill to run out, were his conscience to fail, there was no countervailing political authority or power that could rectify his misrule:"The wickednesse therefore of the King can neuer make them that are ordained to be iudged by him, to become his Iudges" (78). This

[15]Renaissance political thinkers usually began with this definition. A descriptive source is pseudo-Aquinas who stated that a monarchy is "unjust" (*iniustum*) when the "private good of the king" (*bonum privatum regentis*) is sought before the "common welfare" (*bonum communum multitudinis*): *De regimine principum ad regem cypri*, in *Selected Political Writings*, ed. A. P. D'Entrèves, trans. J. G. Dawson (Oxford: Oxford University Press, 1959), 14–15. (I have altered some of the wording in this translation.) This text is actually by Ptolemy of Lucca. For details on authorship, see Quentin Skinner, "Political Philosophy," in *The Cambridge History of Renaissance Philosophy*, ed. Charles B. Schmitt, Quentin Skinner, Eckhard Kessler, and Jill Kraye (Cambridge: Cambridge University Press, 1990), 395–452. For a definition of tyranny, see also Aristotle, *Politics*, 4, 8: 1295a. A seminal study on the dramatic representations of tyranny in this period is Rebecca W. Bushnell, *Tragedies of Tyrants: Political Thought and Theater in the English Renaissance* (Ithaca: Cornell University Press, 1990).

[16]Sommerville notes that James's respect for positive law allowed some to think he was tending to favor a monarchy limited by positive law but, finally, as he continued throughout his works to insist that it was "sedition to dispute his prerogative," his absolutism was quite consistent; "Introduction," xxvi. On James's *The Trew Law* and *Basilicon Doron* specifically, see Jenny Wormald, "James VI and I, *Basilikon Doron* and *The Trew Law of Free Monarchies*: The Scottish Context and the English Translation," in *The Mental World of the Jacobean Court*, ed. Linda Levy Peck (Cambridge: Cambridge University Press, 1991), 36–54.

was an important assertion, one that engaged (perhaps inadvertently) anti-absolutist critique. It reflected the fact that although the authority and power of a monarch were considered to come from God, they were always vested in a merely mortal person, a character who was not subject only to death and disease, but whose goodwill, as history could show, was often in notoriously short supply. A monarch who answered only to divinity made all law practically contingent. He himself was certain to experience law only on the posthistorical day of judgment; his errors on earth had a de facto legitimacy and could not be challenged or corrected.[17] The failure to account fully for the monarch as no more than a human being, subject to passion and liable to sin, proved to be the point of greatest moment in anti-absolutist argument. As Patrick Collinson has observed, the term "absolute" had a certain flexibility and allowed for interpretation: Queen Elizabeth considered herself an absolute monarch, and Sir Thomas Smith found no inconsistency in representing England as a "republic" and her monarch as "farre more absolute" than the Duke of Venice.[18] This latitude made possible a debate on matters of government that was dedicated, in part, to the formulation of terms and principles.

Opposition to absolutism came from diverse quarters and it reflected historical conceptions of monarchy. Generally speaking, political thought in Jacobean England was constitutionalist rather than republican, and it drew on the notion of a mutually beneficial union of monarch and people in which the government of the former was enhanced and made possible by the counsel and consent of the latter, insofar as they were represented in Parliament and especially by the Commons. The point on which constitutionalists most insisted—

[17]In his recent study of the Stuart monarchy, Glenn Burgess notes that absolutist theory could reassure prospective subjects by insisting that the monarch, however above positive law, was nevertheless under divine and natural law. James, in particular, was aware that an absolute monarch who ruled tyrannically was in danger of being deposed, a prospect that Burgess imagines might have encouraged him to be prudent. *Absolute Monarchy and the Stuart Constitution* (New Haven: Yale University Press, 1996), 25; see also 41, 45, 99. But the prospect of deposing a tyrant was not much better than suffering a tyrant and, in any case, entailed suffering and aroused fear of bloodshed. In short, there was little in absolutism that could be made to appeal to popular sentiment.

[18]Patrick Collinson, *De Republica Anglorum, Or, History with the Politics Put Back* (Cambridge: Cambridge University Press, 1990), 19; quoting Sir Thomas Smith, *De republica Anglorum*, ed. Mary Dewar (Cambridge: Cambridge University Press, 1982), 85.

that the powers of the monarch were limited in some respects by positive law—was certainly contested by a few thinkers. But most agreed
that although the monarch could act absolutely in some capacities
by virtue of the prerogative, he could not do so in all situations. Debate
increasingly addressed the notion of some sort of contract between
ruler and ruled.

The Trew Law had represented the monarch's coronation "Oath,"
by which he promised to serve his people, as a promise not a contract
(81). James stated that if this "Oath" was broken, the people could do
no more than pray for the monarch's reform; he also described the
monarch's "free and absolute" authority and power over the property
and persons of his subjects as total and godlike. But early in James I's
reign, it was evident that many of his new subjects were troubled by
such a view of the monarchy. They claimed that the authority and
power of an English monarch were legally determined, at least with
respect to the property of subjects, and that tradition supported them
in this view. Radical thinkers imagined that a monarch who failed to
observe the terms of his office could be deposed. Reasoning that as the
authority and power of the monarchy had "resided originally in the
people as a corporate entity and was conferred on kings by their people for certain purposes only" (chiefly defense of the realm), they
declared that "under some circumstances the people might choose to
revoke the authority they had granted away in order to discipline an
erring ruler" (Burgess, *Ancient Constitution*, 110–11). More representative of anti-absolutist sentiment, especially after the accession of James,
was an insistence on the subject's right to property, the so-called liberties of the subject. Many in the Commons thought the people held
some kinds of property that the king could not take without their consent, a consent that they understood would be based on their judgment
that his demands on the people were justified by what the people
would get in return. A kind of contractualism could also determine
those relations in which the monarch's authority and power were traditionally decisive and others in which they were incontestably
absolute. Whether protecting the realm, or making law in Parliament
or by virtue of the prerogative (as in requiring certain customs duties),
a monarch was expected to use his wisdom for the benefit of his people. In effect, he was to act as a judge in—as well as a party to—a case

in equity, to fashion a rule in which his own interests were consistent with those of the commonwealth. In such relations the situation of the subject remained somewhat indeterminate, of course. But because he could assume the monarch's goodwill, he could also trust that he would get equitable treatment.

Constitutionalists also represented the monarch as divine, but in a different and more limited sense than did James's *Trew Law*. The fact that kings ruled with "divine right" merely meant that their office derived its power from God and passed to them as their inheritance. Divine right was not incompatible with theories of government that limited the monarch's absolute power to the exercise of the prerogative. In fact, as the right of succession, divine right tended to deny rather than support absolutist imperatives. As John Neville Figgis puts it, when Henry VIII overlooked divine right in the matter of the succession and instead determined himself who should inherit the throne, "absolutism triumphed at the expense of legitimism." [19] In general, however, Tudor rule was characterized by an increasing reliance on the monarch's will as absolute chiefly to guarantee its independence from the power of the papacy. When William Tyndale announced that "the kyng is in thys worlde without lawe," he implied what James would eventually claim, that the power of the monarch was suprahuman and godlike.[20] But as I have suggested, claims made in "thys worlde" were

[19]John Neville Figgis, *The Divine Right of Kings*, 2d edition (Cambridge: Cambridge University Press, 1934), 85. For an introduction to the constitutionalist thought and institutions, see Margaret Atwood Judson, *The Crisis of the Constitution: An Essay in Constitutional and Political Thought in England, 1603–1645* (New York: Octagon Books, 1971); for a study of constitutionalism in light of classical republican theory, see Charles Howard McIlwain, *Constitutionalism: Ancient and Modern* (Ithaca: Cornell University Press, 1940). See also the comprehensive critique of regarding absolutist theory as institutionalized by the English monarchy under James I in Burgess, *Absolute Monarchy*, 15–62.

[20]Quoted in Figgis, *Divine Right*, 94; for other examples of Tudor obedience literature, see 95–100. Sir John Hayward, who would later support the absolutist policies of James I, made obedience a feature of an anti-divine right position on the succession in 1601, asserting that a prince might legitimately "work violence against his subiects." [Sir John Hayward], *An Answere to the first part of a certaine Conference concerning succession published since under the name of R. Dolman* (London, 1603), L$_{iiii}$; STC 12988. For an analysis of absolutist theory see J. P. Sommerville, *Politics and Ideology in England, 1603–1640* (New York: Longman, 1986), esp. 115–27, and Francis Wormuth, *The Royal Prerogative 1603–1649: A Study in English Political and Constitutional Issues* (Ithaca: Cornell University Press, 1939). For Hayward in particular, see Sommerville, *Politics*, 70–71; and Burgess, *Absolute Monarchy*, 72–76.

subject to review. The issue of obedience cut two ways. Not to risk his immortal soul, the subject had to know that his king commanded him to perform only godly acts.[21]

The notion of the monarch's status as godlike was not, in any case, fixed. Early in the reign of Elizabeth, it was formulated in such a way as to limit rather than promote absolute rule and to address not the question but the nature of the succession. Its formulation drew on the medieval notion of the monarch's "two bodies": a body natural and a body politic. Only the latter was immune from death and therefore in a sense divine. The decision in the celebrated case of the Duchy of Lancaster, 1561, which prevented Elizabeth from invalidating a grant made by Edward VI because, although a minor, he had acted in the capacity of his "Body politic," provided a necessary definition. As Plowden noted, this body was devoid of the "naturall Defects and Imbecilities which the Body natural is subject to"; it was identified not with the monarch's person (his natural body) but with his office and was therefore eternal. Most important, it was protected by positive and especially common law.[22] In effect, it was a body whose abstract and mysterious nature could be imagined as controlling the will of the monarch which was understood to be absolute and irresistible where positive law was lacking, but which could not change positive law where it already existed. In this perspective, what was divine about the monarch was therefore not his person, but rather the nature of the monarchy he inherited, coextensive and coexistent with the state. It was the transtemporal office not the person of the monarch that was imbued with a numinous authority and power.

[21]A distinction was often made between the monarch's absolute authority and power in "things indifferent" to the subject's salvation and the subject's rights of conscience in things that were matters of faith. James I claimed a subject could disobey a monarch's commands when "directly against God" (*Trew Law*, 72), that is, in matters of faith and doctrine. But some literature, especially sectarian, tended to overlook this distinction and claim a comprehensive right of resistance; see Sommerville, *Politics*, 34–35. For a study of obedience (especially in *King Lear*), see Richard Strier, *Resistant Structures: Particularity, Radicalism, and Renaissance Texts* (Berkeley: University of California Press, 1995), 165–202.

[22]Edmund Plowden, *Commentaries or Reports* (London, 1761), 213. For a study of the theory of the monarch's two bodies in Elizabethan drama, see Marie Axton, *The Queen's Two Bodies: Drama and the Elizabethan Succession* (London: The Royal Historical Association, 1979). For medieval political thought, see Ernst Kantorowicz, *The King's Two Bodies: A Study in Medieval Political Theology* (Princeton: Princeton University Press, 1959).

By distinguishing the office from the person, the fiction of the monarch's two bodies engaged a discourse critical of monarchy and often inspired by sectarian agitation on the continent as well as by Protestants opposed to Mary and later, by Catholics opposed to Elizabeth. Constitutionalist rule (particularly as it was formulated by Sir Edward Coke after the accession of James I) was traced to a concept of feudal reciprocity that gave subjects, like their vassal prototypes, a standing they lacked in James's *Trew Law*. Popular expression of such a rule was relatively easy to find. As Annabel Patterson has shown, both first and second editions of Raphael Holinshed's *Chronicles* (1577 and 1587) report numerous occasions in which monarchic authority and power were restricted by liberties possessed by the people. These liberties were often represented as inhering in the very ancient *lex terrae* or law of the land and as expressed not only in the Magna Carta but in the older laws of Edward the Confessor.[23] Republican theory, more overtly contractual, further informed the concept of a monarchy limited by positive law despite the fact that it addressed the government of a republic, a kingless, and therefore un-English state. Treatises such as Francesco Patrizi's *De institutione reipublicae*, translated by Richard Robinson as *A morall methode of ciuill policie*, 1576, were taken not as a pretext for revolution but rather as an approach to reform, insisting as they did on government under positive law and not by the will of a particular man.[24] In one notable instance, republican rule acquired an essentially English character: John Hooker's *The order and usage how to keepe a parlement in England in these daies*, 1587, gave sovereignty not to the monarch or Parliament but to the Commons, without whose consent "the King . . . cannot with his Lords devise, make or establish any law."[25] Popular government was, in any case, well established in practice. As Patrick Collinson has observed, that vast proportion of the population classified as "the middling sort" regularly served as "the bottom line of early modern government" in small towns and villages

[23] Annabel Patterson, *Reading Holinshed's Chronicles* (Chicago: University of Chicago Press, 1995), esp. 99–127. For an account of popular liberties, see Sommerville, *Politics*, 145–88.

[24] For a study of republican theory in Tudor/Stuart England, see Markku Peltonen, *Classical Humanism and Republicanism in English Political Thought, 1570–1640* (Cambridge: Cambridge University Press, 1995).

[25] Patterson, *Holinshed's Chronicles*, 126; citing Vernon F. Snow, *Parliament in Elizabethan England: John Hooker's Order and Usage* (New Haven: Yale University Press, 1977), 26.

where they functioned in essentially republican settings. Thus republicanism flourished as a practice before it acquired a political register or even much notice in theory.[26]

For those seeking to articulate the terms of constitutional rule, however, the treatise that proved most descriptive was Sir John Fortescue's *De laudibus legum anglie*, 1468–70, in print in Richard Mulcaster's English translation as *A learned commendation of the politique lawes of Englande* in 1567. Its original purpose was to establish the terms of the monarchy as Fortescue knew it, but Jacobeans could interpret his text as defining a monarchy that defied absolutist claims and rested on a foundation of popular rights and liberties. *A learned commendation* reads as if it were the antagonistic pretext for James's *The Trew Law*, so fully does it reject the idea that an English monarch rules by his own will alone.

Fortescue asserted that it was only outside England—in France and elsewhere on the continent—that "the princes pleasure hath the force of a lawe" (i.e., that he is absolute). Such kingdoms are "roiall" monarchies. By contrast, those kingdoms in which the monarch is entirely under positive law are "politique." England's monarchy is both royal and politic; in practice, it is "mixed." As royal, it is exercised where no positive law obtains and through the prerogative; as politic, it acts in and through Parliament—that is, with the consent of subjects. The distinction chiefly affects the status of property; in politic governments, the people "do frankely & freely enioye and occupye their owne goods beynge rueled by such lawes as they themselfs desyer, and the Kynge of Englande can not alter nor change the lawes of his royalme at his pleasure."[27] In short, property entails possession under the law that guarantees its "free and frank" enjoyment.[28] The English subject has a

---

[26]Collinson, *De Republica Anglorum*, 33. For the "middling sort" and Shakespeare's plays, see Theodore Leinwand, "Shakespeare and the Middling Sort," *Shakespeare Quarterly* 44 (1993): 284–303.

[27]Sir John Fortescue, *A learned commendation of the politique lawes of Englande* (London, 1567), D$_{ii}$^{v}; STC 11194. Henry VIII had noted that "the judges have informed us that we at no time stand so high in our estate royal as in the time of parliament; when we as head and you as members are conjoined and knit together into one body politic." This comment reflects the judgment in Ferrer's case, and is quoted in Judson, *Crisis of the Constitution*, 83.

[28]*A learned commendation*, D$_{iii}$, D$_{iii}$^{v}. Fortescue goes on to note that a "roiall" monarchy does not necessarily destroy the "fredom" of subjects; it does so only if the king falls "into

liberty that allows him to reject the monarch's request for his property if he judges this request not to be in the interest of *salus populi* or the health of the people.

Fortescue's argument ends in a paradox that will speak to James's claim to a freedom in absolutism, especially in relation to rights of property. By Fortescue's reasoning the monarch who appropriates his subjects' property in the manner of a "free and absolute" monarch is precisely unfree. Because his "kyngelye power muste bee applyed to [and with] the wealthe of his kyngdome," he will be powerless if his kingdom is poor.

> Truelye suche a kynge maye well bee called not onelye feeble, but eeuene verye feblenes it selfe: nor is not to bee iudged free beeinge tyed with so manye bandes of feeblenes. On the other syde that kynge is free and of myghte that is hable to defende his subiectes aswell agaynste straungers as agaynste his owne people and also theire goodes and possessions not onely from the violente and unlawefull inuasions of their owne countrey menne and neighbours butte also from his own oppression and extortion thoughe such wilful lusts and necessities doe moue him to the contrarie. For who can be more mighty or more free then

tyrannie," D_{iii}^{v}. A "politique" monarchy reconfigures the body politic: its central organ is not the head (the monarch), but the heart (the people), and the nerves (the law); D_{vii}^{v}; D_{viii}. Fortescue's second treatise, *On the Governance of England*, 1471–78, and in print in 1537, establishes that the people's right to property is guaranteed by a general law that requires their consent to be governed. A politic monarchy does not permit a king to "rule his peple bi oother lawes than such as thai assenten vnto. And therfore he mey sett vpon thaim non imposition withowt their owne assent"; *On the Governance of England*, ed. Charles Plummer (London: Oxford University Press, 1926), 109. Donald W. Hanson sees Fortescue's idea of monarchy as comprising a "double majesty" but not a limited monarchy: the king is absolute; in certain spheres, however, and notably in matters involving of property, he must govern with the consent of his subjects. Donald W. Hanson, *From Kingdom to Commonwealth: the Development of Civic Consciousness in English Political Thought* (Cambridge: Harvard University Press, 1980), 217–45. For a history of the concept of an "ancient constitution," the contributions of Fortescue, and the definitions of Sir Edward Coke, see J. G. A. Pocock, *The Ancient Constitution and the Feudal Law: A Study of English Historical Thought in the Seventeenth Century: A Reissue with a Retrospect* (Cambridge: Cambridge University Press, 1987). For further commentary on Fortescue, see David Harris Sacks, "The Paradox of Taxation: Fiscal Crises, Parliament, and Liberty in England, 1450–1640," in *Fiscal Crises, Liberty, and Representative Government, 1450–1789*, ed. Philip T. Hoffman and Kathryn Norberg (Stanford: Stanford University Press, 1994), 6–77, 9–13. See also Burgess, *Ancient Constitution*, 37–38; and Sommerville, *Politics*, 88–89.

he that is hable to conquere and subdue not onely others but also himselfe? (L_{viii}^v; L)

Here Fortescue transformed a political problem, how a monarchy is governed, into a moral problem, how a king governs himself, and made them complementary. The terms of freedom and servitude, wealth and poverty move into paradoxical relations that set the king's desires against his best interests. Finally, these terms underwrite a community of benefits that draw monarch and people together in a single entity in which the freedoms of both are secured. The state as a person is imagined as a body whose health depends on the harmonious workings of its internal organs. If the monarch impoverishes his subjects, his subjects will not provide for him; their poverty is his deprivation.

As I have mentioned, the subject's uncompromising obedience to political authority required by absolutists was called into question in one important respect: it depended on the belief that the monarch's will was consistently good and responded to the dictates of divine and natural law. Why this belief made obedience problematic is obvious: such law, whether written in Scripture or inscribed on nature, was highly interpretable. A subject might well have difficulty in determining whether or not a monarch was obeying it. Furthermore, neither divine nor natural law declared whether a conscience that challenged political authority had any kind of formal or institutional identity. This indeterminacy made the subject's conscience a liability to himself. As long as resistance to authority on the grounds of God's law had no clear reference to a corporate body or action, it could not identify an institution programmatically situated to challenge the absolutist assumption that the ruler spoke with the voice of God. Logically, this should have been an institution comprising all Christian people, but in Reformation Europe, Christendom was a divided body and had several and often contradictory voices. Writers contending with absolutist practices in Tudor England rose to the challenge by fashioning idealized bodies politic in the terms provided by constitutionalist theory. Adapting for their arguments a view of the monarchy as mixed—in Fortescue's sense of the term—they invested assemblies representing the people with the power of conscience working against monarchic presumptions.

The monarch is not God, declared the radical John Ponet in 1556. His "authoritie and power" are established by God, and attached to his office not his person: "not for that they be naturally Godds, or that they be transubstantiated in to Goddes ... but for thautoritie [*sic*] and power which they receaue of God, [they are] to be his ministers here in earthe."[29] The idea that a ruler was merely an officeholder allowed his subjects to consider him as no more than human. As Patrizi observed, "a Civil and well instituted common weale" is not only "safer" than a monarchy, because it is impossible to find "one prince whiche embraceth all vertues"; it is also a "continuall and almoste an immortall state of lyfe."[30] To Protestants under Mary I, the only godly form of government was one that allowed a conscientious review of its execution, that made sure it was "profitably ordayned for the common wealth" (Ponet, 26). Stating that the monarch was no more than an officeholder, Ponet gave further definition to his notion of monarchic authority and power in figurative language that, varying the terms of humanist philosophy, addressed common daily experience.[31]

A king was like a husband not a lover; the former's role was a feature of the "ordinaunce" of marriage, the latter was merely a "persone" functioning anarchically; a king was like a "stuard" who managed property he did not own: as a trustee, a king governed a common wealth owned by the people (41, 95). The analogy between the household and the state allowed Ponet to develop what was implicit in the images of husbandry and stewardship, that is, the idea that political relations were mutually dependent, whether or not they could be contractually defined. This idea is, admittedly, not expressed in language consistent with the kinds of abstractions usual in political argument; Ponet's dra-

[29][John Ponet], *A Shorte Treatise of politike power, 1556,* in Winthrop S. Hudson, *John Ponet (1516–1556): Advocate of a Limited Monarchy* (Chicago: University of Chicago Press, 1942), 10–11.

[30]Francesco Patrizi, *A morall methode of ciuill policie,* trans. Richard Robinson (London, 1576), fols. 1ᵛ–2; quoted in Peltonen, *Classical Humanism,* 50.

[31]On the use of figurative speech in early modern political thought, see Kevin Sharpe, "A Commonwealth of Meanings: Languages, Analogues, Ideas, and Politics," in *Politics and Ideas in Early Stuart England: Essays and Studies* (New York: Pinter, 1989), 3–71; and Andrew Gurr, "Paradigms or Conceits? Metaphors of State in Sixteenth-Century England," *Literature & History,* 3d series, 3, 1 (1994): 1–15. See also my "The Household and the State: Transformations of an Analogy from Aristotle to James I," *Modern Language Quarterly* 54, 3 (1993), 307–26.

matic language sketches relations in rather personal terms. But it conveys not only what a ruler must do, but also what he must suffer if he does not do it. When Ponet describes the monarch's duties as his "labour," his "diligence," his "trouble," and terms them a servitude, he inverts the usual hierarchy of rule and suggests how the subject is in some sense a superior. "Princes" should "knowe themselues mortal men, no Goddes; seruauntes no maisters: and who must make accompt for all their doings, for all soules, men, women, and children: thinke their office and ministerie a heauye burthen bicause God hathe saied it shalbe so" (96 97). Arguing that God's "lawe testifieth to euery mannes conscience that it is naturall to cutte awaie an incurable membre which (being suffred) wolde destroie the hole body" (108), Ponet asserts that it is perfectly licit to kill an evil governor, a "tyrane," who is actually "a monstre and cruell beast" (101).

Huguenots writing on the continent during the next two decades, supported their anti-absolute critiques by particularly bold analogies. Arguing against the absolutism of the so-called politiques, they referred to the status of the wife to specify the rights of the people. They were essentially property rights: the public wealth (what was owned by the state or the royal domain) was hers and she was the people. The royal domain came to her husband, the monarch, as her dowry (*dos*); in the manner of a husband, the monarch could touch only its interest. The commonwealth was also represented as an estate, the patrimony or inheritance of the people; the king only managed it. When the commonwealth was imagined as a ship, the people owned it and its cargo, the king was merely its pilot (Caesar had *imperium*, the subjects had *proprietas*).[32] Philippe de Mornay's influential treatise condemning tyranny, *Vindiciae contra tyrannos*, published in Edinburgh in 1579, denied that the

---

[32]For this language of marriage, dowry, and the possibilities of a political "divorce" between a marital monarch and a uxorial people, see François Hotman, *Francogallia, 1573,* ed. Ralph E. Giesey, trans. J. H. M. Salmon (Cambridge: Cambridge University Press, 1972), 255–57. For the images of political "marriage" and "divorce," see also *De iure magistratum in subditos* (Leiden, 1576), F6ᵛ, F7; this treatise is attributed to Théodore Bèze, and appeared first in French as *Du droit des magistrats sur leurs subjects* (Magdebourg, 1574). The image of the ship of state appears in Philipe de Mornay's *Vindiciae contra tyrannos*, 126; for a full citation see note 33. For Huguenot thought, see Skinner, *Foundations*, 2: 302–38. For the influence in England of anti-absolutists on the continent, see Sommerville, "English and European Political Ideas."

monarch had any divine authority and power. His was merely a "function" (*functio*) of government.[33] Citing the civilist, Bartolus of Sassoferrato, de Mornay claimed that a monarch was not a master but a "brother" to his subjects (121); no more inherently privileged than they, he could be deposed by them (98). Similar analogies—the state as a corporate body, as a family—appeared in the great expositions of government published later in England, Sir Thomas Smith's *De republica Anglorum* and Richard Hooker's *Of the Lawes of Ecclesiasticall Politie*, but without the radical inflections they had exhibited in polemical works against absolutism. These defenses of the Tudor polity show the persistence of figured language in the literature of government, even at its most magisterial.[34]

What was lacking in many sixteenth-century treatises on politics—a discussion of the place of positive law in maintaining the status of both monarch and people—was supplied by commentary on the monarchy after the accession of James. The English habit of seeing the monarchy in terms of law enabled those challenging absolutist conceptions of the monarch as godlike to propose for it an alternative kind of transcendence that would ensure the mystical continuity of the body politic without risking the abusiveness possible in absolutism. Crucial to many of the arguments against the monarch as supreme legislator, a creature of a suprahuman kind, is the image of the law as his superior, not divine and natural law (as James would have it), but the positive law protecting the property of subjects and vested in the common law courts.

The idea of positive law as transcending the will of the monarch had the effect of equalizing the positions of monarch and subject in much the way calling them brothers did. This was especially the case when the monarch and subject were each pictured as persons who

[33]Stephano Junio Bruto Celta [Philippe de Mornay], *Vindiciae contra tyrannos sive de principis in populum populique in Principem, legitima potestate* (Amsterdam, 1610), 141. The monarch was also "administrator fisci," the people was "proprietarius vere," 97. Portions of the texts of Hotman, Beza, and de Mornay appear in English translation in *Constitutionalism and Resistance in the Sixteenth Century: Three Treatises by Hotman, Beza, & Mornay*, ed. Julian Franklin (New York: Pegasus, 1969). De Mornay was known in the Sidney circle; portions of his *De la vérité de la religion chrestienne*, 1582, were translated by Sir Philip Sidney. Completed by Arthur Golding, it appeared in editions of 1587, 1592, 1604, and 1617.

[34]Smith argues for role of Parliament; Hooker mentions consent of people, suggesting terms of marriage contract but disallowing "divorce." See Jordan, "The Household," 322–26.

inherited their patrimony under the common law. As Sir Edward Coke wrote in his *Reports* of 1604, "The king is under no man, but only God and the law; for the law makes the King: therefore let the King attribute that to the law which from the law he hath received, to wit, power and dominion: for where will and not law doth sway, there is no King."[35] Coke's dictum is consistent with his representations of the law as transtemporal, eternal in time if not actually outside time. It suggests that by providing for the succession, the law assures the life of the body politic. Inasmuch as that body is preserved by the succession and therefore expresses divine right, the law that guarantees it has a presumptive compatibility with the word of God. The *Reports* of 1605 enlarges further on the importance of the common law. Not only the means of inheritance, it is itself an inheritance, the "birthright and the most ancient and best inheritance that the subjects of this realm have, for by them he [the subject] enjoyeth not only his inheritance and goods in peace and quietness but his life and his most dear country in safety" ("To the reader," *Reports*, the fifth part, vol. 3, f. iii). In this formulation, the law itself becomes a property, one that belongs to the subjects of the realm. By representing positive law as an inheritance of the body politic, Coke and others called into question the premise of absolutism—that the monarch alone spoke with the voice of God.

Conflicts within the families and states of Shakespeare's romances can, of course, be understood entirely in personal terms, but they acquire a second reference if they are read as metaphors expressing aspects of contemporary political debate. As such, they illustrate the precarious situation of a ruler who has lost the support of his subjects and the moves that are necessary to restore the body politic to health. Oppositions of a binary nature—divine and natural law on the one hand,

---

[35]Sir Edward Coke, "To the reader," *Reports*, 7 vols. (London, 1776–77), the fourth part, vol. 2, f. xix. Cf. *Richard II*: "Take Herferd's rights away . . . /Be not thyself; for how art thou a king/But by fair sequence and succession?"; 1.1.195,198–99. The seminal study on Coke's thought is J. G. A. Pocock's: see his *Ancient Constitution*, esp. 30–69. For a study of Coke on absolutism, see Burgess, *Absolute Monarchy*, 165–208; and Sommerville, *Politics*, 86–100. For Coke's notion of English law as a factor in the construction of a national identity, see Richard Helgerson, *Forms of Nationhood: The Elizabethan Writing of England* (Chicago: University of Chicago Press, 1992), 70–104.

positive law on the other; the exchange of benefits and material goods; art as deception and art as education; freedom and servitude—create the politics of this drama. But the issues it comprehends are less resolved than explored.

Critics have often sought for evidence to identify Shakespeare with one party or another. It is unclear, however, that the plays allow for a position more specific than one rejecting tyranny and warning against its basis in absolutism. The transformation of the acting company of which Shakespeare was a member during the reign of Elizabeth (the Chamberlain's Men) to one under royal patronage at the accession of James (the King's Men) does not seem to have affected Shakespeare's representation of rule and misrule. The subjects of his Jacobean tragedies and romances resemble those of his Elizabethan histories: as a whole, these plays represent governments under which a people prosper and those in which they do not. The histories, perhaps because they dramatize passages in historical record, are characterized by imagery more or less conventional in political thought; the tragedies and romances, concentrating on configurations of patriarchy both in families and kingdoms, deploy a denser poetic medium and display a degree of allusiveness that the histories do not have. But at issue in all these plays is the abuse of rule. How or to what extent Shakespeare's dramatization of this topic in the romances was intended to reflect the particular practices of James is unclear. Some audiences may have seen the irresponsibility of Pericles, the witlessness of Cymbeline, the "Affection" of Leontes, and the bookishness of Prospero as indices of their king's character and will, but the associations are suppositious at best. The most that can be said is that the plays celebrate a rule by law over a rule determined by the will of a single man.

The investigation of Shakespeare's partisanship has been further clouded by the use of an inappropriate terminology. Twentieth-century critics have sometimes seen absolutism as an extension of feudalism.[36]

---

[36]See Franco Moretti, who claims that "Absolutism" is a "utopian late-medieval Project," *Signs Taken for Wonders: Essays in the Sociology of Literary Forms* (Thetford, Norfolk: Thetford Press, 1983), 56. See also Perry Anderson, *Lineages of the Absolute State* (London: Verso, 1979), 18–19. Fortescue, however, who was a good late-medieval projector, provided early modern constitutionalists with what they took as solid legal argument against absolutism, that is, the elements of feudal contract as the basis for relations beween monarch and subject. While it is plausible to claim that Shakespeare would not have produced drama that

But absolutism, which exempted a ruler from all law, was conceptually incompatible with feudalism, which organized political authority and power in the quasi-contractual dependencies of monarch and vassals. The Laws of the Confessor and the Magna Carta were invoked by constitutionalists, not by their absolutist adversaries.[37] Postmedieval monarchies, even when conceived according to the Tudor model, had to go on tolerating the exercise of the vestigial rights of the people supported in the common law. Instances of this puzzling relationship abound in contemporary fictions. When, for example, Cymbeline agrees to continue to be a vassal of Rome by paying her tribute, his action is not understood as the absolute triumph of Rome. The play rather builds on the fundamentals of feudalism to illustrate the equivocal nature of empire and its forms of dependency.

The romances were performed during a period in which what had appeared to be a settled form of government was coming under increasing challenge from different points of view. James's professions of absolute rule, despite his concessions to law, could quite obviously be considered a challenge to the mixed monarchy first described by Fortescue and subsequently transformed by constitutionalists to include a more specific emphasis on popular liberties, especially in relation to property. James had succeeded a queen whose public statements often celebrated her love for her subjects, and whose actions were construed as symbolic of her duty to them. Conversely, the

was designed specifically to provoke criticism of James (or Elizabeth), it does not follow that he was indifferent to the kind of abuse the monarchy was capable of or that his plays did not represent such abuse in conventionally political terms. Alvin Kernan's recent reading of Shakespeare's Jacobean plays assumes a degree of complicity on Shakespeare's part that the evidence in the playtexts does not, I think, support. See Alvin Kernan, *Shakespeare, the King's Playwright: Theater in the Stuart Court, 1603–1613* (New Haven. Yale University Press, 1995).

[37]Nicholas Fuller, for example, regarded the "liberty of the subject" as established by "Magna Carta" and guaranteed by Parliament which alone could deprive him of his goods; *The Argvment . . . In The Case of Thomas Lad and Richard Mavnsell* (London, 1607), B[v], B2; STC 11460. As Margaret Heinemann points out, anti-absolutist argument is historically conservative and rests on claims to "the traditional rights of Englishmen as they had existed at some earlier time"; *Puritanism*, 16–17. For the Magna Carta in general, see John Guy, "'The Imperial Crown' and the Liberty of the Subject: The English Constitution from Magna Carta to the Bill of Rights," in *Court, Country, and Culture: Essays on Early Modern British History in Honor of Perez Zagorin*, ed. Bonnelyn Young Kunze and Dwight D. Brautigam (Rochester: University of Rochester Press, 1992), 65–87.

republicanism proposed by radical thinkers disturbed established assumptions about monarchy as the best form of government. The idea of a universal franchise for all male citizens and their corresponding legislative power went counter to constitutional notions of a representative lawmaking body, and the English "people" was considered to consist of men who voted in the interests of all their dependents; the enfranchised were supposed to represent their households.[38] Such theory finds some correpondence in the romances. Characters doing manual work, and obviously not themselves representative of a "people" who vote, generally suit their behavior not to republican ideals, but to the constitutionalist model of the disenfranchised, represented through their surrogate superiors. They do not express a wish to make their government better or more to their liking by getting the franchise. But they do register protest that is indirectly political: they want to have the value of the work they do acknowledged.[39] And sometimes their work is shown to have a decisive power: it is clear that the mariners of *The Tempest* sail the King of Naples' ship, not the Master or the court party. Apart from their pay, their due is assumed to be the good government they receive (or will receive) from their king. Whether this recompense will actually be forthcoming in the future the play gestures to is finally an unanswered question. *Pericles*, however, ends with a revolution; the "city"

[38]The disenfranchised included "day labourers, poore husbandmen, yea marchantes or retailers which have no free lande, copiholders [i.e., those who rent rather than own their dwelling], all artificers as Taylers, Shoomakers, Carpenters, Brickemakers, Bricklayers, Masons, &c"; Sir Thomas Smith, *De republica Anglorum*, ed. Dewar, 76. The general qualification for the franchise enacted in 1430, the 40 shilling freehold, was practically invalid; all kinds of men and even some women voted in the first decade of the seventeenth century. As a category, however, the poor manual worker appears to have been regularly disenfranchised. See Derek Hirst, *The Representative of the People? Voters and Voting Under the Early Stuarts* (Cambridge: Cambridge University Press, 1975), esp. 17–19, 29–31, 93–96.

[39]The shepherds of *The Winter's Tale* aspire to be "gentlemen born," but their wishes have no obvious political reference. For a study of Shakespeare's entertainment of republican ideas, particularly in *Coriolanus*, see Annabel Patterson, *Shakespeare and the Popular Voice* (Oxford: Basil Blackwell, 1989), 120–29. See also Catherine Belsey's analysis of popular sovereignty, and English political thought and practice in relation to tragedy in *The Subject of Tragedy: Identity and Difference in the Drama* (New York: Methuen, 1985), esp. 93–125. For republicanism in England, see Peltonen, *Classical Humanism*, and J. G. A. Pocock's study, *The Machiavellian Moment: Florentine Political Thought and the Atlantic Republican Tradition* (Princeton: Princeton University Press, 1975), esp. 333–60.

(i.e., the citizens) of Tharsus overthrows the tyrannical king, Cleon, and his queen, Dionyza.[40]

Like absolutism and republicanism, the constitutionalism implicit in mixed monarchy was also an inherently vexed system of rule whose contradictions almost inevitably gave rise to debate. Nor was it thought to enjoy a monopoly on good government. If an absolute ruler could defy divine law, so could a mixed monarchy or, for that matter, a republic. Action in the romances reflects the unsettled character that these various "isms" possessed.

In the plays' final moments, their rulers appear to accept that they must govern and be governed by positive law, but they have been schooled in this discipline by the interventions and counsel of subordinates and the divine forces these subordinates are often allied with: Cerimon and Diana in *Pericles*; Posthumus and Jupiter in *Cymbeline*; Paulina and Apollo in *The Winter's Tale*; and Ariel, Juno, and Ceres in *The Tempest*. The romances thus depict a politics that insists on its essentially *human* subjects, whether rulers or ruled, whose actions elicit divine influence chiefly because they taken in the shadow of mortality. Shakespeare did not, in any case, mystify the operations of authority and power undertaken by men and women. His romances make decisions about rule difficult because they represent its problems not as obscure or remote but rather clear and present. No abstraction, no formula, no dictum is offered to trivialize or dismiss the challenge of government.

---

[40]William Shakespeare, *Pericles*, ed. F. D. Hoeniger (New York: Routledge, 1990), Epilogue, 11–14.

CHAPTER 2

Pericles

*P*ERICLES CONFORMS MORE CLOSELY TO THE NORMS OF ROMANCE THAN do its later companion plays. Its narrative character is illustrated by its opening scene, in which a Chorus, "ancient Gower," describes the play to follow as "an old song" (1.Ch.1). Dramatized in episodes that often lack realistic motivation, it is unified by a focus on its hero, a prince of Tyre. Scenes dramatizing Pericles' adventures are punctuated by moments of dumb show that advance the plot, but omit any reference to matters of character or causality. The plot itself is typical of Greek romance: it tells of the fate of the hero, his unfortunate exile, his loss of family, and his eventual return to a place he considers home. By contrast, the manner in which these events are represented recalls the narrative techniques of medieval romance; the enactment of conflict relies on visual and emblematic moments that ask for an explanatory context or setting, often by association with imagery or figures of thought. In this sense, *Pericles* is stylistically archaic, an evocation of an ancient and a medieval world. Its modality invites interpretation as an act of nostalgia and reflection. Its invocation of memory is also an appeal to conscience.

The story of Shakespeare's Pericles is one of a journey, but it departs from the normative form of Greek romance in which the hero

ends where he has begun. Pericles' point of origin in 1, his kingdom of
Tyre, becomes the home of Marina, his daughter and heir, in 5. The
move replacing the hero by his child registers a principal theme of
the play: a ruler, who is never more than a human being, may achieve
a kind of immortality, not in his person but through the generation that
secures his office. Given this emphasis on dynasty, dramatic conflict
inevitably centers on issues of courtship and marriage, on domestic
government, and especially on the obligations of fathers and husbands.
Action begins with a troubled courtship and closes with a happy one.
The terms of their failure and success have a broad reference not only
to the conduct of family life but to its analogue, the government of the
state. Causality—why failure, why success—is conveyed by repeated
references to the riddle whose answer is incest. Instituted to perpetu-
ate a tyranny in Antioch, incest threatens anarchy in Tyre. Equitable
rule is established in Pericles' kingdom only at the end of the play.

The motif of incest runs through the entire play. Hoping to marry
the princess and heir to the throne at Antioch, Pericles abandons this
courtship when he discovers she is actually a wife to her father, the
king. Reacting to the terrors of tyranny even after his return to Tyre,
Pericles further resolves to absent himself from his own kingdom and
people, at first by actual exile, and at last psychologically, by deep apathy and aphasia. Without an effective prince and head of state, Tyre
verges on anarchy, a condition made more likely during Pericles' several periods of exile. Fortune, malice, and his own errors of judgment
conspire to remove his wife, Thaisa, from the scene; and, at last in utter
despair, he reacts to the supposed death of his daughter, Marina, by
abdicating all responsibility for ruling Tyre. The terms by which he
recovers his family and his throne are corrections of those that have
earlier established incest: they represent the natural law of generation.
This is also the law that forestalls the presumption of godlike rule and
prevents tyranny. As long as Pericles fears tyranny and tolerates anarchy, he is unable to do what will prevent them: establish a dynasty. The
domestic order concluding the play gestures toward a political order
that has been absent in earlier scenes of misfortune, trial, and exile.

The play's narrativity, its representation as an old song, determines
much of its rhetorical complexity. Its Chorus, "ancient Gower," repeatedly intervenes to gloss his matter as if he were reading from a book of

obscure meanings. In a sense the play dramatizes two stories—one of Pericles, the second of "Gower" reading the story of Pericles.[1] As a character, "Gower" is also a double. He opens the play with an equivocation: he has returned to life "from ashes," as if a Phoenix, and yet also "assuming man's infirmities," that is, presumably, as mortal (1.Ch.2–3). His song has had and supposedly will have restorative properties (8); what, exactly, it is medicine for is as yet unclear. What we do know is that "Gower's" identity is overdetermined, even at this early moment in the play.

As both a man and a Phoenix, "Gower" embodies a reality and a fiction. The former is palpably experienced, the second is understood as a metaphor of dynastic continuity. Together, they fashion the enigma of the monarchy, the complex figure of the monarch's two bodies—his body natural which dies, and his body politic which is reborn through time. "Gower" thus enters the discourse of absolutism. He is that curious construction of man and, by virtue of his perennial vitality, of divinity literalized in James's description of a "free and absolute" monarch. He is also, however, the singer of "restoratives": that is, an image of monarchy reflecting upon history to remedy its errors. His is therefore a monitory role. Indeed, by offering restoratives, "Gower" functions as a monarch was supposed to, as the kingdom's physician.[2] His therapeutic song seems manifestly a cure when, in 5, heavenly music is made

[1] The authorship of *Pericles*, who its writer is (if not Shakespeare) and what stories he is reading, is a vexed question. For a detailed discussion, see *Pericles, Prince of Tyre*, ed. J. C. Maxwell (Cambridge: Cambridge University Press, 1965), and William Shakespeare, *Pericles*, ed. F. D. Hoeniger. Evidence suggests that Shakespeare (with whoever was his collaborator) follows two sources quite carefully: John Gower's *Confessio Amantis*, and Laurence Twine's *A Patterne of Painefull Aduentures*, 1607.

[2] The comparison of heads of state with physicians and shipcaptains is Platonic. For Renaissance treatments of the king as physician, see [John Ponet] *A Short Treatise of politike power, 1556,* in Winthrop S. Hudson, *John Ponet (1516–1556): Advocate of a Limited Monarchy* (Chicago: University of Chicago Press, 1942), 18; Barnabe Barnes, *Fovre Bookes of Offices, Enabling Privat persons from the speciall service of all good Princes and Policies* (London, 1606), ¶iiii, STC 1468; George Buchanan, *De iure regni apud Scotos or, A dialogue concerning the Due Priviledge of government in the Kingdom of Scotland* (London, 1689), 57 (cf. Latin editions published in Edinburgh in 1579, 1580, and 1581). Edward Forset considers both monarch and magistrate to be "physicians"; see Edward Forset, *A Comparatiue Discovrse of the Bodies Natvral & Politique* (London, 1606), L–L_{ii}, STC 11186. Thomas Floyd regards only "Judges" as physicians; see Thomas Floyd, *The Picture of a Perfit Common wealth*, E7ᵛ; STC 11119. For Barnes, see Markku Peltonen, *Classical Humanism and Republicanism in English Political Thought, 1570–1640* (Cambridge: Cambridge University Press, 1995), 153 passim.; for Buchanan, see

mysteriously audible to Pericles at the moment he recognizes Marina. The fact that "Gower" is also a dramatic representation of a historical figure, the poet John Gower, points to another set of interpretive coordinates. Audiences may look to the poet's works as authority for the song his stage character will sing. More important, perhaps: they will be prompted to search for reasons to see a figure of monarchy linked to music and poetry.[3]

"Gower" states that his song's story begins at Antioch with the incest of Antiochus the Great, who took his daughter to wife. The story was a familiar one and in fact Shakespeare's *Pericles* follows Gower's version of the story of Apollonius which appears in the eighth book of his *Confessio Amantis*. Gower dedicated all of his poem to his king, Richard II, to promote better government and return peace in the kingdom. His prologue makes the point. Lamenting the "hate," the "double face" of law, and the disappearance of "ryhtwisnesse" that plague the kingdom, and wishing to defer to the "comun vois, which mai noght lie," Gower urges his king to listen to counsel: "Although a man be wys himselve,/Yet is the wisdome more of tuelve."[4] As one "To whom no consail may be hid," the king is like a god in knowing all; implied, however, is also that he is actually a man and needs not only to listen to counsel but to seek it out, to invite speech not silence. Gower's poem has thus a presumptive link to the speech of the counselor. "Gower's" song, a physic for king and kingdom but administered by a figure of monarchy, is a kind of self-counsel, the song of an inner voice or conscience.

Rebecca W. Bushnell, *Tragedies of Tyrants: Political Thought and Theater in the English Renaissance* (Ithaca: Cornell University Press, 1990), 40–56; for Forset, see Glenn Burgess, *The Politics of the Ancient Constitution: An Introduction to English Political Thought, 1603–1642* (University Park: Pennsylvania State University Press, 1992), 156–657, and *Absolute Monarchy and the Stuart Constitution* (New Haven: Yale University Press, 1996), 70–71. For an early image of the sick body politic, see Plato, *Republic* 5, 462D–E. For the role of "Gower," see, among others, Richard Hillman, "Shakespeare's Gower and Gower's Shakespeare: the Larger Debt of *Pericles*," *Shakespeare Quarterly* 36, 4 (1985): 427–37, and F. David Hoeniger, "Gower and Shakespeare in *Pericles*," *Shakespeare Quarterly* 33, 4 (1982): 461–79.
[3]For the association of James I with the figure of the "musician-king," see Robin Headlam Wells, *Elizabethan Mythologies: Studies in Poetry, Drama, and Music* (Cambridge: Cambridge University Press, 1994), 63–80.
[4]John Gower, "Prologus," *Confessio Amantis* in *The Complete Works*, ed. G. C. Macauley, 4 vols. (Oxford: Clarendon Press, 1901), 2: 157–58.

Generation and the Body Politic

The incest of Antiochus, king of Antioch, speaks to a multiple and self-reflexive error and its consequences. By being a king's error, its domestic character is given a political dimension.

> This king unto him took a peer,
> Who died and left a female heir . . .
> With whom the father liking took,
> And her to incest did provoke.

> (1.Ch.21–22, 25–26)

A fact of misgovernment within the family, Antiochus's incest is made graver by the authority and power that allows its perpetuation. By masking its reality in the rituals of courtship, he both preserves and hides a tyrannic will. His incest prevents a succession, but its masking permits the illusion that a succession is possible. Antiochus's marriage is preserved by the feigned and false courtship of his wife, publicly known as his nubile daughter. This wife and his female heir, who is named the Daughter, is always to be courted but never to be married in a legitimate sense.

Antiochus obviously defies natural law. Incest places the father in a position that, by confounding the order of generation, defies the human condition of living in time and presumes a kind of timelessness, an immortality within history. It also denies inheritance. It therefore posits a world without property or what early modern English lawyers referred to as the distinction between meum and tuum. Like the god-king Saturn, who swallowed his offspring to ensure that he would keep his throne, Antiochus, by marrying his daughter and heir himself, prevents any son-in-law from succeeding him. Saturn's reign was termed a Golden Age where property was unknown. Its negative formulation is as a state in which all property belongs to the ruler. Adopting the extreme measures of the mythical Saturn but in a later age—one in which property is not only known but an object of intense desire—Antiochus fosters a pseudo-Golden Age of high and brutal irony. Figured in the garden of the Hesperides in which Pericles imagines the Daughter to be situated, the riches of this Golden

Age are entirely illusory. Antiochus himself, like Prospero later, is a master of illusionism, a creator of vivid impressions of a reality that is, in fact, nonexistent.[5] He is the sinister version of a type that appears throughout the romances: a ruler whose heir is female and whose descendants must be the offspring of a son-in-law.

Antiochus's pretensions to immortality are sustained by measures preventing resistance to his rules of courtship. Compounding his sin against natural law, he makes incest the pretext for what is, in effect, a proclamation that denies the suitor justice. He who does not answer Antiochus's riddle correctly cannot marry the Daughter and must die; but he who answers the riddle correctly, knowing its secret, cannot marry the Daughter either (although he has been promised to her) and must also die. The suitor is therefore doomed.

As one who pays suit to Antiochus, Pericles reflects elements of his character and rule.[6] Pericles knows the conditions of courtship, yet he thinks "death no hazard." He sees the king's daughter "apparell'd like the spring," imagines she is one of the daughters of the heavenly Hesperus, the evening star, and despite his knowledge that the gods have made him "man" and therefore subject to death, he is inflamed with a desire to possess her and to taste what she protects: "the fruit of yon celestial tree," the product of the Hesperides' garden.[7] The riddle itself conveys what threatens Pericles. Spoken by the Daughter—the "I" of the verse who is never given a proper name—the riddle's answer is

[5]James represented himself as a king who had returned the Golden Age to Britain; Antiochus's illusionary garden of the Hesperides may have suggested that James's representation was to be regarded as suspect. For an account of the iconography of magic in the Jacobean "Golden Age," see Vaughan Hart, *Art and Magic in the Court of the Stuarts* (New York: Routledge, 1994).

[6]Many critics have suggested that Pericles is a mirror of Antiochus. See especially Hillman, "Shakespeare's Gower," 434–45; Gerald Barker, "Themes and Variations in Shakespeare's *Pericles*," *English Studies* 44 (1963): 401–7; and Alexander Leggatt, "The Shadow of Antioch: Sexuality in *Pericles, Prince of Tyre*," in *Parallel Loves: Spanish and English National Drama 1580–1680,* ed. Louise and Peter Fothergill-Payne (Lewisburg: Bucknell University Press, 1991), 167–79.

[7]Antiochus's invitation also implies a reference to Eden, whose immortal fruit was forbidden. For an analysis of this iconography, see Mary Judith Dunbar, "'To the Judgement of Your Eye': Iconography and the Theatrical Art of *Pericles*," in *Shakespeare, Man of the Theater,* ed. Kenneth Muir, Jay L. Halio, D. J. Palmer (Newark: University of Delaware Press, 1983), 86–97. On the riddle as sacred parody, see Richard A. McCabe, *Incest, Drama, and Nature's Law, 1550–1700* (Cambridge: Cambridge University Press, 1993), 186.

incest. For Pericles to desire her puts him in danger of Antiochus's anger; for him to desire Incest makes him Antiochus's double. Describing herself, the Daughter says:

> I am no viper, yet I feed
> On mother's flesh which did me breed.
> I sought a husband, in which labour
> I found that kindness in a father.
> He's father, son, and husband mild;
> I mother, wife, and yet his child;
> How they may be and yet in two,
> As you will live, resolve it you.

> (1.1.65–72)

An obvious parody of the Virgin, the Daughter as Incest also speaks to a degradation of political relations insofar as they can be read by analogy to those of the family.[8] The firm distinctions qualifying obvious parallels between the institutions of the household and the state proposed by philosophers following Aristotle were often overlooked in later literature on monarchy, particularly by writers who endorsed absolutism. In any case, the analogy provided that if the king was a father, then his subjects were his children, and his wife was some form of popular collectivity. In question was the status of these dependents.

Huguenot theorists had specified that this "wife" was the people and her "dowry" was the property they brought to the king, a status that allowed them a role in government. Sir Thomas Smith, writing the *De republica Anglorum* in 1583, regarded the commonwealth as the culmination of an evolution from a monarchic patriarchy through an "aristocracy," in which husband and wife have joint rule as equals in freedom, but over subjects who are children, to a "polity" or "democracy," in which "ech man in turne might be receaued to bear rule and have his part of the honour, and . . . of the profit which came by administration of the common wealth." Subjects as represented collectively in Parliament and in union with the monarch, took precedence over the monarch alone, and together they shared the "most high and

[8]These relations are discussed in historical detail and from a psychoanalytic point of view by Bruce Boehrer, *Monarchy and Incest in Renaissance England* (Philadelphia: University of Pennsylvania Press, 1992).

absolute power in England" (*De republica*, 58, 59, 62, 78). Thomas Floyd, speaking descriptively in 1600, simply declared that the "commonwealth"—the people and the totality of their property—is the "mother of vs all"; the King rules as a "Father ouer his people," and is presumably married to the commonwealth whose office is generative (*Perfit Common wealth*, B_v, B2, $C6_v$). Speaking before Parliament to urge a union of the kingdoms of England and Scotland on March 19, 1604, James declared himself the "Husband" and "the whole Isle . . . [his] lawfull Wife".[9] In literal terms, both subordinates in this relation had rights in natural law against their superior husband and father; notably, a wife had rights in property and in governance; a child had rights to nurture and support. Far from absolute and above positive law, the patriarch was bound to care for his wife and children.[10] A conflation of their roles, tending to infantilize the wife and alienate the child, obviously jeopardized their respective rights. In analogical terms, incest signified an unnatural political power. Like the power of tyranny, which acts only in its own interests, the power of an incestuous patriarchy abuses its metaphorical dependents.

The wording of the riddle conveys the effects of incest understood as a figure of misrule. It thwarts generation in an economic as well a

[9]James VI and I, "Speech to parliament, March 19, 1604," in *Political Writings*, ed. Johann P. Sommerville (Cambridge: Cambridge University Press, 1994), 136.

[10]For a formulation in Roman law, see the *Corpus Iuris Civilis*, "De alendis liberis, ac parentibus": "si patrem tuum officio debito promerueris: paternam pietatem tibi non denegabit. Quod si sponte non fecerit: aditus [competens] judex alimenta pro modo facultatem praestari tibi jubebit. Quod si patrem se negabit: quaestionem istam imprimis idem judex examinabit" [If you promise your father to behave according to your duty, he will not deny you his fatherly duty. But if he does not live up to his pledge, a judge will order to be given you what is needed to keep you. But if he denies he is a father, the judge will examine this question first]. *Codex*, lib. 5, tit. 25, 4, in *Corpus Juris Civilis*, 2 vols. (Lyon, 1758–60), 2: 432. For this quotation, I am indebted to J. P. Sommerville. For a discussion of natural rights, see Richard A. Tuck, *Natural Rights Theories: Their Origin and Development* (Cambridge: Cambridge University Press, 1979). In England, Sir Thomas Smith had noted that children are not "in the power of the father," *in potestate parentum* but rather they are "parts of the father," *partes parentum*; a father cannot kill a child or take his property (*De republica Anglorum*, ed. Mary Dewar [Cambridge: Cambridge University Press, 1982], 134). John Cowell, commenting on the laws of England in his *Institutiones juris Anglicani*, 1605, concurred: a father may take the profits of his children's work until the child is twenty-one, but he must provide him with food and clothing; if a child inherits land, a father cannot have its profits; he must give an account of it when the child is twenty-one. John Cowell, *The Institutes of the Lawes of England* (London, 1651), C; STC C6641.

sexual sense. Here reproduction shadows production; by reserving his Daughter as his wife, Antiochus guarantees that she will not bear off-spring outside the royal household and that the resources she embodies will not be put to work by agents other than himself. Her serpentine nature indicates the sterility of the commonwealth in which the monarch is the only proprietor. By "feeding on mother's flesh," the Daughter likens herself to a young viper, who was said to eat its way out of its mother.[11] She turns on what should sustain her, the corporate body of the people of which the monarch is the head, and rather than creating wealth, she consumes it. As a whole, the riddle points to the strange union of tyranny and anarchy that the play continues to represent.

Pericles' reaction to the riddle, easily solved, reveals a practical consequence of a godlike rule that is typically suffered by its subjects. His thoughts revolt at what he now knows, but his ability to act on this sentiment is compromised by his own vulnerability. His speech becomes equivocal, a response to his double-bind. He must tell Antiochus that he has guessed the meaning of the riddle and has passed the trial of courtship, yet he must not give its answer openly because this would reveal the king's secret. Hoping to convey understanding without offending, Pericles tells Antiochus:

> Few love to hear the sins they love to act;
> 'Twould braid yourself too near for me to tell it.
> Who has the book of all that monarchs do,
> He's more secure to keep it shut than shown . . .
> Kings are earth's gods; in vice their law's their will;
> And if Jove stray, who dares say Jove doth ill?

(1.1.93–96, 104–5)

---

[11] A "serpent [that eats] out the bowels of the parent . . . which perisheth by them that were cherished by her" was an image of "princelie prodigalitie" in one contemporary text. See Barnes, *Foure Bookes*, C$_{ii}$^{v}, C$_{iii}$. Cf. Shakespeare: "Civil dissension is a viperous worm/That gnaws the bowels of the commonwealth," *I Henry VI*, 3.1.71–72; see also *Richard II*, 2.1.39–40. For the image of eating, see Anthony J. Lewis, "'I Feed on Mother's Flesh': Incest and Eating in *Pericles*," *Essays in Literature* 15, 2 (1988): 147–63. For the riddle itself, see P. Goolden, "Antiochus's Riddle in Gower and Shakespeare," *Review of English Studies*, n.s. 6, 23 (1955): 245–51. Its analogy to political disorder is discussed in my "Eating the Mother: Property and Propriety in *Pericles*," in *Creative Imitation: Essays in Honor of Thomas M. Greene*, ed. David Quint et al. (Binghamton: Medieval and Renaissance Texts and Studies, 1992), 331–53.

His words make explicit the conditions of absolute rule when it is inspired by the interests of the ruler not his people. Not only does it end in injustice, but its effects go unremarked. Secrecy is its precondition. Excusing incest with a pious generality, "All love the womb that their first being bred," Pericles also excuses his silence by asking for leave to "love [his] head." He leaves Antioch "lest [his] life be cropped" (1.1.108, 142–43). The danger he is in is reimagined in comic terms when Thaliard, Antiochus's henchman, arrives in Tyre to kill Pericles. Having been told by Antiochus not to ask for reasons why he, Thaliard, is to commit this murder, Thaliard links the subject's ignorance of his king's secrets to the subject's obedience to his king's commands. Not to know why one is commanded to do a thing is not to reflect on whether it is licit: "I perceive he was a wise fellow . . . that . . . he might know none of [the king's] secrets," for "if a king bid a man be a villain, he's bound by the indenture of his oath to be one" (1.3.1–8). To admit such knowledge would engage the subject's conscience. Once engaged, he could be led either to sin or to resistance. In both cases, he risks his life. Here speech is the precondition of conscientious action. It can inspire the subject and counsel the monarch. Silence, by contrast, protects the tyrant and, in a sense, the subject.

Of course the speech of subordinates was generally regarded as a contentious matter. Within the household a wife was supposed to be mute, but the frequency with which she was commanded to silence, not to mention how often she was ridiculed as a scold, suggests that in practice women spoke a good deal. In decorous settings, she was often portrayed as her husband's counselor, urging him to good action, only desisting when she offended his sense of status. English treatises urge the complementarity of the married couple. The "wife's" political double, the great body of the commonwealth, had a similar function. Represented by the Commons, the people were to speak of affairs of state and after debate to assent to the monarch's will.[12] What

---

[12]John Guy points out that the subjects' right to speech could be imagined as a wife's duty to counsel her husband: Bacon's dictum—that "sovereignty is married to counsel"—illustrates an aspect of the conjugal relation between monarch and people. John Guy, "The Rhetoric of Counsel in Early Modern England," in *Tudor Political Culture*, ed. Dale Hoak (Cambridge: Cambridge University Press, 1995), 292.

was less clear (and this was also the case for a wife) was whether the Members had an absolute right or merely a revocable privilege to such speech. Opinion depended on the relative value of speech: to protest might be superfluous, to advise might be essential. Those who focused on the benefits of subjects' speech could point to the long history of the right to speak in Commons: Holinshed claimed that this right was granted to the first councils or parliaments.[13] Shortly after the accession of James, and four years before the production of *Pericles*, the Commons had occasion to insist on their right to speech and to assert that it was a check on tyranny. What they assumed in order to make this judgment was first, that they were to counsel the king; and second, that without being able to speak they would not know what counsel to give him. The conditions they demanded illustrate some of the political meanings attached to speech that is addressed to the monarch.

In early April of 1604, James voided the election of Sir Francis Goodwin to the House of Commons because he was an outlaw. When the Commons protested, James, as "an absolute king," demanded a conference between the "House," i.e., the Commons and the Judges, to be reported by his Council. An unidentified Member responded with these words: "The Prince's command is like a thunderbolt, his command upon our allegiance like the roaring of a lion; to his command there is no contradiction."[14] The conference took place a few days later and James eventually agreed to let the election stand (claiming to the Commons that their "privileges" had never been in question), but on this occasion their earlier intervention was reported somewhat differently. Now the Member asserted that although James's voice "was the voice of God in man, the good spirit of God in the mouth of man," it was not the voice of God himself: "I do not say the voice of God and not of man; I am not one of Herod's flatterers" ("[11 April, 1604]," *Constitutional*, 214). The Member was clearly at pains to point out that to divinize the monarch is to flatter him, and even that the monarch who represents himself as a god is a kind of Herod. Both statements reveal

[13] Annabel Patterson, *Reading Holinshed's Chronicles* (Chicago: University of Chicago Press, 1995), 107–9.
[14] "[5 April, 1604]," in *Constitutional Documents of the Reign of James I*, ed. J. R. Tanner (Cambridge: Cambridge University Press, 1930), 213.

a concern to clarify the language of monarchy, to distinguish its literal from its figurative meanings.

Several weeks later, in the written protest that this confrontation elicited, the monarchy was represented in an even clearer light. The "Form of Apology and Satisfaction" told the king that what he had termed "privileges" the undersigned Members considered "rights": hence they did not depend on the king's "grace." They were the "rights of all your Majesty's said subjects and the whole body of this your kingdom." They were the subjects' "due inheritance," just as much as "lands and goods." The people were named a corporation; their body had a collective right to its property which was an inheritance and guaranteed over time. Its principal guarantee was speech, which must be free from public "disgrace" ("Apology," *Constitutional*, 220–22.) Both rights were essential to the future of the commonwealth:

> What cause we your poor Commons have to watch over our privileges[15] is manifest in itself to all men. The prerogatives of princes may easily and do daily grow: the privileges of the subject are for the most part at an everlasting stand. They may be by good providence and care preserved, but being once lost are not recovered but with much disquiet. If good kings were immortal as well as kingdoms, to strive so for privilege were but vanity perhaps and folly; but seeing the same God who in his great mercy hath given us a wise King and religious doth also sometimes permit hypocrites and tyrants in his displeasure and for the sins of the people, from hence that the desire of rights, liberties and privileges, both for nobles and commons, had its just original, by which an harmonical and stable State is framed, each member under the Head enjoying that right and performing that duty which for the honour of the Head and happiness of the whole is requisite. (222–23)

The "Apology" pointedly dismisses any notion of the king's divinity as a dangerous fiction. It represents his mortality as the finitude of his

---

[15]The change in diction is remarkable; the "Apology" is clearly representing what the Commons possess not what they must request. For a study of the political significance of the "Apology," see J. H. Hexter, "Parliament, Liberty, and Freedom of Elections" in *Parliament and Liberty from the Reign of Elizabeth to the English Civil War*, ed. J. H. Hexter (Stanford: Stanford University Press, 1992), 21–55.

actual life, and indeed the condition of postlapsarian man. If monarchs were consistently "good," subjects would not need to insist on rights. Both Thaliard and Pericles are silenced by Antiochus, the first because he is a subject, the second because he is in Antioch. The reason Pericles continues to fear Antiochus once in Tyre engages the matter of speech more abstractly. Less a consequence of a particular word or statement (the terms of the riddle), Pericles' continued dread of Antiochus depends on his belief that a ruler's language realizes his actual power, that his word is felt as an action.

The Subject and the Monarch's Two Bodies

Apparently convinced that Antiochus will pursue him to Tyre, invade his country, and destroy his people, Pericles determines on exile. Intent on killing him, Antiochus will then bypass Tyre, or so Pericles thinks. His absence from his kingdom will constitute his "care" of his subjects (1.2.30). The paradox here hardly needs stating: having represented himself as the people's defense, the "tops of trees" that "fence" and defend their "roots" (31–32), the possibility of an invasion by a foreign tyrant forces Pericles to deny what he has declared is his office and function. He decides to abandon the Tyrians to their alien enemies, although to do so risks anarchy within the kingdom. Helicanus, Pericles' counselor, knows that to foresee "peace" in the absence of a head of state is flattery (45–46), but he acknowledges Pericles' motives: "justly . . . you fear the tyrant,/Who either by public war or private treason/Will take away your life" (103–5). The decision to go into exile is made more ambiguous by Pericles' mistrust of his own people, who, he declares, will not have the courage to fight in the event of an invasion, who will be "vanquish'd *ere* [i.e., before] they resist" (28); a mistrust that Helicanus does not seem to share. When Pericles asks what the Tyrians would do if their kingdom was invaded even in his absence, Helicanus replies: "We'll mingle our bloods together in the earth" (113), hardly a description of a cowardly people. Escaping the reasoning supporting exile (his presence will cause an invasion) is Pericles' doubt that were Antiochus to attack Tyre, its people would be incapable of resistance. Why Pericles lacks confidence in his subjects implies a twofold rupture in the mutuality he outlined earlier: he—the tops of trees—is obliged to "fence" his and their kingdom, but instead he leaves it open to an enemy; they—the roots of that tree—are supposed to give sap to his greenery, but instead he assumes that their contribution to defense is inadequate. In short, rule in Tyre has lost its quasi-contractual character: the kingdom, root and branch, is cut in two. If Pericles has misjudged the situation, overrating the power of Antiochus and underestimating his own, there is reason to ask why. I suggest that his error, literalized in his subsequent wandering, originates in solecism.

Put simply, Pericles has misunderstood the nature of Antiochus's rule, and, by extension, the rule of the monarch or prince. Accounting for his own silence at Antioch, he had termed kings the gods of earth whose will was law. Speaking of Antiochus as "Jove," he—like the frightened Member who pictured James's command as a "thunderbolt"—imagined his absolute power as invincible.

> Kings are earth's gods; in vice their law's their will;
> And if Jove stray, who dares say Jove doth ill?

$$(1.1.104-5)$$

Unlike the writers of the "Apology," Pericles does not recognize metaphor. He attributes to the figured language of monarchy a real correlative—a solecism made attractive by James's self-imaging but not in any case inevitable. Erroneously assessing the power of Antiochus, a tyrant but not divine, Pericles overlooks the contestatory nature of all government and refuses to entertain resistance. In other words, he attributes to his own subjects the passivity they would (necessarily) have were they ruled by a divine being whose word was (necessarily) law. His engagement with the people of Tharsus, the first port of his exile, illustrates a related kind of miscalculation.

Tharsus is a city whose people lack the most basic of substances: food. Its mothers are about to eat their children, a situation that obviously inverts the terms of Antioch's emblematic tyranny but has the same outcome. Tharsus consumes itself; it will have no generation. Pericles' response is, like his exile, fraught with ambiguity. He feeds the Tharsians with grain he has on his ship. Ostensibly a charitable act, his gift implies a commerce not in goods that can be priced, but in benefits that have a value beyond the mechanics of the market. In this case, Cleon, the king of Tharsus, promises the loyalty of this people as a return for Pericles' generosity.[16] Whether and how a monarch was to dispense largesse rather than be a careful husband or steward was, however, a topic of political debate that involved more than matters of style.

Prudent writers tended to prefer a modest rather than a magnificent monarch for obvious reasons: royal gifts came from the pockets of the people. Michel de Montaigne's argument is representative. "Liberality it selfe in a soveraigne hand is not in her owne luster," he observed: "private men have more right, and may challenge more interest in her . . . [A] King hath nothing that is properly his owne; hee oweth even himselfe to others." In fact, his generosity may be close to "tyrannie": "If the liberality of a Prince be without heedy discretion and measure, I would rather have him covetous and sparing. Princely vertue seemeth to consist most in justice."[17] Seneca, on whose *De beneficiis* Montaigne drew, made a sharp distinction between benefits that are extended among private persons and those that are public affairs. The latter are not really benefits because they lack the necessary intentionality. A public or "comon" feast, for instance, is designed to get public approval and indicates a weakness in the giver: "he did it but too feede his owne humor."[18] Huguenot writers had used the figure of the merchant ship to distinguish its owners (the people) and cargo (their wealth) from its pilot (the monarch). In England, where James's largesse was notorious, at least one representation of the monarch's ship of state suggested that he was not its only owner.

[16]Shakespeare's sources clarify what he leaves obscure. Gower states that Apollonius owns what he gives to the Tharsians; Twine has Apollonius accept payment for it initially but then reimburse the Tharsians: *Narrative and Dramatic Sources*, ed. Geoffrey Bullough, 8 vols. (New York: Columbia University Press, 1977), 6: 383, 432. Shakespeare's Pericles speaks of "our" Tyrian ships, a locution that refers ambiguously to a proprietorship that is both his and his people's. For a discussion of the figure of royal merchant in *Pericles*, see Steven Mullaney, *The Place of the Stage, License, Play, and Power in Renaissance England* (Chicago: University of Chicago Press, 1988), 135–51.

[17]"Of coaches," in *The Essayes of Michael Lord of Montaigne, Translated by John Florio*, 3 vols. (London: J. M. Dent, 1928), 3: 134–35.

[18][Seneca], *The woorke of the excellent Philosopher Luciius Annaeus Seneca concerning Benefyting*, trans. Arthur Golding (London, 1578), 1.14, C_{ii}; STC 22215. On the influence of Seneca and the question of benefits generally, see Linda Levy Peck, "Benefits, Brokers, and Beneficiaries: The Culture of Exchange in Seventeenth-Century England," in *Court, Country, and Culture: Essays on Early Modern British History in Honor of Perez Zagorin*, ed. Bonnelyn Young Kunze and Dwight D. Brautigam (Rochester: University of Rochester Press, 1992), 109–27.

A year before *Pericles* played at the Globe, Robert Wilkinson preached at the marriage of Lord Hay on the subject of the Union by alluding to the "traffique" that was about to occur between the two kingdoms.[19] But his enthusiasm had a certain bite in it, too: to him, James's ship of state was also a "wife" in virtual command. She was the good wife of Proverbs 31:14, who, "like a Merchants ship . . . bringeth her foode from affare." Although not its captain, she behaves as if she were: "She commands and countermaundes each man to his charge . . . as if none but shee were captaine, owner, Maister of the Ship, and yet she is not master but the mastersmate, a royall shippe she is . . . and if shee bee a Merchants too, then is she the Merchants roy-all" (B4ᵛ). Wilkinson's equivocation—"as if . . . and yet"—reveals the uncertain status of the monarch in relation to the commonwealth. Absolutists such as Cowell, whose *Interpreter* also appeared in 1607, maintained that the monarch owned the property of all his subjects, but this was not a common or popular view.[20] If Pericles' gift to the Tharsians is regarded as specious—as the language generally describing the ship of state suggests—what is at issue in this episode is the provenance and proprietorship of the substance that is given away, and Pericles in Tharsus is a kind of reflection of Pericles in Tyre. Just as he could not imagine his Tyrian subjects as supplying the means and the force to defend themselves, the substance of their resistance to a tyrant invader, so also does he regard his right to their property as absolute. His subjects cannot give him anything because he already has every-thing. In his own eyes, he is, de facto, the sole proprietor of Tyrian property. But that he is so de iure is unclear, as the following action

---

[19]Robert Wilkinson, *The Merchant Royall* (London, 1607), F; STC 25657. For this reference, I am indebted to Lori Anne Ferrell's unpublished paper: "Misogyny, Patriarchy, and Protestant Identity in Jacobean England." The occasion of the sermon was the marriage of Lord Hay, a Scot residing in London and "one of James's most prodigal courtiers and beneficiaries." James's favoritism toward his Scottish subjects was especially remarkable: "During the first few years of his English reign, James bestowed upon Scots £10, 614 in pensions, £88, 280 in 'ready money,' £133,100 in old debts, and £11,093 in annuities . . . [James] made himself unusually accessible to his Scottish associates and thus gave the impression that these men were exercising undue influence in the formulation of royal policy, so much so that contemporaries referred to the 'Scottish government' of England." Brian P. Levack, *The Formation of the British State: England, Scotland, and the Union, 1603–1707* (Oxford: Clarendon Press, 1987), 195.

[20]See "subsidie," John Cowell, *The Interpreter* (Cambridge, 1607), Rrr1; STC 5900.

illustrates. The trial that he undergoes after leaving Tharsus, his shipwreck, and landing naked and destitute on the shores of Pentapolis, comments further on his problematic proprietorship.

Still evading Antiochus, Pericles emerges from the sea no more than an "earthly man" whose "substance" must yield to "Wind, rain, and thunder"—in other words, possessing no more than his natural body which is subject to natural forces (3.1.1–2). But this body is also subject to conditions imposed by the economic life of men. In words that recall the despair of King Lear, who had declared that "humanity" eats itself, "like monsters of the deep" (4.2.46), the first of three fishermen (who are about to help the wrecked Pericles) claims that men live as fish in the sea:

> the great ones eat up the little ones. I can compare our rich misers to nothing so fitly as to a whale: 'a plays and tumbles, driving the poor fry before him, and at last devour [*sic*] them all at a mouthful. Such whales have I heard on a'th' land, who never leave gaping till they swallow'd the whole parish, church, steeple, bells, and all. (2.1.28–34)

To the first and master fisherman, scarcity is a fact of nature. Fierce competition for resources leads to the consumption of resources, resources that may even include the property and persons of those who are competitors. An ingenious reflection of the fate of Jonah the Prophet by the third fisherman, Patchbreech, responds to this image of misrule by hinting at the importance of political speech. Were he in the whale's belly, Patchbreech promises, he would "jangle bells" to force the whale to cast up his prey (41). In other words, unlike Jonah who waited for God to deliver him (Jonah, 1.1–2; 3.1–4), Patchbreech would "cry against" oppression and so find relief. His protest has a more than abstract reference. Patchbreech declares that were King Simonides of his mind—which he is not—he would purge the "drones" that "rob the bee of her honey," and confound the parasites that consume the wealth of the kingdom.[21] This speech, innocuous enough when made to fellow fishermen, is immediately silenced when the first fisherman,

[21]Hoeniger points to parallels between Shakespeare's image of a rapacious fish, Patchbreech's protest, and a passage in John Day's *Law-Tricks*; see *Pericles*, 172–73. The image of the sea as an analogue to anarchy also appears in Ponet, *Politike power*, 10.

addressing Pericles (who has admired the analogy in an aside), prudently praises Simonides' "peaceable reign and good government." These exchanges on the subject of property in and of the sea—a "finny subject" as Pericles notes—draw attention to the actual transactions that then take place between the fishermen and Pericles.

Responding to Pericles' request for help, the first fisherman makes him a gift of his gown and welcomes him, as a man in want, to his house. The second and third fishermen show him a suit of rusty armor that they have just hauled up in their nets. Recognizing it as his father's—it has gone down in the wreck—Pericles "begs" the fishermen for it and states he, their "debtor" until his fortunes mend, will pay them "bounties" then. They agree to the bargain and insist that he remember his promise of "certain condolements, certain vails" (2.1.135–51). These transactions, clearly of two kinds, occur at a moment of crisis and also of transition.[22] As an "earthly man," Pericles is given charity; as a monarch temporarily without the resources of his office, his father's armor signifying the royal inheritance jeopardized by exile and then more recently by a "wat'ry empire," he becomes the debtor of workers who have secured this inheritance from a medium—the sea—that is notoriously transformative. The nature of Pericles' debt is enhanced by the actual privation of the three fishermen; they live in a cannibalistic world. The scene also hides a warning: the voice of Patchbreech may rise above the conciliatory words of the first fisherman and expose the dark side of a government that by swallowing the resources of whole parishes, prevents subjects from having anything to give or exchange.

The gown and the suit of armor each clothe Pericles, but their provenance and function are conceptually distinct. Together they express the relations comprised by a mixed monarchy. Plowden's formulation of the monarch's two bodies separated the monarch's person from his office. How each body was to rule was debated by absolutists and constitutionalists throughout the early years of James's reign, but consis-

[22]Gower and Twine represent Apollonius as rescued by only one fisherman and clothed with only a cloak. In common law, the armor would have been regarded as the fishermen's property unless someone showed up who could prove ownership. See Edmund Plowden, Eysten v. Stubbs, *Commentaries or Reports* (London, 1761), 465–66.

tently in view were the "liberties of the subject"—liberties that were bound up with the possession of property. Fortescue had stated that the monarch's political rule was restricted by and inseparable from his dependence on the consent of the Commons for revenue beyond what was provided by his domain and his prerogative. Under James, the idea of the people's liberties was made more specific. For Pericles to have reacquired his Tyrian inheritance from subjects he will gain in Pentapolis (in the future to which the play looks) obviously points to the eventual union of these kingdoms. In a symbolic sense, it indicates how the rule of a monarch, as expressed in Parliament and therefore as a function of the body politic, depends on the substance of his people. By 1608 the relations between these two bodies were clarified, to a degree, by a decision in common law that in a backhanded way went far to limit what the monarch could do in his body natural and independent of his body politic. The decision was a subtle one but its effects—touching also on the question of the Union of the Kingdoms—were comprehensive.

The decision was rendered in the case of a Scotsman, Robert Calvin, a *postnatus* (i.e., a Scotsman born after 1603) who claimed land in England by inheritance. The question was whether he was an English subject. If he was not, his claim was void. Sir Thomas Fleming decided for Calvin on the grounds that nationality was determined by allegiance to the monarch which followed the body natural and was not determined by a presence in the body politic. Allegiance was a matter of natural law, not positive law. It was a "quality of mind," and not a local obligation.[23] By discussing nationality and allegiance, Fleming's decision also delineated the relatively narrow scope of the powers attached to the body natural, expressed for the most part by the prerogative, and, by contrast, the greater importance of the powers of the monarch in his body politic, powers that constitutionalists claimed had to be consistent with positive law. Reporting on Calvin's case, Sir Edward Coke wrote: an "attainted" man (convicted of a crime) lost the king's "legal protection" (in positive law); hence he could be denied the right to bring a suit. He did not, however, lose that "protection which

[23]The Case of the Post-nati, *State Trials*, ed. T. B. Howell, 22 vols. (London, 1811–26), 2 (1816): 614, 623.

by the law of nature is given to the King for that is *indelibilis* &
immutabilis . . . and therefore the King may protect and pardon him" for
a particular crime. The decision had very clear consequences for the
prospect of a Union, inasmuch as it denied James the right to make the
antenati (Scotsmen born before 1603) subjects of England by virtue of
the prerogative.

In a more theoretical way, Calvin's case also implied a distinction
between the subject's relation to the body natural of the monarch and
the subject's standing in the body politic. If the subject's allegiance was
to the body natural and consisted of a "state of mind" not an element
in positive law, then it was enforced only by the law of nature, by a
consciousness of that relation and the moral obligation it entailed. It
left unaffected what a subject possessed in positive law: those rights or
"liberties" were guaranteed by "judicial and municipal laws."[24] Allegiance could (and should) result in professions of loyalty, acts of charity, and benefits of considerable value, but its character as an expression
of natural law was, in a sense, indeterminate. The subject's standing
in the body politic, however, was far more specific and, after the accession of James, increasingly a topic of discussion. Characterized by
property and the ethos of the market, it made possible a relation with
the monarch that admitted negotiation, the calculation of a quid pro
quo, and a kind of contractualism. Clothed by the master fisherman,
Pericles benefits from a sympathy for the purely human body natural
and a charitable state of mind. Armed by the second and third fishermen with a property that (although his) they have worked for, he
becomes a party to an agreement in which he is made viable politically by the real substance of subjects. This comes not as a gift but with
an agreement to furnish recompense. Both gift and agreement could

[24]Sir Edward Coke, Calvin's case, *Reports,* 7 vols. (London, 1776–77), the sixth part, vol.
4, ff. 13^v, 14. For a detailed analysis of Calvin's case, see Bruce Galloway, *The Union of England and Scotland, 1603–1608* (Edinburgh: John Donald, 1986). Burgess notes that Calvin's
case distinguished allegiance to the person of the king, or his body natural, from allegiance
to the state, "an artificial body that must be constituted 'by a law precedent.'" Inasmuch
as the prerogative allowed "royal action in areas where the common law had no force," it
was associated with the body natural of the monarch that functioned independently of the
state and its law; *Ancient Constitution,* 128, 142. In other words, "Fleming in 1608 [i.e., in
Calvin] was placing his conception of absolute power unremarkably into an English tradition of discretionary and inseparable prerogatives, confined but not governed by law";
Absolute Monarchy, 83.

have been withheld, of course; but the first, responding to the common condition of mankind, conformed to natural law, while the second, more narrowly tailored to the unique mission of a prince, participated in the propriety of positive law.

Pericles' courtship of Simonides' daughter, Thaisa, is a logical extension of these emblematic exchanges on the seashore at Pentapolis. Successful because he triumphs in a tournament of arms, his courtship gets him a royal daughter and the succession to another kingdom. It also quite obviously inverts the terms of his courtship at Antioch. Promoted by Simonides, who mocks incest by pretending to discourage Pericles but is actually delighted by his daughter's "absolute" desire to marry a "knight of Tyre" (2.5.19–22, 43), Pericles' marriage ends in generation, the conception of Marina. Exogamy is made a feature of a more comprehensive politics when Simonides praises the godlike generosity of monarchs in a setting that has already established the transience of earthly rule. Seeing that Simonides resembles his father, Pericles had earlier reflected on his own uncertain inheritance, his difference from his father (a difference just barely moderated by his bargain with the fishermen), and concluded: "Time's the king of men;/He's both their parent and their grave" (2.3.45–46). The fishermen's complaints and bargain that were so powerful a determinant of action earlier in the scene are recalled by association with the impresa Pericles bears at the tournament, a "wither'd branch, that's only green at top," glossed as "*in hac spe vivo*" ([in this hope I live], 2.2.42–43).[25] The hope he celebrates lies in his ability to win Thaisa and, more symbolically, in the Tyrian tree from which this branch has split, a tree with its roots in the people of Tyre and to which he expects to be regrafted (cf. 1.2.31–32). His first hope is realized in Pentapolis; his second only at the end of the play.

The Physician's Art

With the death of Antiochus, the anarchy Helicanus feared would come to Tyre in the absence of its head of state becomes a threat to

---

[25]For a source for this image, see Alan R. Young, "A Note on the Tournament Impresas in *Pericles,*" *Shakespeare Quarterly* 36, 4 (1985): 453–56. The imagery of tree trunk and branches is prominent in *Cymbeline* where it refers to the reunion of the king with his children.

its future (2.4.23–39; 3.Ch.26–29). Pericles is accordingly sought for, found, and summoned home with the pregnant Thaisa. He is prevented from reaching Tyre by a second storm during which Thaisa gives birth to Marina, and is erroneously pronounced dead by Lychorida, the nurse and midwife in charge. Sailors, following their custom of casting the dead into the sea, demand that the supposed corpse go overboard (locked in a casket with identifying papers); and the ship makes for Tharsus with the infant, who needs immediate nourishment. These apparently rational actions are subsequently called into question by the fact that Thaisa, washed up at Ephesus in her casket, is not dead (the judgment of those attending Marina's birth was premature), and Marina, left to be nursed in Tharsus by the supposedly grateful Cleon, becomes years later the object of Dionyza's murderous anger (Marina's situation as foster child was imprudently protracted). These events, brought about by errors in timing or temperance, find a correspondence as images of anarchy, a correspondence already realized by the storm in which Tyrian rule and its succession are jeopardized.[26]

Pericles, certainly a victim of fortune, is clearly also complicit with misfortune. Although Lychorida counsels "Patience," he immediately agrees to observe the sailors' "custom" which he has earlier thought "superstition":"as you think meet," he tells them (3.1.19, 26, 50–54). His command of his men is ambiguous:[27] he obeys, without much reflection, what is in effect a positive law of the sea, improvising upon its custom only to provide Thaisa's "corpse" with a watertight casket. Had he defied the sailors and been patient, had he been resolute in his judgment of their custom as ill-founded, he would have dismissed it and so have secured both wife and daughter. Seen as an instance of government, the

---

[26]The imagery of shipwreck often presumed a political reference; e.g., Suffolk's accusation of Gloucester for turning "peers" into "bondmen to [his] sovereignty," "racking" the commons, and "costing" the "public treasures"—actions that together explain why "the commonwealth hath daily run to wrack"; *2 Henry VI*, 1.3.124–31. Cf. Thomas Floyd who pictures the "tyrant" as a "battered or crazed ship [that] by letting in of water not only drowneth her selfe but all that are in her"; *Perfit Common wealth*, C12ᵛ.

[27]At the height of the storm, of course, the ship is commanded by the sea and the winds. In Marina's retelling, the hierarchy of state in overturned completely: Pericles hauls ropes, a man is swept overboard, and the shipmaster's commands "treble their confusion" (4.1.52–56; 64). For the role of Fortune, see Elena Glazov-Corrigan, "The New Function of Language in Shakespeare's *Pericles*: Oath versus 'Holy Word,'" *Shakespeare Survey* 43 (Cambridge: Cambridge University Press, 1990), 131–40.

situation on shipboard takes on the appearance of an enigma. Pericles has not been a tyrant captain; his will has deferred to the sailors' law. That law has, however, led to dreadful error. The enigma—neither the monarch's will nor positive law are wholly adequate to secure the future—was a common topic in political literature and notably in Plato's *Politicus*.

The treatise appeared in Latin translations throughout the sixteenth century, and expressed a general preference for a government that depends on written texts rather than on "the kingly art" (*scientia civilis*; *scientia imperandi*; *ars Regia*).[28] This art is less successful in creating and maintaining a just state than is law for the same reasons later advanced by Fortescue and the writers of the "Apology": it is practiced by a human being. At the same time, law is not a perfect political instrument.

The debate concerning the nature and scope of a ruler's art is contextualized in discourse that represents art as the expression of a philosophy. Perhaps most familiar were the qualified rejections of the art of the philosopher for the purpose of practical government in Plato's *De republica*, where he who possesses such an "art" (*ars*) is deemed "useless" (*inutile*) because the people are beyond reform; they are generally "dishonest" (*improbi*; *Opera* 2, 489D). In the best of all worlds, such a man would govern. As it is, he who possesses the true art of government must "turn completely to his own affairs" (*in rebus suis solide versatur*, 496D). In Sir Thomas More's *Utopia*, this position is substantially adopted by Hythloday, who insists that a philosopher "cannot remedie the follie of the people."[29] These arguments spoke to the relative

---

[28] *Platonis opera quae extant omnia*, 3 vols., trans. Jean de Sevres (Geneva, 1578), 2: 293C, 295B, 300E. In his analysis of the *Politicus*, Charles Howard McIlwain points out that the law is theoretically secondary to political wisdom in that it is only an imitation of the wisdom of a perfect ruler; actually it is superior to the will of any particular ruler who will, inevitably, lack wisdom from time to time; Charles Howard McIlwain, *Constitutionalism: Ancient and Modern* (Ithaca: Cornell University Press, 1940), 31–36. For an analysis of rule by law in relation to contemporary republican theory, see Peltonen on Patrizi, who insisted that it is impossible to find "one prince whiche embraceth all vertues," and therefore is always a reliable source of justice. *Classical Humanism*, 50; quoting *A morall methode of ciuill policie*, 1576, f. 1. For Plato on tyranny, see Rebecca W. Bushnell, *Tragedies of Tyrants*, 9–19. When citing Sevres' Latin text, I have altered inflections whenever appropriate.

[29] Syr Thomas More, *A Most pleasant, fruitfull, and wittie worke, of the best state of a publique weale, and of the new Yle called Vtopia*, trans. Raphe Robinson (London, 1597); G4, G4ᵛ. More's character "Morus," an exponent of compromise rather than principle, had warned that one is not to "leaue and forsake the commonwealth; [one] must not forsake the ship in a tempest, because [one] cannot rule and keep downe the windes"; G3.

impotence of persuasion, reason, and the appeal of a just society to a people generally given to self-interest. When the art in question was imbued with a political authority and power, however, the question of its effectiveness was answered differently. A kingly art is inevitably coercive, whether or not it is constructive. The case for a government by law in *Politicus* rejects government by "kingly art" as tending to misrule and even tyranny.

The apologist in *Politicus*, named the Stranger, agrees with young Socrates that kingly art may at its best be inspired. In any case, it is expressed by bending and sometimes suspending laws made by assemblies and popular custom. Noting that the law, made in generalities, cannot respond to "differences of men and actions" (*dissimilitudines personarum . . . actionumque*; *Opera*, 2; 294A, B), the Stranger likens the monarch who is bound by the law to the captain of a ship or a physician who must pursue his profession by the book. He is fully competent only when he goes beyond the letter and "makes use of art not written rules" (*servare non scriptis sed arte*; 2; 297A). But his freedom to improvise upon the law is made doubtful by the ways in which his art is or can be fallible: it may be deficient in skill; it may respond to questionable motives. Reconsidering his images from the arts of navigation and medicine, the Stranger notes that there have been captains who have plotted to abandon their passengers in "deserted and desolate places," others who have wrecked their ships and thrown "their freight overboard," and physicians who have mistreated their patients and then gone on to demand payment (2; 297E, 298A). Thus he concludes: despite the fact that written rules are inimical to the exclusive practice of art and cannot result in a "perfectly right government" (*rectissimus gubernatio civilis*) on every occasion, to govern by them and not kingly art is the only reasonable choice (2; 297D). A monarch's rule may be superlative on occasion, but no monarch consistently "excels all others [i.e., all his subjects] in his character of mind and body" (*antecellens caeteros habitu tam corporis quam animi*; 2; 301D). He can draw on the minds and bodies of his subjects, their counsel and aid, and he should, in any case, be governed by their laws.

Plato's case for law is, however, a second best case. Law is a default from a better if impossible way of governing. The Stranger insists that the "counsel of the commonality" be written down (2; 301D, E) and that it be the law by which the state is governed. But he cautions that it will not create the perfect state. Were such a state possible, it would be the creation of that most impossible of faculties, an infallible "knowledge of affairs and intelligence":

> Can we wonder then, Socrates, at all the evils that arise and are destined to arise in such kinds of government when they are based upon such a foundation and must conduct their affairs in accordance with written laws and with custom (*scripti, mores*) and not on a knowledge of affairs and intelligence (*scientia rerum, intelligentia*)? (2; 301E)

In fact, states under law endure despite the law—a situation both evident and marvelous, as the Stranger goes on to observe:

> Ought we not rather to wonder at the stability that inheres in the state? For [lacking a perfect monarch] states so affected [i.e., with the arbitrariness of law] for long periods, disturbed by inconveniences, have nevertheless endured and have not perished.

Having expressed qualified praise for the rule of law, Plato concludes by deploring a government that knows no law. Always fatal in the end, rule by human beings who have no recourse to the traditions and customs of the past is characterized by pervasive ignorance and almost inevitable catastrophe. Mere intelligence, it would seem, is insufficient for the governance of the ship of state.

> Many [states], like ships that founder at sea, are destroyed . . . through the worthlessness of their captains and crews (*improbitas gubernatorum nautarumque*) who have the greatest ignorance of the greatest things (*ignorantia in rebus maximis*), men who have no knowledge of statesmanship (*res civilis*), but think they have in every respect most perfect knowledge of this above all other sciences. (2; 302A)

Were men—kings and their counselors—perfect in skill and judgment, truly godlike, government by their inspired art would be best. As it is, their deficiencies in this respect make it necessary to institute government by law. When the Stranger considers which of the various "not right forms of government" is "the least difficult to live with," he evitably decides on a monarchy circumscribed by law: "When bound by good written rules, which we call laws, [it] is the best" (*copulata bonis constitutionibus, quas leges vocauimus . . . optima est*); a monarchy without law is "hard and exceed-ingly oppressive" (*dura est, & . . . molestissima*; 2; 302 E).

In contrast to Plato's muted apology for legalism, Shakespeare's *Pericles* grants art a wide although not unqualified privilege, especially that art which is devoted to the health of the body politic. The relevant ques-tion to ask of the play is whether the nature and practice of that art can answer legalism's critiques. In what sense, if any, does the romance of Pericles' rule illustrate the norms of a monarchy under law and yet open to the direction of a benign kingly art? This is, presumably, the art alluded to in 1 by "Gower" which is to restore human life and, by ref-erence to its source in Gower, the body politic. It is, arguably, an *ars regia*, designed to enhance royal government and self-government. Defec-tive as exemplified by Pericles' command of his ship, where his judg-ment is overwhelmed by custom, the art of the physician (of state) appears obviously beneficial when practiced by Cerimon, who func-tions as "Gower's" double and Pericles' surrogate in reviving Thaisa.

Cerimon's art is above all the art of a man; it is limited by the ineluctable fact of death. The "Nature" on which Cerimon practices is "conversant with pain" and his first words are of the patient he cannot cure (3.2.7–9, 25). But Cerimon also believes that his "virtue and cun-ning" are godlike endowments. "Immortality" attends them even though they are constrained to respect mortality (27–30). Important, too, is how Cerimon employs his "physic," his "secret art." He is not a simple follower of his "book" and its "authorities." He relies on "prac-tice" which has made him "familiar" with the medicine in nature, "in vegetives, in metals, stones" (31–38). Perfected by experience, his art is proved on Thaisa. Unlike Pericles who cannot remedy the effects of the storm off Ephesus, Cerimon puts right the "disturbance" that "Nature" has brought about in Thaisa by producing a harmony that is both natural and a work of art (38). His cure is music, punningly understood as an "air" (93) and also "heir."[30] Air, what Thaisa needs

[30]This is the first instance of this thematically important pun which occurs in all the later romances. Cerimon's music is made by a "viol," its medicinal properties shadowed perhaps in its echo as "phial"; see Q4. For musical cures in Shakespeare generally, see F. D. Hoeniger, "Musical Cures of Melancholy and Mania in Shakespeare," in *Mirror up to Shakespeare: Essays in Honour of G. R. Hibbard*, ed. J. C. Gray (Toronto: University of Toronto Press, 1984), 55–67.

to recover consciousness, is also her daughter and the succession in the two kingdoms, Tyre and Pentapolis, in which Thaisa is both queen and a figure for the uxorial kingdom to which Pericles is married. Air as the breath of life subsumes the meaning of heir as the product of generation and what is immortal or continuously alive by virtue of generation. The heir Thaisa will live to see, Marina, embodies the materiality of the mystical body politic (the royal succession) and what Pericles later sees in her, the "modest Justice" of a mortal ruler rather than the terrible justice of Jove's thunderbolt. Defined by Cerimon's practice, illustrated by the physician's decorous use of rhetorical figures, the art that revives Thaisa is a modification of the kingly art in the *Politicus*. Informed by writ (his book) and limited by the natural law of mortality (consider the patient for whom "nothing can be minister'd to nature/That can recover him"; 3.2.8–9)—Cerimon's achievements are divine (as Pericles will later acknowledge; 5.3.61–64), but only in a metaphorical sense.

The complex physic that restores vitality to the living but is circumscribed by death is emblematized in Diana, the deity Thaisa chose to worship when she decided to remain in Ephesus. Diana, the goddess of chastity, has a second aspect in Lucina, the deity presiding over childbirth. The prominence of Diana here and at the final reunion of Thaisa and Pericles testifies to the link between chastity and fecundity in the work of generation when it is free from associations with an incestuous and anarchic sexuality. This link is represented again by Marina's defense of her virginity while in the brothel at Mytilene and in her willingness to marry when a suitable match can be made—a defense that also cures the promiscuity of the brothel's patrons. Its more important effect is to free Marina to practice an art that will eventually lead to the restoration of her father and the body politic.

The Art of the Heir

Marina is prostituted by several agents: Boult, who buys her from pirates (4.2); who have seized her from Dionyza's henchman, Leonine; who has obeyed Dionyza, Queen of Tharsus (4.1); who is supposed (by Pericles) to have provided for Marina out of gratitude for his earlier gift of grain (3.3). Of these agents, the most egregiously in error is, arguably, the prince of Tyre. His tenuous attachment to Marina, evident over a period of many years, is the inverse of Antiochus's complete domination of his Daughter.

Pericles' decision to leave Marina in Tharsus has plausibility at first: Tyre's is a "litigious peace" and her presence there would be precarious. But Tyre's unrest is also Pericles' responsibility. Prolonging his exile, leaving his kingdom without a head of state, he remained in Tharsus a year. His vow at parting, that he will not cut his hair from his head before Marina is married (or, in the language of song, his heir from his thoughts), suggests a kind of dementia that not even the ethos of romance can fully account for. (It makes a spectacular showing in the last act of the play.) Marina remains in Tharsus for her entire childhood, a situation that had some precedent in noble families when it was limited to adolescence. As a feature typical of romance, the abandonment of a child is usually an act of fortune; in *Pericles*, however, it is a consequence of Pericles' misplaced confidence in professions of hospitality in Tharsus, and also of the silence of Cleon's subjects who, like the subjects of Antiochus, are bound by the monarchy's secrets. The "common body" that Cleon stated would guarantee Marina's security never knows of Dionyza's plot. Leonine, who is commanded to carry it out, is silent about the outcome (Marina's abduction by pirates) and is himself silenced by Dionyza's poison. In the political logic of the play, it makes perfect sense that Marina's speech in Mytilene to its various subjects, and most of all to Pericles, redeems these misfortunes and misjudgments. She prevails by the several facets of her art: her words convert her would-be clients, and her womanly skills, fetching a price in the markets of Mytilene, satisfy the economy of its brothel. Her "sacred physic" (5.1.74)—her song, both music and speech—later cures Pericles.

The attempted prostitution of Marina in Mytilene recalls the royal incest at Antioch by inversion. There a princess was appropriated by her father. Here a princess is up for sale; she is an item to be had for a price. The parallelism marks the similarity as well as the difference between the *oikonomia* of the ancient household and the economy of the modern market. The condition of both is predicated on scarcity, but it is more acutely represented by the specificity of market exchange. Pander complains that he and his cohorts "have lost too much money this mart by being too wenchless"; and when Bawd observes that their "creatures" are "with continual action . . . even as good as rotten," he replies that what they need is a woman they can sell dearly: "Our credit comes not in like the commodity. . . . If in our youths we could pick up some pretty estate, 'twere not amiss to keep our door hatched" (4.2.4–5; 8–9; 28–31). Had they been able to secure an estate in youth, they would not now be in trade. As it is, Pander's intention is clearly to ruin estates, both in the sense of land and of rank. Marina's resolve to "keep her virgin knot untied" (4.2.146) is made practically effective not because she gets protection from the positive laws of Mytilene and not only because her speech, invoking divine and natural law, is powerfully convincing. She remains a virgin because her art responds to material needs that support the market economy in which she must participate.

To each of her adversaries, she speaks a different language. The style of her "divine preaching" correlates with Jacobean notions of rank and class, with office and work. Her "gentlemen" suitors espouse virtue immediately: "I'll do anything now that is virtuous, but I am out of the road of rutting forever" (4.5.8–9). The governor of Mytilene, Lysimachus, moved by Marina's appeal to his honor ("if you were born to honor, show it now" [4.6.91]), instantly reforms his "corrupted mind" and condemns the "house" he has just entered: "Your house, but for this virgin that doth prop it,/Would sink and overwhelm you. Away" (4.6.119–20), he tells the pimps. But neither he nor Marina forget the market. When Lysimachus offers Marina gold, not once but twice, she does not and, indeed, cannot refuse it (113). Her preaching has to be gainful as well as self-defensive. Lysimachus's gold will go to Pander and Bawd for her keep, and her status as a property will never be more than mitigated by the decorum of courtship: Lysimachus will not think of marrying her until he is sure she is of "gentle kind and noble stock" (5.1.67–69).

The brothel-keepers are similarly implicated in processes of exchange. Boult, whose arguments on the limits of virtue are the most pointed, cannot easily renounce bawdry; it is what he sells to keep alive. Marina's words to him need to be qualified by material factors that allow for no more than a modest shift in practice. Boult tells Marina that he cannot leave his pimping: "What would you have me do, go to the wars, would you? where a man may serve seven years for the loss of a leg, and have not money enough in the end to buy him a wooden one?" (4.6.169–72). Marina tells Boult that he could "do anything"—"Empty/Old receptacles, or common shores, of filth;/Serve by indenture to the common hangman" (4.6.173–75), but these alternatives merely emphasize why he might choose to remain Pander's doorkeeper. Marina only succeeds in getting Boult to open the doors of other (lawful) "houses" to her practice of a licit trade. She too engages in commerce, although of a benign kind. Having demonstrated her art, she now sells it as a valuable commodity and uses her gain to buy her livelihood (she continues to give money to the brothel-keepers). Even the most refined of her practices, "the sacred physic" that heals Pericles, is paid for by Lysimachus (5.1.73–74); in this sense, her "feat" is aptly named "prosperous and artificial" (72).

Marina's art, dedicated to the inculcation of virtue and the observation of a divine and natural law, has no persuasive or moving force outside real and material settings. Her practice suggests that an art of government—of the self or society—is never independent of an economy. While its materialism cannot be understood as dismissing the value of gifts, it does suggest that items exchanged are always susceptible to pricing. The brothel scenes elaborate the economics of work exemplified by the fishermen of Pentapolis; the economy of the state and the body politic is naturally and pervasively one of scarcity. Pericles' earlier gift of grain to the Tharsians, so brutally recompensed by Dionyza's treachery,[31] is further perspectivized when Helicanus, negotiating as surrogate for a demented Pericles aboard a Tyrian ship, buys grain from Lysimachus at Mytilene. Their deal is both a "courtesy" and an exchange of commensurables (5.1.54–55).

But despite Marina's traffic in goods, her art proves to be the most valuable of the play, a "sacred physic" of state that restores Pericles to his senses. Its scope is universal and revealed by a cosmic harmony. Like the therapeutic song of "Gower" and the two kinds of "airs" of Cerimon, Marina's music acts upon a body that is identified as a member of a body politic. The song she sings to Pericles, still Prince of Tyre despite

---

[31] This is the only benefit that remains unmatched or is betrayed by treachery in the romances. In general, benefits are subsumed in acts of kindness and between kin; they are elements in the larger pattern of human exchange where they have a privilege all their own.

his obvious pathology, draws from him the first sound he makes since learning of her death (5.1.8), and begins to impose its measures on the "tempest" that has been tearing apart "his mortal vessel" (4.4.29). The figure of music as "air" and its homonym "heir" makes Marina's art an image signifying generation and therefore the rectification of incest. In political terms it subsumes the principal elements of the plot which has organized the action of the play to this point. It evokes the figure of a rule that is harmonious by being historical as well as transhistorical. Temporally incarnate in one ruler, preserved dynastically by divine right, it also comprehends the continuous vitality of the body politic. Her song is also speech, a speech that breaks the silence of the subject about her misfortune (and, to the extent that Pericles has failed to rule, her abuse) and can thus inform and counsel. It proceeds by enigma, like the riddling discourse that began the play.

Presented with puzzles of identity, with a sameness that is also a difference, Pericles begins to understand himself. Marina's claims to "equal grief" and "equivalent derivation" call into question what appear to be the most stable of distinctions between nation or race, and rank or class (5.1.88, 90–91). She appears to be of Mytilene and lives by her work; he is of Tyre and lives by and for his subjects. She describes herself as "bound in servitude" (96), a condition that in a classical sense applies to Pericles as an officeholder. The similarity Pericles sees between Marina and what he remembers of Thaisa also registers the apparent difference between this likeness, which he considers lost to him, and the young physician who is to cure him. His "woe" transforms his masculine spirit into one that labors to deliver grief to the world, to sever its burden from his consciousness (105–6). The experience of her speech is of a food that starves (112–13); its nourishment of perception creates a hunger for understanding. As art, its effect is to engage sensuous and intellectual pleasures, faculties that both feel and know. When Pericles tells Marina that "I will make my senses credit thy relation" (123) his reference is double: his five senses will make him believe that she is kin; and his good sense will make him authorize her story.

By recognizing that Marina is his daughter and like but not in fact her mother, Pericles replicates the goodwill of his own father-in-law, Simonides. Before the play is over, he will marry Marina to Lysimachus (and cut the hair from his head). More important, this recognition metaphorically brings him back to the only life he can experience, which is as a mortal. Marina "begets" him who did "beget" her—an enigma whose augmented meaning depends on distinguishing a rebirth of the mind and spirit from physical reproduction. The effects of her art are more profound than those of Cerimon, who took Thaisa from her coma, in that they induce a conscientiousness beyond mere consciousness. In Pericles, Marina's words evoke the sensation of a "Most heavenly music"—perhaps to signal that the natural law of generation is manifest analogically in the measures or times of the cosmos.[32] Certainly the "crowned Truth" that Marina has exemplified is of generation: the fact that kinship is a temporal event and that the sameness inherent in dynastic continuity is also a difference between parent and child. She is therefore also a figure of the divine law of mortality that applies to monarch and subject. In that sense, her maternity speaks to the sonship and brotherhood of all human beings. It recalls the most ambiguous of the relations described by the Antiochan riddle: the daughter as her father's mother. In its original formulation, the figure would seem to allude to the tyrannical patriarch's condition as anarchic infant. Here it speaks to the condition of the subject under the natural law of generation, a law that by specifying the human condition as mortal and not divine would equalize monarch and subject in a fraternal relation, each "brother" also a "son" of a commonwealth and under her law.[33]

Marina also has an emblematic character: she is a "modest Justice" and "Patience" (121, 138), figurations that recall Lychorida's advice to Pericles during the storm in which Thaisa "dies" ("Patience, good sir, do not assist the storm;" "Patience, good sir, even for this charge"

[32]It is possible that Marina's music was also intended to refer to positive law. Cf. Richard Hooker, speaking "not only of the law of nature and of God, but very nationall or municipall law consonant thereunto. Happier that people whose lawe is their King in the greatest thinges, than that whose King is himself their lawe. Where the King doth guide the state, and the lawe the King, that commonwealth is like an harpe or melodious instrument, the stringes wherof are tuned and handled all by one hand, following as lawes the rules and canons of Musicall science." The Laws of Ecclesiastical Polity, the eighth book, 3.3, in The Works of Richard Hooker, ed. W. Speed Hill, 6 vols. (Cambridge: Harvard University Press, 1981), 3: 341–42.

[33]De Mornay speaks of subjects as brothers of the king: "Subditos non esse regis servos, sed fratres," Stephen Junio Bruto Celta [Philippe de Mornay], Vindiciae contra tyrannos sive de principis in populum populique in Principem, legitima potestate (Amsterdam, 1610), 121.

[3.1.19, 26]). She is an image of the Patience that is forced on Pericles during the long interval between the loss and recovery of his kin. And she embodies the modest Justice that such suffering necessarily creates, a justice that holds back from extremes, is equitable in its interpretation of writ, and that is open to merciful interventions. An emblem of these virtues, she performs the "prosperous and artificial feats" that cure the prince and the body politic.

The action of the play ends in a scene that represents discrete and legitimate relations between Pericles, his wife and his daughter. Unlike relations at Antioch, they no longer imply and presume the monarch's divinity. Established by speech, they defy the silence necessary to preserve the monarch's secrets. Prompted by Diana in a vision, Pericles is told to "reveal" his "crosses" [i.e., the story of his trials] and "give them repetition to the life" (5.1.243–44). Voices are everywhere at Ephesus. Thaisa hears Pericles' "voice"; he recognizes her "voice" (5.3.13, 34), and their stories are mutually credited. Embracing Thaisa, Pericles acknowledges that she is not reborn but rather has never died: the "burial" she has in his arms is the second he knows of, neither literally true (44–45). His language plays with death and rebirth as metaphor, with Cerimon as a "mortal officer" who is "like a god" in what he can do. These figures do not delude. They describe the elements of a history that ends in the physical separation of parents and children and thus also looks forward to their future dynastic integrity. Pericles does not return to Tyre (as Apollonius does in Twine's *Patterne of Painefull Adventures*), a feature of plot that qualifies the sense of a return typical of romance. His place in Tyre is taken by Marina, as he takes the place of Simonides, his father-in-law, at Pentapolis. The tyrannical states, which remain outside the empire established by his dynasty—Antioch and Tharsus—are scenes of tyrannicide, whether by divine intervention (the heavenly fire that consumes Antiochus), or popular insurrection (the subjects who burns the palace of Cleon and Dionyza). The course of history is not without its divinities, but they are never to be confused with their human agents or factors.

CHAPTER 3

Cymbeline

S HAKESPEARE COMBINED "MATTER" FROM TWO QUITE DIFFERENT GENRES
to create *Cymbeline*: fragments from Holinshed's chronicle histories
of England and Scotland; and Boccaccio's wager story in his tale of the
merchants, Bernabo and Ambrogiuolo, as revised in the anonymous
Frederyke of Jennen. As an account of a historical moment, *Cymbeline*
dramatizes the conflict between the British king, Cymbeline, and his
lord, Augustus Caesar, the Emperor of Rome, over the payment of tribute money. As a tale of merchant intrigue, the play represents com-
peting notions of fidelity in marriage. Because a party to this dispute is
a princess and heir to the British throne, Imogen (Cymbeline's daughter), the wager story touches on dynastic issues and is linked to the history of Britain. The conflict over tribute engages questions of empire.
At the play's conclusion, Britain remains a vassal state of Rome, but she
retains the fundamental liberties she would have were she independent
of Rome. Elements of romance—the reuniting of lovers, the return
of lost children—cohere in a final prospect of a westering empire that
will gather together its people, British and Roman, in generative unions
rather than by violent conquest.

The "matters" of both chronicle and story refer to contemporary
ideas of contract. Imogen's marriage to Posthumus and Cymbeline's

tribute to Augustus Caesar are guaranteed by verbal agreements; they remain valid through time and independent of the circumstances in which they were first made. The words of betrothal joining Imogen and Posthumus, and the words of Cassibelan (Cymbeline's predecessor) agreeing to an annual tax ensure the continuity of mutual dependencies. The factor that makes these words have the power to bind parties together—conscience—is also the factor that guarantees to each party a kind of freedom. The idea of contract that was shadowed in images of the monarch's body politic in *Pericles* is registered in relations between husband and wife, and lord and vassal in *Cymbeline*.

Threats to mutuality derive from abuses that, like incest and tyranny, jeopardize or deny the standing of subordinates. Like Pericles, Cymbeline is frightened by a tyrant—in this case, his wife, the Queen, who is his children's stepmother.[1] Her power is unauthorized and therefore unaccountable, but in effect she governs Britain. The nature of her unofficial rule is manifest in her desire to make her son, Cloten, Imogen's consort. Her plans to bring about an incestuous marriage defy Imogen's own wish to marry not only outside the family but a man whose ancestry is obscure. By the end of the play, however, the dynastic future of Britain will have been guaranteed twice over, first by the death of Cloten and the recognition of Imogen's marriage to Posthumus; and also by the discovery of Cymbeline's male heirs, Imogen's brothers, Guiderius and Arviragus, who have been lost and are thought dead. This conclusion succeeds in fusing otherwise discrete narrative elements: Imogen, the heroine of the wager story and the exponent of spousal fidelity, is displaced from the succession by the heroes of chronicle, Guiderius and Arviragus, who exemplify the instinctive or artless courage conventionally attributed to those who were thought to be natural rulers.

The art of government that was so prominent a topic in *Pericles* is demonstrated by characters who hold subordinate office: Cornelius, the

---

[1] For the effeminate character of stage tyrants, see Rebecca W. Bushnell, *Tragedies of Tyrants: Political Thought and Theater in the English Renaissance* (Ithaca: Cornell University Press, 1990), 63–69. Cymbeline's Queen has been associated with tyrannical women rulers by several critics. David M. Bergeron argues for Tacitus's Livia as a model: David M. Bergeron, "*Cymbeline*: Shakespeare's Last Roman Play," *Shakespeare Quarterly* 31, 1 (1980): 31–41. Patricia Parker discusses parallels with Amata: "Romance and Empire: Anachronistic Cymbeline," in *Unfolded Tales: Essays on Renaissance Romance*, ed. George H. Logan and Gordon Teskey (Ithaca: Cornell University Press, 1989), 189–207.

court physician, and Pisanio, Posthumus's servant. Cymbeline himself, dominated by the Queen, is witless for most of the play. The British body politic is therefore figuratively without a head and, in the imagery of plot, no more than a trunk. The state regains its head when Cymbeline begins to rule on his own as the action concludes in 5. His state (of mind), although precarious, appears to be guaranteed by surrogates, his children, and the prospect of their legitimate succession. Subordinates, especially Pisanio, act to restore competent government although they lack the confidence of Cerimon and the grace of Marina. Both physician and servant are in danger of the Queen's power and protest her tyranny in asides in the opening scenes of the play. They resort to deception in order to be faithful to what they see as a more imposing truth. Neither, however, manages to control the consequences of their trickery. The devices they put into play have effects they cannot know and in this sense they work in the dark. Belarius is a special case. Once a trusted courtier but an outlaw for the time of the play, his mode of operation, which fuses the resources of art with the disciplines of nature, is more obviously under divine direction. Unlike the deities in *Pericles* whose roles are limited, *Cymbeline*'s Jupiter is a *deus ex machina* who directs the action of the play in a manner that conforms to Christian conceptions of salvation history.

In general, characters choose courses of action that end in unexpected ways. They are mistaken in what they assume and misguided in what they do. A confusion of purpose and motive is especially apparent in Cymbeline, whose errors are not altogether the result of senility or his queen's malicious manipulation of evidence. The practice of government (and self-government) is enigmatic, perhaps inherently so, because it often engages incompatible loyalties. Describing his relations with the Queen after her death, he depicts his role as a faithful husband as at odds with his obligations as a father. As a husband, "it had been vicious to have mistrusted her," his wife; yet as a father, "it was folly" not to have studied her actions and so detected their treacherous intentions toward his daughter, an obvious target for her stepmother's envy. Voicing this dilemma (quite after the fact), he calls for divine intervention: "The Heavens mend all."[2] Were this the only instance of such

[2]William Shakespeare, *Cymbeline*, ed. J. M. Nosworthy (New York: Routledge, 1991), 5.5.65–68.

an invocation it might stand as an index of Cymbeline's continued incapacity. But the play's most resourceful character, Pisanio, resigns himself to providence when, having no news of either master or mistress, he does not know how to act or advise others to act: "The heavens must work," he insists (4.3.41). And, more important, it is the divine will that allows the British a victory over their Roman invaders. Outnumbered and fearful, the British are rallied and Cymbeline is rescued improbably by four "peasants" of whom one, Posthumus (in disguise), states that had "the heavens" not fought, "all [had been] lost" (5.3.3–4).

Chronology and chronicle provide the drama of Cymbeline's return to rule with a thematics of providence. Histories of ancient Britain represented his reign as coinciding with the rule of Augustus Caesar, a time of universal peace and the birth of Christ, when all the world was to be taxed. Mankind was then to live under a new dispensation. The action depicted in *Cymbeline* celebrates events that were supposed to have occurred at a time when a Christian idea of divine justice and love was not yet understood but rather about to revealed.[3] This crisis inevitably affects how human agency is portrayed. What is identified as divine is not some supernatural agent that defies natural law or makes positive law irrelevant, but the voice of the individual conscience speaking words that have meaning, and arguably new meaning because of the historical moment in which they are spoken, the moment of the incarnation of the Word in the reigns of Cymbeline and Augustus Caesar.

This sacred event, implied throughout *Cymbeline*'s dramatization of its historical matter, affects the play's representation of rule and especially of the ruler's supposed divinity. Ideas of earthly government are treated in light of the Augustinian distinction between the politics of man and that of God. A sense of "time when" informs all moments

[3]For this chronology, see Edmund Spenser's *The Faerie Queene*, 2.5. See also Raphael Holinshed, *Chronicles of England, Scotland, and Ireland*, 6 vols. (London, 1802), 1: 478–79; Geoffrey of Monmouth, *De origine et Gestis Brittanorum* (Paris, 1508), Book 1, Chapter 26; quoted in Robin Moffet, "*Cymbeline* and the Nativity," *Shakespeare Quarterly* 13, 2 (1962): 206–18; and John Stow, *The Chronicles of England* (London, 1580), 35; quoted in Lila Geller, "*Cymbeline* and the Imagery of Covenant Theology," *Studies in English Literature* 20 (1980): 241–55. See also Patricia Parker, "Romance and Empire." For a study of the romances as vehicles for eschatological concerns, see Cynthia Marshall, *Last Things and Last Plays: Shakespearean Eschatology* (Carbondale: Southern Illinois University Press, 1991).

in which government is at issue. In the "time" represented as the time of the action in the play, imperial rule is vested in the Roman Augustus Caesar, the first of a succession of emperors to claim that he was a god; monarchic rule is illustrated by the tyranny of the Queen seconded by Cymbeline—a rule above positive law. Both emperor and king govern in the expected light of a different order of government about to be instituted by the birth of Christ, a "Caesar" whose rule, being eternal, would in some sense abrogate the rights of emperors and, more generally, call into question justifications of imperialist conquest. In the "time" understood as the time of the play's production (conveyed by the Italian setting of the wager), the image of the ruler as godlike was recognizably contemporary, a feature of Stuart self-representation. Shakespeare's contemporaries knew that the imperial government of Rome was to be identified with the earthly city, Augustine's image of all things subject to decay and death. The spiritual government of the faithful and invisible church was, by contrast, an emblem of the truth of history which was eternal and itself a world without end. The difference between the two governments of heaven and earth invariably raised the question of obedience. From St. Paul, in his famous thirteenth chapter of Romans, to such reformers as Luther, Calvin, and the English Protestants and Catholics debating monarchic rule, writers generally agreed that a subject was to obey divine law before any kind of positive law. But what divine law covered or how a refusal to obey positive law might be expressed was unclear. In *Cymbeline*, this uncertainty is most prominently registered by Britain's relation to Rome.

When Shakespeare's Cymbeline at last agrees to pay Augustus Caesar's tax, his action has already been complicated by associations that establish a basis for guaranteeing the very thing tribute money might appear to deny—the liberties of the subject. Cymbeline's gesture of deference to the emperor is loaded with paradox: Cymbeline, a king, is shown to be in a subject role; he, a victor in a battle with the emperor, submits to an imperial order. He is also prospectively an "emperor" in the west: in the prophetic vision announced at the end of the play, his domain supersedes Rome's. Finally, he also represents a king of Britain in a play produced in a moment in history when the actual King of England and Scotland, nominally Britain, was regularly identified as a latter day "Caesar," a proponent of a *pax Britannica*, and the head of a new empire to take the place of Rome as Rome had taken the place of Troy.[4] Cymbeline himself is an antagonistic double: as Cymbeline, he is a subject who pays a tax, and as prospectively a "Caesar," he is the emperor who collects it. The means by which these aspects of his character are fused and resolved, and the terms by which the actual characters of king and emperor become allies at the end of the play, illustrate a mutuality between the monarch as tribute-taker, and the subject as tribute-giver. A harmony of interests is brought about less by a contract between parties than by what makes contracts binding: the faculty of conscience. At the moment in time the play represents, conscience is being created in the sense that Christians were to understand it in doctrine, that is, as intrinsically free of any political obligation.

The Marriage Contract

The play's opening scene conveys the most important feature of a contract: its status as a promise and therefore as a matter of conscience. At immediate issue is Imogen's betrothal. As the gentlemen who know court gossip reveal, Cymbeline's courtiers resent his decision not to honor this betrothal, to imprison Imogen, and to exile Posthumus (1.1.1–3). The king's promotion of Cloten as Imogen's prospective consort is clearly incestuous; her situation, were it to be determined by the wishes of Cymbeline and the Queen, would resemble that of the Daughter in *Pericles*. Although Posthumus is the foster son of Cymbeline, who "breeds" him after he is orphaned (1.1.42), his marriage to Imogen violates no natural law.[5] It is further justified by perceptions of

[4]Much of the iconography represented in James's coronation procession reflected the imperial theme of his monarchy. See especially Graham Parry, *The Golden Age Restor'd: The Culture of the Stuart Court, 1603–42* (New York: St. Martin's Press, 1981), and Jonathan Goldberg, *James I and the Politics of Literature: Jonson, Shakespeare, Donne, and Their Contemporaries* (Baltimore: Johns Hopkins University Press, 1983). See also David M. Bergeron, *English Civic Pageantry, 1558–1642* (Columbia: University of South Carolina Press, 1971). For particular references to *Cymbeline*, see J. P. Brockbank, "History and Histrionics in *Cymbeline*," *Shakespeare Survey* 11 (1958): 42–49; and Glynne Wickham, "Riddle and Emblem: A Study in the Dramatic Structure of *Cymbeline*," in *English Renaissance Studies Presented to Dame Helen Gardner*, ed. John Casey (Oxford: Clarendon Press, 1980), 94–113.

[5]Cloten's wish to marry Imogen as a way of getting rich recalls the connection between incest and greed in *Pericles*, 1.1. For a study of Posthumus's character and identity in light

worth made mysterious by allusions to kingship and dynasty. The courtiers celebrate Imogen's "election" of Posthumus as a response to his "virtue"—"the regions of the earth" do not have his "like" (20–21, 53–54)—which is furthermore signified by his ancestry that cannot be "delve[d] to the root" (28) but is identifiably royal: his father is Leonatus and he is Posthumus Leonatus, one of the "lion's whelp." In scriptural prophecy *leonatus* is identified with Judah, the progenitor of the house of David: "The sceptre shal not depart from Iudah ... and the people shal be gathred vnto him" (Genesis 49.10). By being displaced from the succession by Cymbeline's sons at the end of the play, Posthumus will be seen merely to have figured what they will actually ensure: a proper dynastic succession. But his character as a metaphor of monarchy is respected throughout the action of the play.[6] It is matched by Imogen's character as the "Arabian bird," the chaste Phoenix who is perpetually reborn. It is also, like the character of Cymbeline, double and self-reflexive. Just as Cymbeline is both king and subject, so Posthumus is *leonatus* and *postnatus* or the Scottish subject born after the accession of James, who, in the time of the play's production, is about to be integrated into the English body politic.

But illicit as Cloten's suit may be, promoted as it is by the Queen in defiance of natural law, Imogen's marriage to Posthumus is not valid in all respects. It was evidently not celebrated in a public ceremony, *per verba de praesenti*, that is, witnessed by family and friends as expected of a woman of property, and preceded by a written contract determining

of a psychoanalytic view of family relations, see Meredith Skura, "Interpreting Posthumus's Dream from Above and Below: Families, Psychoanalysts, and Literary Critics," in *Representing Shakespeare*, ed. Murray Schwartz and Coppélia Kahn (Baltimore: Johns Hopkins University Press, 1980), 203–16.

[6]In addition to being the "lion's whelp," Posthumus is also an "eagle" (1.2.70). Posthumus's lineage is ambiguously established by allusions to different mythical pasts. Frances Yates, citing Geoffrey of Monmouth's *History of the Kings of Britain* who states that Imogen is the wife of Brut whose heraldic animal is a lion and whose mother died in childbirth, declares that Posthumus Leonatus is a figure of the Trojan Brutus; Frances Yates, *Shakespeare's Last Plays: A New Approach* (London: Routledge & Kegan Paul, 1975), 49–50. See also David Bergeron, who states that Posthumus is "the most Roman of the British characters"; "Cymbeline," 36. Leah Marcus assumes that Posthumus as a figure of the Scottish *postnati*; Leah Marcus, *Puzzling Shakespeare: Local Reading and Its Discontents* (Berkeley: University of California Press, 1988), 106–46. This identification is confirmed by Posthumus's character as a "lion's whelp" and therefore (in the imagery of Scripture) a "Judah" who, in contemporary treatises on the Union, signifies the Scottish inheritance of the English throne by James VI and I.

dowry and dower or jointure. Rather, it was a clandestine marriage marked only by a verbal agreement to be married, *per verba de futuro*. Typically, this was a procedure chosen by persons who either had little property or wished to defy parental wishes. Clandestine marriages were not legally binding before consummation; in effect, the fact of consummation in a clandestine marriage served the same function as the act of agreeing to marriage before witnesses in a public marriage.[7] Exiled in Rome, Posthumus insists that Imogen is a virgin (2.4.161–62) and so reveals that she is not unequivocally his wife. This was presumably known at court—it gives the Queen's encouragement of Cloten's suit a certain standing. Despite its provisional status, however, the marriage of Imogen and Posthumus is indissoluble in their eyes. *Verba de futuro* signified not only a promise to marry (i.e., to consummate the union), but also to accept the obligations of a married couple. As I have suggested, the association of moral factors in cases of contract, and especially in verbal contracts not substantiated by writ, is made notably powerful by the play's reference to sacred history—the Word of God.

In English legal practice, contracts of all kinds had been considered to have a conscientious dimension for centuries. In 1602, conscience became an explicit issue with respect to a kind of contract that relied on the spoken word for its power to enforce behavior. Such contracts were verbal in contrast to written, and entered into without legally recognized witnesses. They were inherently weak and susceptible to challenge. But as Sir Edward Coke reported, the decision in Slade's case, an action for debt that depended on a verbal contract, made their promissory force decisive. Coke's reasoning underscored the power of the spoken word that—even when unwitnessed or undocumented— had legal authority.

Actions for debt were usually based on a writ or on a verbal agreement for which witnesses could be produced. When a verbal agreement

---

[7]For details on marriage law, see Lawrence Stone, *Road to Divorce: England, 1530–1987* (Oxford: Oxford University Press, 1990), esp. 51–58; see also his *The Family, Sex, and Marriage in England, 1500–1800* (New York: Harper and Row, 1977), esp. 30–37. On the play's representation of sexuality in general and some aspects of the marriage contract in particular, see David M. Bergeron, "Sexuality in *Cymbeline*," *Essays in Literature* 10, 2 (1983): 159–68. See also Ann Thompson, "Person and Office: The Case of Imogen, Princess of Britain," in *Literature and Nationalism*, ed. Vincent Newey and Ann Thompson (Liverpool: Liverpool University Press, 1991), 76–87.

had been made in the absence of witnesses, the defendant typically resorted to a procedure, known as an "action of debt," that allowed for a trial by "wager of law." In such a trial, the defendant would summon a number of oath-takers who would swear not to the facts of the case, but that the defendant's claim that he owed nothing to the plaintiff was good; they would swear either that he had paid the plaintiff or that no contract existed. The problem with this procedure is obvious: the word of an oath-taker could be bought. To remedy this abuse, Coke focused on the salient feature of contracts entered into without writ or witnesses, namely that their legal remedies were open to perjury. He stipulated that a plaintiff in a case involving a verbal contract, a spoken word, could resort to another kind of procedure than "wager of law." He could bring an "action upon *assumpsit*." In these cases the thing assumed referred to the thoughts and intentions of the parties to the contract. Their contract, although not substantiated by evidence in the ordinary way, was nonetheless considered to be valid because it had a place in conscience. "*Assumpsit*" prohibited the defendant from relying on testimony of oath-takers and required that he submit to an investigation of evidence to determine what would have been clear if the contract in question had been documented or witnessed. To assess the meaning of a contract in light of conscience meant, paradoxically, that the consciences of parties to that contract were to be made the subject of scrutiny. As Coke noted, this change in procedure was necessary because the "wager of law" could no longer protect the interests of the plaintiff (assuming it ever had): "experience proves that mens consciences grow so large that the respect of their private advantage rather induces men (and chiefly those who have declining estates) to perjury."[8] In effect, Coke made a verbal agreement to perform an action the equivalent of a promise to perform an

---

[8]Sir Edward Coke, Slade's Case, in *Reports*, 7 vols. (London, 1776–1777), the fourth part, vol. 2, f. 95. For a history of contract law, see A. B. W. Simpson, *A History of the Common Law of Contract: The Rise of the Action of Assumpsit* (Oxford: Clarendon Press, 1975), esp. for "wager of law," 137–40, and for Slade's case, 295–99. See also Theodore F. T. Plucknett, *A Concise History of the Common Law*, 5th edition (Boston: Little Brown and Company, 1956), esp. 647–48 on actions for debt. For a study of the verbal contract as a literary trope, see J. Douglas Canfield, *Word as Bond in English Literature from the Middle Ages to the Restoration* (Philadelphia: University of Pennsylvania Press, 1989). For the representation of contractual and performative language in the romances, see Maurice Hunt, *Shakespeare's Romance of the Word* (Lewisburg: Bucknell University Press, 1990).

action: "every contract executory imports itself an *assumpsit*, for when one agrees to pay money or to deliver anything, thereby he assumes or promises to pay, or deliver it" (the fourth report, f. 94). Whereas the "wager of law" had demonstrated how fragile was the moral force behind taking an oath, *assumpsit* made a verbal contract legally binding by transforming it into a matter of conscience.

Assumpsit was no more than a second best solution (like a government by laws rather than by "kingly art"). Coke (like Plato) would have preferred a society more open to ideals. Remarking generally on the moral decay of the times, he stated: "I am surprised that in these days so little consideration is made of an oath, as I daily observe, *Cum jurare per Deum actus religionis sit* [for to swear by God is an act of religion, i.e., of faith]" (f. 95ᵛ). Coke's belief that an interest in private gain rather than in public justice determined the course of the law made a virtue of skeptical inquiry.

Conscience is a factor in decisions made by many of the characters in *Cymbeline*, none of whom are as affected by their outcomes as Posthumus and Imogen when they respond to the promises made at their betrothal. These include a promise to keep faith, not only by not being unfaithful but also by not losing faith in the other's fidelity. The couple sharply differ in their understanding of these promises. Neither is adulterous. But while Imogen does not doubt Posthumus's fidelity, Posthumus does doubt hers. The terms defining his doubt suggest mercantile relations—what they lack is any reference to conscience. It is no accident that they are initially "Italian" terms and associated with the mentality of the merchant, the money lender, and the trader in currency bought and sold on foreign exchanges, activities prone to actions for debt.[9]

Iachimo is all calculation: to him, Posthumus appears to be "of crescent note," like a bill of exchange that increases in value as its term nears expiration. His "endowments" can be "tabled" in a "catalogue"; at the same time, he is subject to devaluation; his "weight" by marriage, relying on a "word" not "matter," is hypothetical (1.5.1–15). Iachimo's view of women is comparably objectifying: they are all for sale. Upon

[9]For a subtle interpretation of the complexities of the market in nubile women as it is represented in literature, see Lorna Hutson, *The Usurer's Daughter: Male Friendship and Fictions of Women in Sixteenth-Century England* (New York: Routledge, 1994).

his arrival in Rome, Posthumus exhibits a different mentality, suggesting a nobleman's largesse: he expects to be his friend Philario's "debtor" for "courtesies." Philario responds in the same vein by stating that his "poor kindness" is "o'errated" (34–36).[10] Speaking of his marriage while still in Britain, Posthumus used a similar language expressing value; he had declared Imogen's "loss" to herself and therefore his gain as "infinite" (1.2.51). The language of incommensurability here is intended to convey how inadequately any reference to measure can comprehend value; it implies a distinction between a price that is calculable and a worth that is beyond calculation. Why Posthumus does not continue to use this language is partly anticipated by the gifts he and Imogen have exchanged in Britain. Hers to him is a diamond ring, a token of their betrothal that she sees as without any term or condition as long as she is alive (1.2.42–45); his to her is a bracelet, a "manacle of love," which is to signify the same thing but looks rather like a device to secure property (1.2.53). Once in Rome, Posthumus is easy prey for Iachimo who tempts him from his faith by language that prices Imogen's diamond and, by association, her fidelity. Posthumus replies that she, a "gift of the gods," cannot be priced, but the little "religion" that holds him back for a moment soon gives way before an urge to equate Imogen and her virtue with a sum of money (1.5.67–73; 79–82, 133–34). The fact that his wager is for a considerable sum does not obscure the lack of faith and bad conscience that has motivated it. His wager has removed his wife from an inner world of feeling and faith and placed her in a market of items and objects. Once at stake, Imogen becomes an object of calculation, not only priced but also theoretically subject to market fluctuations.

At this point Posthumus's situation becomes contradictory. Seeking to prove he is not a cuckold, he allows himself to become indebted to Iachimo for attesting to his status as an honorable husband. Iachimo, in turn, poses as a witness who will provide relevant

[10]Their relations are similar to those Pericles expects when he gives grain to Cleon, who betrays his host's trust (4.Ch.). Here Posthumus allows himself to be betrayed. In *The Winter's Tale*, Leontes, afflicted with suspicion, will see himself as betrayed when in fact he is not (1.2). In all these cases, Shakespeare is dramatizing the conflict between economies of gift on the one hand, and of the market on the other. Each sponsors a form of exchange but the mode in which the exchange is carried out differs.

evidence. Because he will not be questioned by a jury, he actually functions as an oath-taker—a function that, as Coke noted, was highly susceptible to perjury. In the case at hand, Iachimo's self-interest is obvious: he is also a party to a second contract, the wager he makes with Posthumus (in effect, charging him with being a cuckold). This contract effectively breaks the terms of Posthumus's earlier contract of betrothal with its promise of spousal trust and fidelity. The language of the second contract is explicit: Iachimo and Posthumus make a "covenant," a "match," a "bargain," a "wager"; they draw up "articles" set down by "lawful counsel" (1.5.140–66). Posthumus elects to defend himself from the threat of a bankrupt marriage (the first contract) by the word of an oath-taker who stands to benefit from that bankruptcy (the second contract). In the course of events, he is shown to be unfaithful by doubting his wife's fidelity. She, by contrast, is revealed to be faithful to all her vows. When Iachimo attempts to tease Imogen out of believing in Posthumus, he is unsuccessful. She rejects his speech as an "assault" on the honor of a gentleman (1.7.145–50). The details of the episode expose the corruption possible when the value of a human relationship is subjected to mercantile negotiation.

Iachimo's intention is quite obviously to win the wager. As soon as he knows he cannot do so (Imogen will not be seduced), he resorts to deceit. Like the oath-taker Coke objected to, his word is a fiction that serves his own interests. This much is clear when, emerging from the trunk in Imogen's bedchamber, he inventories her possessions. Even her "mole cinque-spotted" becomes a "voucher" (2.2.48–49).[11] His lust is not the lover's who longs for the horses of the night to run slowly, but rather the merchant's who wants a quick return on his investment: "Swift, swift, you dragons of the night, that dawning/May bear the raven's eye" (58–59). The process by which Posthumus is duped into believing Iachimo's perjury reveals the extent to which he shares Iachimo's mentality.[12]

[11]For another view of the inventoried female body, see Patricia Parker, *Literary Fat Ladies: Rhetoric, Gender, Property* (New York: Methuen, 1987), 126–54. For a comprehensive assessment of the ways in which mercantile practice affected theatrical representations of value and price, see Jean-Christophe Agnew, *Worlds Apart: The Market and the Theater in Anglo-American Thought, 1550–1750* (Cambridge: Cambridge University Press, 1986).

[12]Posthumus's suit is later assumed, both literally and figuratively, by Cloten, who incarnates the spirit of mercantilism more even crudely than Iachimo. He buys music in order to "pen-

The initial reasons Posthumus states for doubting Iachimo's word and the supposed evidence he gives to prove Imogen's adultery remain good at all stages of the interrogation and not just at its outset. If a servant could have reported the contents of her bedchamber and stolen her bracelet, a maid could have described her "mole" (2.4.133–36). Posthumus's failure to persist in doubt reflects his fundamental distrust of women. Like Iachimo, he sees them merely as objects—they have a price but no unique value. His state of mind is expressed as a dream of parthenogenesis, a unique and unpartnered generation in which the male is the only parent and the "woman's part" excised altogether. "Is there no way for men to be, but women/Must be half-workers?" he asks. As the answer is no, he insists that generation produces only "counterfeits" (153–58)—coins appearing to correspond to a price but actually of adulterated value. By indicating that he thinks of a woman as a property without generative agency, Posthumus also reveals that he could not have kept his own promise to keep faith in marriage, a revelation that in retrospect makes his parting from Imogen all the more pathetic. Aboard his ship bound for Rome, Posthumus eventually vanishes from the horizon of sight, but clearly not from her mind (1.4.8–16). Perspectivism conveys the difference between Posthumus's perception of Imogen's worth which fluctuates circumstantially (in this case, with space), and Imogen's inner vision of Posthumus who retains his worth despite contingency. The sense of this difference is again evident later in the play when the character of Cymbeline's lost sons is at issue. They exhibit a royalty quite independent of place. "Place," as their guardian Belarius explains, only "lessens and sets off" (3.3.13)—it has nothing to do with an inherent virtue.

Posthumus's wager obviously affects Imogen's status as heir, the British succession, and the kingdom as a whole. Iachimo's fictionalized picture of Posthumus in Rome—he "slaver[s] with lips as common as the stairs/That mount the Capitol"—politicizes adultery (1.7.105–7). Although a fiction—Posthumus is not adulterous—the image hides a

etrate" Imogen (that is, he buys an "air"), and he sees marriage as a way to get rich (2.3.7–8, 11–12, 81–82). He tells Imogen that her "contract" with Posthumus is null because he is a "base wretch" and she cannot be allowed the "enlargement" available to "meaner parties" who "knit their souls . . . in [a] self-figur'd knot" (2.3.116–18); that is, her marriage must find its social and material correlatives.

truth. Having priced Imogen, Posthumus engages in a kind of prostitution. Like Marina at Mytilene, Imogen is up for sale. Rejected by her
husband and abandoned by her father, Imogen's state is metaphorically
"headless." Its vulnerability is further suggested by Iachimo's "trunk."
Having told her to seek revenge for Posthumus's supposed adultery
or else lose her "great stock," Iachimo emerges from his trunk to com-
pile evidence that will reduce her moral stock to nothing in Posthumus's eyes. Important to the play's imperial theme is the image of a
royal "stock" figuring Cymbeline's dynastic interests—interests that the
play will depict as embracing the translation of empire from Rome to
Britain. Cymbeline's "trunk" is what remains after the branches of his
family tree, his sons and his daughter, are lopped off, lost or abandoned;
when they return, the king's "stock" is revived.

The language of arboriculture was current in defenses of the
Union of England and Scotland in the interest of creating a British
empire. In general, these texts pictured the Union as an extension of
the monarchy that would occur when the two branches of the kingdom, England and Scotland, were regrafted to a central trunk. A common authority was Zechariah, who celebrated the union of Judah and
Israel as their return to the "tree" of Joseph.[13] A second reference in

---

[13]Bishop John Thornborough argued that England and Scotland were "at first both but one.
[But] . . . it pleased God, for sinne of people, to breake those Bands . . . *to dissolue the broth-
erhoode of Israell and Iuda*" and invoked Zechariah 11.14: "Then brake I asunder mine other
staffe, euen the Bandes, that I might dissolue the brotherhode betwene Iudah and Israel."
Explaining Zechariah, Thornborough refers to Ezekiel 37.19: "Thus said the Lord God,
Beholde, I wil take the tre of Ioseph, which is in the hand of Ephraim, and the tribes of
Israel his fellowes, and wil put them with him euen with the tre of Iudah, and make them
one tre, and they shalbe one in mine hand." Later, James is represented as a single "Vine,"
divulged by "the inserting and fast grafting of each branch and al fruite into his owne Royal
person, as into a fruitfull and flourishing vine, even into the head of the whole body" (cf.
Jeremiah 23.5–8). Bishop John Thornborough, *The Ioiefull and Blessed Reuniting the two
mightie & famous kingdomes, England and Scotland into their ancient name of great Brittaine* (London, 1605), A-A2ᵛ; STC 24036. In an earlier treatise Thornborough asked: "Are not diuerse
boughes from one tree, and all they of one and the same substance? And may not diuers
people vnder one Prince, though they are deuided in persons, yet be vnited in lawes?"
Bishop John Thornborough, *A Discovrse Plainely Prouing the euident vtilitie and vrgent neces-
sitie of the desired happie vnion of the two famovs Kingdomes of England and Scotland* (London,
1604), C3ᵛ; STC 24035. Thornborough is briefly described in Markku Peltonen, *Classical
Humanism and Republicanism in English Political Thought, 1570-1640* (Cambridge: Cambridge
University Press, 1995), 191, 215. For Jacobean arboriculture, see also Barnabe Barnes who
notes that the "auncient tree" of Britain has been grafted with Danish, French and Saxon

the most prominent of these defenses, Bishop John Thornborough's *The Ioiefull and Blessed Reuniting the two mighty & famous kingdomes, England and Scotland into their ancient name of great Brittaine*, 1605, alludes to the *conditions* in which such a truncated tree can be revived. The text implies that it flourishes only by God's will. Thornborough refers to Daniel who describes the regeneration of Nebuchadnezzar. Imagined as "tree of great height," that king is reduced to a "stump," a sign that God punishes overweening ambition. Daniel prophecies the revival of the royal "tree" "after that thou [the king, Nebuchadnezzar] shalt knowe that the heauvens haue the rule." He is to "breake of [his] sinnes by righteousnes, & [his] iniquities by mercie to the poore" (Daniel 4.11–27). Thornborough understood that James, supposedly both mindful of heaven's rule and charitable, had already respected Daniel's conditions: "great Britain" is "for the height of his honor, like the tall and goodly Cedar, in whom the dream of Nabudchodonorser [*sic*] hath beene verified. . . . Out of the Stumpe of the rootes . . . the tree is growne vp againe to former beauties" (C4ᵛ, D). To find Cymbeline's stock revived, however, Shakespeare's audiences have to wait for the end of the play.

The move to defer resolution is, of course, characteristic of romance. In this case, the interval between Cymbeline's loss of Imogen (supposed to be his heir and only living child) and his recovery of her and his sons is marked by various trials. They conclude when, having lost his queen, he regains his headship in marriage and in his kingdom. His relations with his subjects become "gracious," predictive of the Christian era that is about to begin, and also in line with the requirement that a Christian king act for his people. The moment at which his reformation is apparent coincides with his agreement to pay Augustus Caesar. By honoring this contract, a verbal contract made in circumstances that no

branches; collected in the person of James, "these seuerall plants graciously sprout out on high, like the sweet Cedars in *Salomons* forrests: which shortly by transportation or inoculation of their sprigs into other kingdomes may beare rule and preheminence in all the goodliest gardens of the world." Barnabe Barnes, *Fovre Bookes of Offices, Enabling Privat persons from the speciall service of all good Princes and Policies* (London, 1606), Lᵢᵢᵢᵛ. For the iconography of the cedar in *Cymbeline*, see Peggy Muñoz Simonds, *Myth, Emblem, and Music in Shakespeare's Cymbeline: An Iconographic Reconstruction* (Newark: University of Delaware Press, 1992), esp. 241–43.

longer obtain, Cymbeline exhibits his willingness to respect its promissory character and its guarantee in conscience.

Two Caesars

Caius Lucius, speaking for Augustus Caesar, asks Cymbeline for tribute on the basis of an agreement made years earlier by Cassibelan, Cymbeline's uncle, to pay Rome an annual sum in recognition of Julius Caesar's conquest of Britain (3.1.2–9).[14] In theory, a victor's rights following conquest were absolute (as *The Trew Law* had stated). Over time, of course, they invited modification or, worse, provoked outright revolution. The conflict over tribute in *Cymbeline* ends in a negotiated settlement. Although the British have won, the Romans are paid. By way of justification, the idea of imperial rule is reconceived to preserve the liberties of the subject. Initially, however, the British monarchy chooses resistance. The Queen and Cymbeline argue two quite different cases.

The Queen states that Cassibelan's word is meaningless because Rome never actually conquered Britain. Caesar's was but "a kind of conquest." In reality, "he was carried [by the British]/From off our coast, twice beaten" (3.1.23, 26–27). This protest is based on what most audiences would have recognized as a patent lie; the story of Roman Britain in some form or another was widely disseminated. The Queen's misrepresentation of what was held to be fact is comparable to a tyrant's silencing of the subject. She presumes that her word will not be questioned, even on the basis of contradictory evidence. Cymbeline denies tribute on subtler grounds. He bases his position on the prior and fundamental freedom of the British people, a freedom that permits them to cancel any contract limiting that freedom provided they have the will and the force to do it. His argument makes the word of his ancestor subject to a kind of contingency; it holds good only in certain circumstances:

[14]Cymbeline's refusal to pay tribute is not mentioned in Holinshed's chronicles. See Jean Warehol Rossi, "*Cymbeline*'s Debt to Holinshed: The Richness of III.i," in *Shakespeare's Romances Reconsidered*, ed. Carol McGinnis Kay and Henry E. Jacobs (Lincoln and London: University of Nebraska Press, 1987), 104–12.

> You must know,
> Till the injurious Romans did extort
> This tribute from us, we were free. Caesar's ambition,
> Which swell'd so much that it did almost stretch
> The sides o'th'world, against all colour here
> Did put the yoke upon's; which to shake off
> Becomes a warlike people, whom we reckon
> Ourselves to be.
>
>   Say then to Caesar,
> Our ancestor was that Mulmutius which
> Ordain'd our laws, whose use the sword of Caesar
> Hath too much mangled; whose repair, and franchise,
> Shall (by the power we hold) be our good deed,
> Though Rome be therefore angry.
>
> (3.1.47–59)

Following Caius Lucius's pronouncement of "War and confusion/ In Caesar's name," Cymbeline declares that the British will follow the example of the "Pannonians and Dalmatians [who] for/Their liberties are now in arms" (74–75). This is suggestive language. It implies that British freedom entails more than independence from the Roman yoke, that it is provided for in British law and as much to be exercised *by* the British subject as in behalf *of* a subject Britain.

The notion of a double freedom—of the British people and the British subject—drew on a uniquely English understanding of imperialism. To promote support for the Union, James had represented the peace that would follow it as an extension of the peace between England, Spain, and the Low Countries concluded in 1604. He would consequently become a second Augustus whose *pax Britannica* would supersede its Roman prototype. He had also inherited an earlier and historically Tudor imperialism whose ideological function was not to harmonize but rather to divorce English from continental and especially Roman interests. Published by Henry VIII as a feature of reformation policy, the doctrine that the English monarch was an "emperor without a superior" was a means to justify the liberties of the English subject under Elizabeth. After 1559, the doctrine protected the vast properties—formerly of the church but confiscated by the Tudors—

that belonged to English subjects.[15] By its association with property, it was seen also to guarantee English liberties. The two imperialisms, British and English, were in a sense contradictory. The imperialism James pretended to was associated with absolutism, at least in some measure. The imperialism of the Tudors was bound up with English liberty and liberties. Linking the two was the question asked by all political systems and, notably, dramatized by the action in *Cymbeline*: the limits of a subject's obedience to authority.

In general terms, the question was framed by reference to Scripture's representation of the historical Caesar and the nature of his rule after the birth of Christ. It asked under what circumstances was Caesar to be obeyed, whether in matters of tribute or other situations. The dicta in Matthew 22 proved enigmatic. When asked whether it was "lawful to giue tribute to Caesar," Jesus had answered: "Giue . . . Cesar the things which are Cesars, and giue vnto God those which are Gods" (19–21). Interpretations of this text usually restricted Caesar's claims to those which did not impinge on the subject's obligations to God. Aquinas prefaced his discussion of obedience by stipulating the fundamental "freedom" of all Christians. In his commentary on the sentences of Peter Lombard, he noted that the dicta in Matthew 22 are preceded by a declaration of Christian liberty:

> It would seem that Christians are not bound to obey the secular powers, and particularly tyrants. For it is said, *Matthew* XVII, 25: "Therefore the children are free (*liberi*)." And if in all countries the children of the reigning sovereign are free, so also should the children of that sovereign be free, to whom all kings are subject.

[15] To illustrate Henrician imperialism, John Guy quotes the preamble to the Act of Appeals: "Where by divers sundry old authentic histories and chronicles it is manifestly declared and expressed that this realm of England is an empire, and so that been accepted in the world, governed by one supreme head and king having the dignity and royal estate of the imperial crown of the same, unto whom a body politic, compact of all sorts and degree of people divided in terms and by names of spiritualty and temporalty, be bounded and are to bear next to God a natural and humble obedience; [the king is] also institute and furnished by the goodness and sufferance of Almighty God with plenary, whole and entire power, pre-eminence, authority, prerogative and jurisdiction": 24 Hen. VIII, c.12; "'The Imperial Crown' and the Liberty of the Subject: The English Constitution from Magna Carta to the Bill of Rights," in *Court, Country, and Culture: Essays on Early Modern British History in Honor of Perez Zagorin*, ed. Bonnelyn Young Kunze and Dwight D. Brautigam (Rochester: University of Rochester Press, 1992), 65–87. For an extended examination of *Cymbeline* in light of Stuart church/state relations, see Donna B. Hamilton, *Shakespeare and the Politics of Protestant England* (Lexington: University of Kentucky Press, 1992), 128–62.

Christians have become the sons of God as we read in the *Epistle to the Romans* (VII,16); . . . Christians then are everywhere free, and are thus not bound to obey the secular powers.[16]

As Aquinas recognized, however, there is a countervailing argument in Romans 13.1: "Let euerie soule be subiect vnto the higher powers. For there is no power but of God: & the powers that be, are ordeined of God." To mediate these claims of freedom and subjection, Aquinas went on to qualify obedience so that it was due only when it was truly "of God," and "derived from God" (*a Deo descendit*). He acknowledged that authority (*prelatio*) did not derive from God if it was falsely obtained or wrongly used. In cases in which an authority commands the performance of a sinful act, a subject "is obliged to disobey" ([*tenetur non obedire*]; 182–83). In cases in which an authority exceeds the scope of his office—as, for example, when a master demands payment from a servant which the latter is not bound to make—a subject "need not obey . . . need not disobey" ([*non tenetur obedire . . . [non] tenetur non obedire*]; 184–85). In all cases, the subject's conscience determines the validity of a command and of the authority making it.

Erasmus returned to Romans 13 specifically to explain the conduct of a Christian prince. Discussing tyrannical rule in his *Institutio principis christiani*, 1516, he notes that although Paul had commanded Christians to obey a "pagan prince" (*ethnicus princeps*), he would have devised a different rule to cover a Christian polity had such a thing existed. When Paul spoke, there were no Christian princes. But as Christians, both prince and people were to regard their obligations in light of divine love: "owe no one anything unless you love each other."[17] Paul had ordered Christians to tolerate bad magistrates for the

---

[16]St. Thomas Aquinas, "Commentary on Sentences of Peter Lombard," Book 2, 44.2.2; *Selected Political Writings*, ed. A. P. D'Entrèves, trans. J. G. Dawson (Oxford: Oxford University Press, 1959), 180–81. The *Commentum* appeared in numerous editions from the 1470s. [17]"inter vos nemini quicquid debeatis nisi vt inuicem diligatis"; Desiderius Erasmus, *Institutio principis christiani* in *Opera omnia*, ed. O. Herding, 21 vols. (Amsterdam: North-Holland Publishing Co., 1969–94), 4.1 (1974): 166. This text reproduces that of the *Opera omnia* ed. Froben (Basel, 1540). On Paul's command in Romans 13, Erasmus notes: "id ad ethnicos principes esse referendum, quod ea tempestate nondum essent principes vlli Christiani." For a modern English translation, see *The Education of a Christian Prince*, trans. Lester K. Born (New York: Columbia University Press, 1936). The idea of Christian obligation is expressed to a different purpose by William Tyndale; see his *The Obedience of a Christian Man*, in *The Works of the English Reformers: William Tyndale and John Frith*, ed. Thomas Russell, 3 vols. (London, 1831), 2: 208–9.

sake of civil order, but he had also said that they were privileged to live at the beginning of a new era. To Erasmus, this meant that a Christian prince was to consider his office as he would a "burden" (*quantum onoris*). He was a Caesar whose authority was subject to question and whose power was limited. His pagan prototype had been absolutely free; he, by contrast, was bound by principles that transformed his freedom into something like a servitude. The place of a king, Erasmus wrote, is "a thing of care" and "trial" (*res sollicitata, pericolosa*; 152).

Arguing for a "free and absolute" monarchy, James (and absolutists who later supported him) effectively rejected Thomist and Erasmian interpretations of Scripture and insisted that Paul's words requiring obedience to civil authority were to be taken literally at all times. To imagine that the "Spirit of God," having commanded the people to give their rulers "heartie obedience for conscience sake, giuing to *Caesar* that which was *Caesars* and to God that which was Gods," would renege on this fundamental point of government was a "shameless presumption." It posited an "vnlawfull libertie" of the people.[18] Scripture allowed them rights only in conscience; they could not actively disobey the monarch and remain within the law. Constitutionalists, by contrast, tended to adhere to traditional Christian notions of a polity, which were on the whole consistent with their idea that monarch and people were bound together by mutual dependencies. But their habit of linking the freedom of a subject in conscience to his liberties as a property holder had consequences unforeseen in literature that dealt with general principles.

Inevitably, their language describing freedom of conscience, a Christian liberty, became bound up with the language of property, the liberties of the subject. With the exception of purely doctrinal matters, in no respect did the distinction between the monarch and God have more meaning than in disputes over tribute, subsidies, impositions, and other forms of taxation that were owed to or demanded by the monarch. Invoking Aquinas, Fortescue had limited the monarch's authority and power over the property of subjects and had stated that beyond what the monarch could demand by his prerogative, his revenues were a gift from the people. Moreover, all his revenue was to be spent in the interest of the commonwealth:

[18]James VI and I, *The Trew Law of Free Monarchies*, in *Political Writings*, ed. Johann P. Sommerville (Cambridge: Cambridge University Press, 1994), 72.

Ffor as Seynt Thomas saith, *Rex datur propter regnum, et non regnum propter regem* [a king is given for the kingdom not the kingdom for the king]. Wherfore all that he dothe owith to be referred to his kyngdome. Ffor though his estate be the highest estate temporall in the erthe yet it is an office, in wich he mynestrith to his reaume defence and justice. And therfore he mey say off hym selff and off his reaume ... *servus servorum Dei* [he is a servant of the servants of God]. (*Governance of England*, 127)

The monarch was supported by his people because they had "much ffredome in thair owne godis" (140). Their right to property was the guarantee that he neither want for their support nor they for his.[19] Later commentators were more precise in considering the possibility that the people might refuse such support. In his *Pandectes of the Law of Nations,* 1602, William Fulbecke made the monarch's prudence a condition of his ability to get tribute: "it behoueth euerie Monarch to haue a watch-full care of his subiects good, and to bend the force of his minde to the preseruation and maintenance of their safetie and good estate; so subiects should not grudge to pay vnto them tributes & subsidies and other publike impositions."[20] Barnabe Barnes saw that the monarch's temperance in collecting and spending was the chief assurance of his revenue: a prince is to be "liberall according to strict conscience" (*Fovre Bookes*, C2, C2ᵛ). But such formulations also set limits to the subject's freedom: they left the monarch's prerogative absolute. Were a subject to exercise his freedom by resisting the prerogative, he became an outlaw automatically and a revolutionary potentially. By 1606, a case involving

---

[19] Fortescue compares English with French subjects and finds the former rich, free, and taxable, and the latter poor, lacking justice and likely to rebel: "Ffor nothyng mey make is [i.e., his, the king's] people to arise, but lakke off gode, or lakke off justice. But yet sertanly when thay lakke gode thai woll aryse, sayng that thai lakke justice" (*On the Governance of England*, ed. Charles Plummer [London: Oxford University Press, 1926], 140; cf. Patchbreech's claim, *Per.* 2.1). For the concept of revenue before the Great Contract, 1610, see Sacks, "The Paradox of Taxation," in *Fiscal Crises, Liberty, and Representative Government, 1450–1789,* ed. Philip T. Hoffman and Kathryn Norberg (Stanford: Stanford University Press, 1994), 3–66; and Clive Holmes, "Parliament and Liberty, Taxation and Property," in *Parliament and Liberty from the Reign of Elizabeth to the English Civil War,* ed. J. H. Hexter (Stanford: Stanford University Press, 1992), 122–54.

[20] *Pandectes of the Law of Nations* (London, 1602), S4; STC 11414. Fulbecke was a civil lawyer who appears to have promoted a qualified absolutism; see J. P. Sommerville, *Politics and Ideology in England, 1603–1640* (New York: Longman, 1986), 69, 147, 161; and Glenn Burgess, *Absolute Monarchy and the Stuart Constitution* (New Haven: Yale University Press, 1996), 78–80.

a customs duty, a form of revenue and therefore a kind of tribute from the subject to the monarch, had clearly established this point.

Sitting on the court of the Exchequer, Sir Thomas Fleming decided that John Bate, an importer of currants, had to pay the king a customs duty. This was a consequence of the fact that the monarch's prerogative, absolute and above positive law, had always covered imports and exports; in any case, the tax was against an item not a man and his labor and it did not, therefore, impinge upon his liberties as a holder of property. On the question of liberties in general, Fleming's decision embraced issues beyond the payment of customs duties. It described the character of the prerogative and its practical consequences. As Fleming admitted, the prerogative—by conferring an authority and power beyond determination in positive law—could freely go wrong as much as right. It was, in that sense, a terrible instrument. Faced with the prerogative, a subject only had the recourse provided by petition; having no standing at law, he only could ask for grace:

> And whereas it is said that if the King may impose [i.e., by the prerogative], he may impose any quantity what he pleases, true it is that this may be referred to the wisdom of the King, who guideth all under God by his wisdom, and this is not to be disputed by a subject; and many things are left to his wisdom for the ordering of his power, rather than his power shall be restrained. The King may pardon any felon; but it may be objected that if he pardon one felon he may pardon all, to the damage of the commonwealth, and yet none will doubt but that is left in his wisdom.... [T]o restrain the King and his power because that by his power he may do ill, is no argument for the subject.[21]

[21]Chief Baron Fleming's Judgment, *Constitutional Documents of the Reign of James I*, ed. J. R. Tanner (Cambridge: The University Press, 1930), 343–44. By its exercise of pardon, the prerogative was associated with the powers of the body natural; see the discussion of Calvin's case, Chapter 2, pp. 53–54. Bate's case has received much comment. See Francis Oakley, "Jacobean Political Theology: the Absolute and Ordinary Powers of the Kings," *Journal of the History of Ideas* 29 (1968): 323–46; Sacks, "The Paradox of Taxation," 61–63; and Glenn Burgess, *The Politics of the Ancient Constitution: An Introduction to English Political Thought, 1603–1642* (University Park: Pennsylvania State University Press, 1992), 141, and *Absolute Monarchy*, 80–81. In the context of Jacobean politics, Bate's case characterized the monarch's power as a "mystery"; to the extent that this allowed him not to give a reason for his actions, it gave rise to Parliamentary resentment. See Margaret Atwood Judson, *The Crisis of the Constitution: An Essay in Constitutional and Political Thought in England, 1603–1645* (New York: Octagon Books, 1971), 159–60.

What wisdom a monarch might call on when empowered absolutely was therefore the question. Fleming, like all theorists of the monarchy, had stipulated that the prerogative, the king's absolute power exercised independently of Parliament and positive law, must be used for "the general benefit of the people and is *salus populi*; as the people is the body and the King the head" (*Constitutional*, 341). But he also pointed out that the only faculty promoting monarchic wisdom in these cases was a moral one. Wisdom necessarily depends on the discrimination of better and worse, good and evil—distinctions that have their basis in conscience. This reasoning clearly exposes the subject's vulnerability. *Cymbeline* represents three notable challenges to a superior authority, each by a subordinate who reveals the risks of conscientious action.

Conspicuously unwise in its toleration of the Queen's tyranny, Cymbeline's government is mended, to a degree, by the actions of Cornelius and Pisanio, who disobey or in some way contravene the commands of their superiors. They do so deceptively and without attracting attention. A third, Belarius, represents a more critical case. His abduction of Cymbeline's sons is actually an instance of treason; it makes him an "outlaw" (4.2.138). It also ends by preserving the kingdom in ways for which Belarius is responsible although not always consciously.

Cornelius, recognizing the Queen's "spirit," simply thwarts her plan to poison Imogen by substituting an innocuous for a lethal drug: "She is fool'd/With a most false effect: and I the truer,/So to be false with her" (1.6.42–44). His art, although unnoticed and delayed in its effects, ministers to the body politic. Imogen is not poisoned but merely made comatose for a time. Then disguised as a page, she is found and protected by Romans whose forces would otherwise have been directed against her as the British heir apparent (4.2.355–86). Pisanio exercises his freedom in a series of strategic actions. He tacitly maintains his allegiance to Posthumus despite the Queen's invitation to serve her (1.6.86–87). But he also refuses to obey Posthumus when he is ordered to murder Imogen: "I am ignorant in what I am commanded" (3.2.23). Knowing Imogen's character, he terms Posthumus's accusation of adultery "slander," and drawing on the resources of art as deception, he invents her disguise and means of escape.[22] He

[22]On knowledge and experience as tropes in *Cymbeline*, see Maurice Hunt, "Shakespeare's Empirical Romance: *Cymbeline* and Modern Knowledge," *Texas Studies in Literature and Language* 22, 3 (1980): 322–42.

provides her with male clothing and prompts her to seek service with Lucius, the Roman general in Britain (3.4.174–75). Like Cornelius, Pisanio preserves the body politic by defying the obligation of servant to master. He responds to the "headlessness" of the state by providing its anarchic tyranny with his own surrogate wit made instrumental by art, the play that succeeds in keeping Imogen safe, protected by a surrogate father—the Roman general, Lucius—who replaces the male kin who have rejected her (4.2.394–95).

Unlike Cornelius and Pisanio, who act from a general interest, Belarius is motivated by revenge. His case—which ends in treasonable disobedience—replicates the principal elements of Slade's case, and draws attention to the consequences of perjury. Once loved by Cymbeline, for "when a soldier was the theme, [his] name was not far off," Belarius was "as a tree/Whose boughs did bend with fruit." His prosperity was destroyed by the "false oaths" of "two villains" who accuse him of treachery: their effect was that of a "storm, or a robbery (call it what you will)/[which] Shook down my mellow hangings" (3.3.59–63).[23] Punished with banishment, his property confiscated, Belarius avenges the injury he thinks he has suffered: he steals what properly belongs to the body politic, the king's sons—the succession, and the inheritance of the crown—to bring them up as outlaws in the depths of the Welsh forest. He can imply that he has behaved conscientiously (if not legally) because he believes that Cymbeline has been unjust:

> O Cymbeline, heaven and my conscience knows
> Thou didst unjustly banish me: whereon,
> At three and two years old, I stole these babes,
> Thinking to bar thee of succession as
> Thou refts me of my lands.

> (3.3.99–103)

His claims have some merit: knowing Belarius's virtue, Cymbeline nevertheless trusted the word of oath-takers. But the facts of the case are undeniable. Against Cymbeline's words of banishment, Belarius can invoke only a natural law, grounded in his conscientious percep-

---

[23]For a study of this topos in relation to the play, see Simonds, *Myth*, 182–89.

tion of a right that he cannot pursue in positive law.[24] The question to ask is whether natural law protects him and promotes the interests of the commonwealth.

The action that follows shows how the subject's rights in natural law also work to confer obligations. Paradoxically, by "stealing" the succession, Belarius has also made it secure. Undertaken by outlaws—but to defend British liberty and liberties—Belarius's attack on Roman forces, made critically effective by the help of Guiderius, Arviragus, and Posthumus (disguised as a poor British peasant), illustrates the vast authority of natural law, a law whose force is not derived from courts, cities, or books. Informed by the spirit of pastoral and its communities, this law promotes a character wholly dependent on and in tune with "Nature." This is the character which triumphs in the event of war: faced with the apparently victorious Roman army, Belarius and his company turn defeat into victory and secure the independence of Britain. Belarius's rough art of the chase, the practical art of venatical pastoral, is deployed to physic the British body politic. Exemplified by his foster and Cymbeline's actual sons, his art is also acknowledged by Imogen.

The "Stock" in Pastoral

The filial "branches" to be restored to Cymbeline's dynastic "tree" at the end of the play are the products of a world that is at once harsh (as the princes complain [3.3.32–40]) and salutary. Innocent of urbanity, it is nevertheless a place of a natural courtesy.[25] Guiderius and Arviragus show hospitality to Imogen (posing as the youth, Fidele). They drive Cloten (who has assumed Posthumus's "suit" and seeks to rape Imogen) from their woods. Why their existence in the forest has provided them

[24]The relations between conscience and natural law are described by Robert A. Greene, "Synderesis, the Spark of Conscience, in the English Renaissance," *Journal of the History of Ideas* 52, 2 (1991): 195–219.

[25]When Guiderius and Arviragus object to their exile, Belarius maintains that their life in the forest is better than what it would be at court: "to our comfort, shall we find/The sharded beetle in a safer hold/Than is the full-winged eagle" (3.3.19–21). The image recreates a popular emblem and suggests that Belarius is highly conscious of the fact that he is in charge of princes: this is a beetle who, hiding itself in the eagle's wings, pierces the eagle's eggs and "forestalls any hope of offspring" (*prohibet spem crescere prolis*). For the topos, see Simonds, *Myth*, 143–44.

with such fine sensibilities is partly answered by Belarius's repeated stress
on the inevitable effects of royal blood—it is the princes' nature to be
valiant and courteous (3.3.79–80; 84–85; 4.2.169–81). Their virtue also
corresponds to a primal complementarity in "Nature" whose role in
shaping character is suggested by Imogen's reflections on her own
hunger. A basic need of her body natural, hunger overcomes her fear of
forest creatures and drives her into Belarius's cave in search of food. In
retrospect she recognizes that it has served as a form of moral discipline:

> famine,
> Ere clean it o'erthrow Nature, makes it valiant.
> Plenty and peace breeds cowards: hardness ever
> Of hardiness is mother.

$$(3.6.19-22)$$

"Hardiness" is the quality she later sees in her brothers whom she compares to the "[g]reat men/That had a court no bigger than this case,"
did "attend themselves" [i.e., had no servants], and "had the virtue/
Which their conscience seal'd them, laying by/That nothing-gift of differing multitudes" (3.7.54–58). She extols a toughness of morals and
morale, a deference to principle, and an independence of spirit. Still
later, she remarks that her brothers are "kind creatures" who disprove
the claim that "all's savage but at court":

> Experience, O, thou disprov'st report!
> Th'emperious seas breed monsters; for the dish
> Poor tributary rivers as sweet fish.

$$(4.2.34-36)$$

This nautical cannibalism (recalling the fishermen's complaint in *Pericles*) illustrates the situation of tribute-givers in an empire; they are
consumed by monsters of greed. Imogen's image of a corruption that
emanates from centers of political power is answered with inversion
by Guiderius's beheading of Cloten. Guiderius throws Cloten's head
into a creek: "let it to the sea,/And tell the fishes he's the queen's son"
(4.2.152–53; 184–85). The action both marks and transforms the condition of the kingdom as a headless "trunk." Cloten literally and
Posthumus by association with Cloten's suit are reduced to an image

of the body politic as Cymbeline has shaped it; thus reduced, that body is ready for a new head. Remembering Cloten, Guiderius calls him an "empty purse" because he is a "fool" and lacks brains (85, 114–15), but the epithet also conveys the sense in which Cloten's intrusion into the forest in order to force himself on Imogen constitutes an attempt to impose on what is actually Guiderius's inheritance, the British throne and its commonwealth. Imogen has earlier depicted the court as monstrously consumptive; Guiderius manifests his princely status by exploiting the sea's power to consume courtly monsters, not their country tributaries.

The decapitation of a monarch who has failed to live up to his office was condoned in radical argument; in this case, the action was imagined as a kind of cure for a diseased body politic. Robert Parsons (a Catholic radical who argued for the succession of the Spanish infanta) described regicide in just these terms. Because the "whole body is of more authority then the only head," the "weal publique [may] cure or cutt of their heades if they infest the rest, seing that a body ciuil may have diuers heades by succession and is not bound euer to one as a body natural is." Anyone who tolerated an "infested" head was no more than a "slaue," and the people who failed to resist a tyrant were no better than "oxen and asses . . . *pecora campi*."[26] Guiderius, whom Cloten repeatedly calls a slave, takes the role of the subject as it was envisaged by those who did not stop at regicide. By beheading Cloten, he destroys the tyrannical organ for which Cymbeline is actually responsible and reestablishes the proper succession. Like Belarius, from whom he learned the art of venery, he physics the body politic.

Imogen's stock in pastoral flourishes by way of illustrating the principle her hunger in the Welsh forest has revealed to her: a life in

---

[26][Robert Parsons] *A Conference Abovt the Next Svccession to the Crowne of Ingland* (London, 1594), D8ᵛ, F7ᵛ, F8; STC 19398. For Parsons, see Sommerville, *Politics and Idealogy*, 62, passim. Cf. John Ponet: "Common wealthes and realmes may liue, whan the head is cut of, and may put on a newe head, that is, make them a newe gouernour, whan they see their olde head seke to muche his owne will and not the wealthe of the hole body, for the which he was only ordained"; [John Ponet], *A Shorte Treatise of politike power, 1556,* in Winthrop S. Hudson, *John Ponet (1516–1556): Advocate of a Limited Monarchy* (Chicago: University of Chicago Press, 1942), 61. Some radical thinkers (Protestants under Mary I, Catholics under Elizabeth I) thought that in extraordinary cases the subject alone and independent of an office could act to depose the monarch.

"Nature" creates a valiant subject. The ensuing scenes of battle between Romans and Britons realize her perceptions. The courageous actions of Belarius and his "sons," with the help of Posthumus—all "outlaws" and therefore not part of the body politic, the domain of subjects protected by positive law—demonstrate a salutary "hardiness" that proves to be the salvation of Britain.[27] Their allegiance to Britain is a natural one and a reminder that while the subject is under positive law for reasons of "locale" or "an oath in leet," his allegiance goes everywhere and is a "state of mind." Their plebeian valour is contrasted with the military ineptitude of the gentry on both sides. The weakness of the gentry is exemplified when Posthumus disarms Iachimo, the leader of a squadron of Roman "gentlemen," who explains that the "air" (i.e., also Leonatus, who represents an "heir") of Britain "enfeebles" him, otherwise he could not have been overcome by a "carl," a "very drudge of Nature" (5.2.3–5). Iachimo disparages his own status: "Knighthood and honours, borne/As I wear mine, are titles but of scorn," and he praises the virtue of the lout who revealed this to him:

> If that thy gentry, Britain, go before
> This lout, as he exceeds our lords, the odds
> Is that we scarce are men and you are gods.

(6–10)

This critique of distinctions of rank applies also to the British. When Posthumus describes the decisive stand of the "ancient soldier" and his three allies to a "British lord" who was among the "fliers," he begins by attributing victory to the fact that "the heavens fought." But he ends by ridiculing in doggerel verse that gentleman's wonder at the "strange chance" of the victory: "Nay, do not wonder at it: you are made/Rather to wonder at the things you hear/Than to work any" (5.3.53–55). Posthumus is himself the figure of a common (plebeian as well as universal) virtue. Invoking the "strength of the Leonati" (and indicating his royal status as "Judah"), he assumed the guise of a "peasant" to fight for Imogen and Britain (5.1.22–34).

[27]There appears to have been a compliment to the Scots and King James in the picture of this triumphant triumvirate of country soldiers who defend Britain. Several Scottish families had "wildmen" as figures in their coats of arms. See Simonds, *Myth*, 156–61, and Glynne Wickham, "Riddle and Emblem," 112–13.

The status of subjects in "Nature," the motif of the play's pastoral inter-
lude, was an important topic in a moralized project of empire building
advanced between 1606 and 1608 by Francis Bacon. Its interest to the
drama in *Cymbeline* is chiefly in its association of poverty, both the
monarch's and his subjects', with military conquest and, conversely, of
national wealth with a debilitating consumption. Bacon's arguments
went far to clarify an actually ambiguous situation. Insisting that to tax
subjects—even to achieve an empire—was politically dangerous, Bacon
also thought that imperialist expansion was necessary to avoid civil
strife at home. But, he reasoned, if such expansion could be made to
depend on the valor of the subject, broadly understood as his moral
resourcefulness rather than his property or material resources, empire
could be achieved without risk. Bacon's solution was to refashion for
English subjects the conventional apology for a militaristic ethos typical of republican Rome, which he saw as validated by poverty, in the
interest of promoting an expansion of resources characteristic of imperial Rome. In this way he also accommodated the two notions of
empire—the English Tudor version and the British Stuart version—by
making the subject's liberties rather than the monarch's wealth the basis
for imperial conquest. In 1606, in Bacon's speech on empire to the
Commons, the elements of this argument are evident:

> And for Greatness, Mr. Speaker, I think a man may speak it
> soberly and without bravery, that this kingdom of England, hav-
> ing Scotland united, Ireland reduced, the sea provinces of the Low
> Countries contracted, and shipping maintained, is one of the
> greatest monarchies, in forces truly esteemed, that hath been in
> the world. For certainly the kingdoms here on earth have a
> resemblance with the kingdom of Heaven; which our Saviour
> compareth, not to any great kernel or nut, but to a very small
> grain, yet such an one as is apt to grow and spread; and such do
> I take to be the constitution of this kingdom; if indeed we shall
> refer our counsels to greatness and power, and not quench them
> too much with the consideration of utility and wealth.[28]

[28]Spedding notes that this was Bacon's speech to the Commons on February 17, 1606–7.
"Preface to the True Greatness of Britain," in *The Works of Francis Bacon*, ed. James Sped-
ding, Robert Leslie Ellis, and Douglas Denon Heath, 15 vols. (Boston, 1860), 13: 221–22.
For Bacon on empire, see Peltonen, *Classical Humanism*, 190–228.

Bacon's comparison of the earthly and heavenly empires was a conventional feature of the discourse on the two Caesars. Voiced in the Commons, it functioned as a reminder of the limits of monarchic authority and power, especially over the commonwealth. Developing his argument, Bacon turned the poverty of a kingdom into a richness in morals and morale sufficient for imperial conquest:

> [As Solon said], "if another come that hath better iron than you, he will be lord of all your good." [The] beginnings of the monarchie of the world . . . [were] founded in poverty. . . We should a little disdain that the nation of Spain . . . should of late years take unto themselves that spirit as to dream of a monarchy in the west, according to that device *Video solem orientem in occidente*, only because they have ravished from some wild and unarmed people mines and store of gold; and on the other side that this island of Britain, seated and manned as it is, and that hath I make no question the best iron in the world, that is, the best soldiers in the world, shall think of nothing but reckonings and audits and *meum* and *tuum* and I cannot tell what. (222–23)

Bacon associated both the Spanish "ravishment" of the New World and the "reckonings" of the English subjects with a debilitating age of gold. Neither approach would lead to a global "spreading" which rather depended on an iron-willed soldiery. In a manuscript memorandum entitled *Comentarius Solutus*, probably from the summer of 1608, Bacon noted that he was "finishing" his treatise of "ye Great. of Br. wth aspect ad pol." in order to persuade "K. and peop." of the "cours. of infusing every whear the foundat. in this Ile of a mon. in ye West as an apt seat [;] state people for it" (*Works*, 13: 225–26). Not in print before its final revision as "Of the Greatnesse of Kingdomes" in his *Essays*, 1612, portions of the treatise Bacon refers to as "ye Great. of Br." (and Spedding prints and entitles "Of the True Greatness of the Kingdom of Britain") may well have been in circulation before 1608 when it was due to be finished. This treatise is explicit on the matter of revenue and the benefits of a naturally disciplined way of life.

In measuring a nation's capacity for greatness, Bacon wrote, too much is attributed to "largeness of territory," "treasure or riches," "fruitfulnes of soil," and "affluence of commodities." Greatness is actually the product of the ".valour and military disposition of the people" and requires "every common subject by the poll be fit to make a soldier." It depends as well on "the temper of the government fit to keep subjects in heart and courage, and not to keep them in the condition of servile vassals" (*Works*, 13: 232–33). In other words, greatness follows a monarch's respect for liberties. At the same time, a people's riches are suspect. Bacon insisted that wealth, whether "public" or "private," "maketh men either slothful and effeminate, and so no enterprisers, or insolent and arrogant, and so overgreat embracers, but most generally cowardly and fearful to lose" (248). This line of reasoning suggests that the liberties promoting greatness will not sustain a general affluence. But a monarch should curb his desire to impose upon his subjects: "he that shall look into your [i.e., James's] prerogative shall find it to have as many streams to feed your treasury, as the prerogative of any of the said kings, and yet without oppression or taxing of your people" (251). In sum, Bacon saw that the British empire over which James aspired to rule was to be built not by gold but iron: the wealth of its emperor and people was to be in their courage and spirit of enterprise.

The moral wealth Bacon had in mind seems also to have had a real correlative in the commercial advantages that would follow the Union and the creation of an empire in the west. As he framed this prospect in "Of the true Greatness of the Kingdom of Britain," it entailed peaceful rather than military conquests, processes of naturalization rather than domination, and thus what would appear to be an organic spreading of the imperial "tree":

> There must evermore distinction be made between the *body* or
> *stem* of the tree, and the *boughs* and *branches*. For if the top be over-
> great and the stalk too slender, there can be no strength. Now the
> body is to be accounted so much of an estate as is not separated
> or distinguished with any mark of *foreigners*, but is united specially
> with the bond of naturalization. And therefore we see that when
> the state of Rome grew great, they were enforced to naturalize
> the Latins or Italians, because the Roman *stem* could not bear the
> provinces and Italy both as *branches*: and the like they were con-
> tent after to do to most of the Gauls. (238)

As I have noted, the imagery of tree and branches was a feature of pro-Union argument that drew on scriptural models of prophecy, particularly in Daniel where the monarchic stump puts forth new growth in

light of the monarch's obedience to God and charity to his people.
Bacon's treatment of the figure had a practical advantage over those of
Thornborough and Barnes in that it resolved at a rhetorical level some
of the differences generated by the Union debate in the Commons and
the law courts. Avoiding the easy providentialism of his pro-Union colleagues, Bacon argued more specifically that a British empire divinely
ordained need not depend on taxing the people because, finally, it need
not depend on war and conquest. It could grow through commerce. In
effect, Bacon transformed material relations between the two Caesars
so that they appeared to be harmonious. His vision of a British empire,
like Fortescue's idea of the English monarchy centuries earlier, suggested
that its ruler was most powerful when he guaranteed the liberties of his
subjects. They, in turn, were to find their freedom in a natural order of
things, not in the artifice of the city and the court.

Bacon's imperialism, premised on an equation of real poverty and
moral strength, is shadowed in the paradox concluding *Cymbeline*. The
Britons, victors over their overlords, the Romans, nevertheless remain
vassals of Rome. Cymbeline's decision to pay Roman tribute indicates
that the force of a word, a verbal contract, inscribed in conscience,
can supersede the weight of circumstance, registered in moments of
history. The play concludes by a series of acknowledgments of contracts
broken and then renewed. They are all reviewed in light of the most
imposing of contracts made by the Word of God for the generations to
come and continuously present in *Cymbeline* by a consciousness of the
"time when" the action of the play is represented as having taken place.

Visions of History

Christian thinkers had traditionally supposed that the Word instituted
the form of a polity in which the subject's material liberties were
assured by the more fundamental liberty of conscience he possessed in
common with his superiors. According to English notions of a constitution, conscience bound ruler and people together in mutual dependencies, ratified by laws both natural and positive. Posthumus, whose
wager profoundly disturbs the relation of marriage, is the character who
most fully articulates what conscience means.

Having fought for Britain in disguise, Posthumus allows himself to be captured as a Roman. He has accepted Pisanio's proof of Imogen's death, a "bloody cloth," and, although he accuses Pisanio of a bad conscience (the "bond" of service only requires obedience to "just" commands [5.1.1–7]), he focuses on his own breach of faith. It justifies his imprisonment in a Roman "bondage" whose only release is in death, a "liberty" from the consciousness of sin (5.4.3–11).[29] The language of calculation is voiced again but only to be rejected, not once but twice. Posthumus wishes to render his "whole self" to satisfy a debt that he could legally discharge by the payment of a mere fraction (18–28), but Jupiter, who governs such exchanges, is disposed to provide merciful benefits rather than engage in punitive retribution. Posthumus's dream of the Leonati, his parents, and his brothers, indicates how forcefully a moral arithmetic determines his sense of personal worth. He "sees" them plead with Jupiter to spare him: his pitiable birth, his orphanhood, his virtue in Imogen's eyes, his undeserved exile, and Iachimo's treachery all speak to their claims for consideration. Posthumus experiences the god's answer in a more palpable way.

Jupiter's descent appears anomalous in its fusion of moral decorum and visual hyperbole—the actor playing the god, smelling of sulfur and seated on an eagle, was presumably lowered from the rafters above the stage to the sound of thunder (114–19). The scene makes sense, however, as the moment at which the two "matters" of wager and chronicle, marriage and empire, are brought together. Jupiter settles the matter of the wager, for which Posthumus believes he should die, by rejecting Leonati claims for justice but bettering their requests by displaying mercy. He answers them by a Christian logic: "Whom best I love I cross; to make my gift,/The more delay'd delighted" (101–2). What is exchanged in the balance is the god's benefit of a human life. Posthumus will not only live but prosper. Jupiter's actions also represent the matter of chronicle by their reference to two prophetic accounts of the future British empire.

[29]This "bondage" is what Posthumus recognizes as sin; it is to be distinguished from the obligations of parties to a contract. "Liberty" from the first comes with grace; mutual freedoms are the condition of the second. For a different view, see Judiana Lawrence, "Natural Bonds and Artistic Coherence in the Ending of *Cymbeline*," *Shakespeare Quarterly* 35, 4 (1984): 440–60.

The divine eagle, actually a prop and figuratively the god's power, is a reminder that Posthumus shadows an imperial self. It is also the central figure in the Roman soothsayer's prophecy of victory. Misinterpreted at first, the true meaning of the prophecy is not apparent before the last moments of the play. Jupiter's eagle in 5.4 recalls the first of these interpretations in 4.2. The Soothsayer reports:

> I saw Jove's bird, the Roman eagle, wing'd
> From the spongy south to this part of the west,
> There vanish'd in the sunbeams, which portends
> (Unless my sins abuse my divination)
> Success to th' Roman host.

(348–52)

As the audience can recognize in 5 as it could not in 4, the truth in the Soothsayer's prophecy is mingled with falsehood: the British have in fact defeated the "Roman host." The eagle which has signaled success seems to have altered his Roman and traditional character to embrace a British and novel presence. Plausible in light of figurations of James's own imperial monarchy in contemporary Stuart iconography,[30] the identification of a triumphant British eagle flying west anticipates the conflation of empires, Roman and British, that is imagined in the play's concluding vision of history.

The tablet Jupiter leaves with Posthumus establishes a direct link between the marriage story and its place in the future history of empire. It tells of two fortunes, one of "a lion's whelp . . . to himself unknown," who will "without seeking find, and be embrac'd by a piece of tender air," and the other of "a stately cedar" whose "lopp'd branches . . . which, being dead many years, shall after revive, be jointed to the old stock, and freshly grow." These events will signal the end of Posthumus's "miseries," and the "peace and plenty" of Britain (5.4.138–45). Ignorant of the language of the Union, Posthumus cannot know that "the lion's whelp" or

---

[30]For a literary representation of this iconography, see especially Barnabe Barnes who illustrates James's monarchy by allusions to an eagle and the sun: James is "hyeroglyphically represented by the figure of the sun" and the "Eagle," who looking into the "Sunne," finds "miracles within that sanctified Orbe of bright vertue." The eagle is also "shadowed in Phoebus or Apollo, bearing also with him the thunderbolts of Iupiter (who mystically reueileth soueraigne Maiestie) to grinde, burne, and consume into powder the violence of his enemies"; *Fovre Bookes*, ¶$_{iii}$^{v}, ¶$_{iiii}$^{v}, A.

Judah signifies the Scottish inheritance; or that embraced by "air" (or revived), it will be at one with Britain, and the two, the heirs of Scotland and Britain, will form one empire. Nor could he guess that the "old stock" of a "stately cedar" (a tree of state or royal dynasty), which is about to be revivified by the return of its branches, constructs an image favored by pro-Union apologists. His own situation gives no hint as to how Jupiter's words will be fulfilled. They are not only literally riddling but dramatically enigmatic. Posthumus is being asked to have faith in what he cannot find plausible or even quite understand.

The final scene, dazzling in its revelations, realizes the terms of the prophecy as if to dramatize the work of providence in human history. Those who have been lost are found: Imogen, Belarius, Guiderius, Arviragus. Offenders are recognized and pardoned: Posthumus, Iachimo, Belarius, Guiderius. The courageous are praised and the villains are dismissed. Here, as in *Pericles*, a modest Justice is celebrated. It is realized when Cymbeline exercises his absolute power of pardon and honors Cassibelan's agreement by paying Roman tribute.

When Imogen identifies Posthumus and tries to stop his grief, he sees her merely as a pageboy and knocks her down: "There lie thy part" (5.5.229). His impulsive beating of a subordinate testifies to his continuing tendency to objectify whoever is beneath him in rank or by virtue of gender. Imogen's response is enigmatic but it rectifies their relations:

> Why did you throw your wedded lady from you?
> Think that you are upon a rock, and now
> Throw me again.

> (261–63)

Her words reflect her history as faithful and Fidele. They also imply her chaste sexuality.[31] Posthumus responds appropriately by asking her, now his "soul," to be fruitful (5.5.263–64) and thereby recalls her complaint that Cymbeline, by exiling Posthumus, had "like the tyrannous breathing of the north,/[Shaken] all our buds from growing"

---

[31]Nosworthy sees that the "rock" Posthumus must think he stands on is that to which he anchors later (5.5.394), that is, Imogen herself. Donna B. Hamilton reads these lines as an intervention in the debate on church and state under James I; *Shakespeare and the Politics of Protestant England*, 147.

(1.4.36–37). By calling Imogen his soul, Posthumus rejects the notion of her as a pricey item and renews the terms of betrothal. He also experiences a more pervasive conversion of spirit in which Cymbeline then finds inspiration.

When Cymbeline orders the execution of his Roman captives, including Lucius, in order to appease the kinfolk of slaughtered Britons, he appeals to an ancient code of retributive justice that defied the usual practice of bargaining for ransom. By refusing to negotiate with the Romans, Cymbeline exercises his prerogative to refuse pardon. His wisdom in doing so, however, is called into question when Posthumus pardons Iachimo, who has confessed his part in promoting Posthumus's faithless wager: "my heavy conscience sinks my knee ... [take] the bracelet of the truest princess/That ever swore faith" (414–18). Posthumus becomes exemplary, telling Iachimo: "Kneel not to me:/The power I have on you, is to spare you," to which Cymbeline responds "Nobly doom'd!/We'll learn our freeness of a son-in-law:/Pardon's the word to all" (418–23). By imitating Posthumus, Cymbeline does more than save his Roman adversaries. By associating his "freeness" specifically with pardon, he illustrates the most benign effects of the prerogative, the absolute power of the monarch granted to him by law.

Cymbeline's moment of self-reflection coincides with his recognition of his "son-in-law," not only as his daughter's husband but as one of the "four peasants" whose resistance to an imperial force was the occasion of his own salvation. That Posthumus is acknowledged as Imogen's consort signals in a formal way what the action has already established: Cymbeline has abandoned plans for the incestuous marriage he had earlier envisaged. To have learned his son-in-law's "freeness"—if that is a freedom to resist even the authority and power from which an outlaw has no legal recourse—also constitutes a warning. Even an absolute monarch is absolute only to a point: he is never a god. Beyond positive law, the subject has a footing in "Nature" that makes contingent even the prerogative. Cymbeline as Caesar's subject benefits from this resistance which validates, in turn, his respect for conscience and contract. Cymbeline as king of Britain and prospectively emperor of the west is therefore in a position to arrive at the wisdom Fleming had indicated was the only guarantee that the prerogative would be exercised for the benefit of the subject.

The Soothsayer's interpretation of Jupiter's tablet confirms that what has just happened on stage is the result of providence. It establishes what those characters who had been made helpless by their own confusion (especially Pisanio) had hoped for: the heavens working in and through history. The Soothsayer's *re*-interpretation of his own vision of the Roman eagle's flight west obviously speaks to the fact that Rome has not won the kind of victory he had earlier foreseen, but has secured the tribute she had requested in the first place. It alludes by figures of thought and of speech to the forces both personal and numinous that have resolved the conflict between Rome and Britain. Its explanatory power is the more important because Cymbeline himself gives no reason why the Queen's argument for rejecting tribute, which he did not oppose, is no longer good. Nor does he explain why he is no longer convinced that his own position on very fundamental English liberties and liberty is correct. He simply "promises" to pay Caesar "our wonted tribute" (463). In effect, he repeats Cassibelan's promise—a promise that he must now regard as holding good despite the fact that the circumstances in which it was first made no longer obtain.

Cymbeline's decision to honor his ancestor's verbal contract is plausible only if he has accepted what he earlier rejected: a word given in good faith has a force in conscience. What guarantees its privilege is both in "Nature" and in the Word, the hidden subject of the Soothsayer's new interpretation of the Roman eagle:

> For the Roman eagle,
> From south to west on wing soaring aloft,
> Lessen'd herself and in the beams o' the sun
> So vanish'd: which foreshadow'd our princely eagle,
> Th'imperial Caesar, should again unite
> His favour with the radiant Cymbeline,
> Which shines here in the west.

> (471–77)

British victory and Roman success coincide in a moment at which imperial rule is both enlarged and reduced—enlarged by assimilating a western people, reduced by light from a sun in the west. The eagle's fabled vision—said to be able to look into the sun—becomes one with the radiance it seeks. Literal historicism opens a figuratively contrived perspective on salvation history when the Soothsayer's words are read as puns: thus the Roman eagle "lessen'd" (that is, "lessoned") herself in the "sun" (that is, the Son) and so "vanish'd." The condition of this Roman lesson—the eclipse of Caesar before God—would therefore appear to be the precondition of the *translatio imperii* which is clearly alluded to as Caesar's "favour" to "radiant" Cymbeline. The British king literally pays tribute to the Roman Caesar. Figuratively, however, he pays tribute to that lessoned or instructed emblem of imperial rule by which he must now, that is, in the future the play looks forward to, agree to govern. Under the aegis of the Word, this new imperialism paradoxically guarantees the liberties and liberty on which Cymbeline had originally insisted.

This action of an appropriation turned in on and, in a sense, against itself, exemplifies the process of "enterprise" Bacon illustrated in his "Of the true Greatness of the Kingdom of Britain."[32] It leaves the Britons as "naturalized" Romans, the tribute they owe to Caesar paid not from the abject position of a conquered people but granted in conscientious observance of a contract. Tribute paradoxically signals their freedom not their servitude. It also casts Cymbeline in the self-reflexive light that according to virtually all theories of monarchy, whether absolutist or constitutional, was supposed to show him how to rule. His status as subject, by way of fictions of accident, deprivation, or sympathetic identification, provides a mirror in which he can see the effects of his authority and power. Enabling these exchanges is the contractualism effected by the human word and legitimated by divine law incarnate in the Word.

[32]A later version of "The True Greatness of the Kingdom of Britain" entitled "Of the Greatnesse of Kingdomes," in print in *The Essays*, 1612, returns to the topic of taxation and the need for restraint: "The blessing of *Iudah* and *Issachar* will neuer meet, to be both the Lions whelpe and the Asse laid betweene burthens: Neither will a people ouercharged with tributes, bee euer fit for Empire. Nobilitie & Gentlemen multiplying in too great a proportion, maketh the common subiect grow to bee a pesant and base swaine driuen out of heart, and but the Gentlemans laborer . . . take away the middle people, & you take away the infantery, whch is the nerue of an Armie . . . For it is the Plough that yeeldeth the best soldier; but how? maintained in plentie and in the hand of owners, and not of meere laborers"; *Works*, 12: 377–78. In its final form, entitled "Of the True Greatness of Kingdoms and Estates," published in 1625, Bacon's treatise on empire puts a special emphasis on Rome's peaceful conquests by naturalization: "you will say that it was not the Romans that spread upon the world, but it was the world that spread upon the Romans, and that was the sure way of greatness"; *Works*, 12: 182.

CHAPTER 4

The Winter's Tale

*T*HE MOTIF OF RETURN, A COMMON FEATURE OF ROMANCE NARRATIVE, can provoke a powerful illusionism. The terms of the hero's home-coming and his recovery of things lost (including his morale) may become fused with the terms of pastoral and allow his entertainment of an earthly timelessness. Romance typically describes a career defined by temporal conditions; pastoral promises, or seems to promise, restorations like those of vegetation in spring, always perfect, always complete. Loss in pastoral can, of course, be permanent and definitive, but it is significant that then it gets a special and symbolic acknowledgment. Convention dictates that the shepherd's grave be covered with cut flowers, a mark of the human condition (cf. *Cymbeline*, 4.2.218–28). *The Winter's Tale* exploits these generically distinct notions of time to convey an experience of both finitude and a kind of eternity.[1] The play dramatizes the desire of Leontes, king of Sicilia, for a free and absolute rule and shows it to be consistent with the presumption that he is somehow immortal.

[1] Of the many studies of temporality in *The Winter's Tale*, two are especially relevant to the material in this chapter: Inga-Stina Ewbank, "The Triumph of Time in '*The Winter's Tale*,'" *Review of English Literature* 5, 2 (1964): 83–100; and Michael D. Bristol, "In Search of the Bear: Spatiotemporal Form and the Heterogeneity of Economies in *The Winter's Tale*," *Shakespeare Quarterly* 42, 2 (1991): 145–67.

At the beginning of the play he seems still to believe that he is what Polixenes, king of Bohemia, says each of them, as children, thought he was: "a boy eternal" (1.2.65). At its conclusion, he recognizes the child he thought he had lost, Perdita, who is now a nubile woman. His desire and presumption are represented as the basis of a tyrannical misrule; his dis-illusionment is shown as consistent with an equitable government.

Living by an entirely illusionistic sense of what rule can and should be, Leontes initiates the action of the play in a world that he sees as timeless, comparable to the false Hesperides of Antiochus. It is charac-terized by the effacement of mutual dependencies, those created in marriage and among friends (kin and kind), and by attempts at monop-olistic control of resources. Like Posthumus, Leontes desires partheno-genesis: to be the father of a child who has no mother. His career is finally comedic, however. The play mitigates the inevitable pathos of pastoral illusionism by showing its relation to art and, more extensively, art's relation to nature. Pastoral becomes both a vehicle for the instruc-tion art provides and the model of how that instruction should pro-ceed. In danger of deep despair (comparable to Pericles' apathy), Leontes acquires a renewed vitality—symbolized by the return of his queen and his heir—through the art of theater. Paulina, counselor and surrogate physician, stages what is in effect a play, "the vivification of Hermione," that celebrates what Leontes can feel as a rebirth and yet remain firmly grounded in temporal reality.

The most obvious indication that Shakespeare intended to work a thematics of pastoral into his romance plot are the two major changes he made to his source, Robert Greene's *Pandosto*, a prose narrative that he otherwise follows quite closely. By the end of Greene's romance, his principal characters—the king, Pandosto and his wife, Bellaria (mod-els for Leontes and Hermione)—each die. Their places are taken by Pandosto's heir and her consort. Shakespeare, departing from Greene, portrays Leontes and Hermione in states that figure death—madness and exile—but are not actually lethal. He concludes the action of the play with events that signify life: the king moves from despair to joy, the queen regains her office and her daughter, and the kingdom recovers its dynastic integrity. The simultaneity of these events contrasts with the disjunctions of *Pandosto*. Unlike Greene's Pandosto, who dies for grief over the loss of his wife despite his daughter's return, Leontes retrieves both wife and daughter.[2] Such a reformulation of plot reflects a Shakespearean idea of self-discipline. Leontes can experience a pastoral dimension to his romance—seeing his daughter as like but different from his wife, finding in his "autumn" a kind of "spring"—because he has learned that all human life is actually finite.

Consciousness of time and hence of mortality is expressed initially as the recognition of the difference between youth and age, and then more pervasively in conflicts between different persons or interests. To refuse to recognize differences in general is an allowable trait of childhood; to insist that every difference be definitive and beyond reconciliation is tyrannical. Leontes opens the play by falling quickly and almost inexplicably into the condition of tyrant. He behaves as if neither Polixenes nor Hermione have agency and can differ from him in what they desire without breaking bonds of friendship and marriage. He assumes a powerful uniqueness that he believes is capable of infinite reproduction: neither his children nor his subjects are to exhibit a character or will that are not reflections of his own. Absolute politically, he is different from and indifferent to everyone.[3] He recovers his reason when his megalomania is shown to be a form of impiety, but he regains his sanity—a more comprehensive attribute—only after years of self-reproach. The connection between a pious acknowledgment of a divine as opposed to a merely human will on the one hand, and the acceptance of difference on the other, is established by an act of faith in human beings: Hermione can come alive to Leontes only when he regains his trust in her.[4]

[2]For studies of this source, see Inga-Stina Ewbank, "From Narrative to Dramatic Language: *The Winter's Tale* and its Source," in *Shakespeare and the Sense of Performance: Essays in the Tradition of Performance Criticism in Honor of Bernard Beckerman*, ed. Marvin and Ruth Thompson (Newark: University of Delaware Press, 1989), 29–47; see also Roy Battenhouse, "Theme and Structure in 'The Winter's Tale,'" *Shakespeare Survey* 33 (1980): 123–38; and Charles Frey, *Shakespeare's Vast Romance: A Study of The Winter's Tale* (Columbia: University of Missouri Press, 1980), 50–68.

[3]The concept of constitutional rule is bound up with language describing marital relations. See Bracton, who states that the monarch's law is passed only with the "whole assent of the republic," i.e., the representative assembly (*communis rei publicae sponsio*), a formulation that suggests the passage of legislation can be understood metaphorically, as a perpetual reenactment of a marriage ceremony (*sponsalium*); cited in Charles Howard McIlwain, *Constitutionalism Ancient and Modern* (Ithaca: Cornell University Press, 1940), 71.

[4]For a study of Leontes' career in light of a Christian morality, see Robert N. Watson, *Shakespeare and the Hazards of Ambition* (Berkeley: University of California Press, 1988), 222–79.

Leontes' tyranny is brief by measures of real time. It erupts as Polixenes is leaving Sicilia to return to Bohemia. It ends some days later when Leontes, recognizing his error, is ready to accept counsel, and presumably, to rule in the interests of his whole people. Its effects, however, linger for sixteen years. With Mamillius dead and Perdita abandoned in the Bohemian desert, Leontes' Sicilia is "heirless" and airless, without a future and apparently dead. In the language of dense metaphor usual in the romances, Leontes "killed" his kingdom when, assuming a parthenogenic generation, he denied his wife and daughter agency and therefore, in effect, a separate life. The jealousy that made him suspect every sign of independence as an instance of rebellion directly affects his person (or body natural) as madness, and by extension the state (or body politic) as anarchy. His madness leaves his kingdom "headless." Both Hermione and Perdita are preserved but by different agents and actions.

Perdita is not, however, only the heir to Sicilia's throne. At the conclusion of the play, she is also betrothed to Polixenes' son, Florizel, and therefore figures in a second dynastic succession. Their marriage realizes a union of the kingdoms of Bohemia and Sicilia, a dramatic fact that gains meaning by its representation in the setting of pastoral. Literary tradition identifies two places as the principal scenes of pastoral, Sicily and Arcadia, the latter a region east of the Roman world and located in the Peloponnese. The mythos of the genre links them by the underground river, Alpheus, whose source is in Arcadia but whose "spring," the nymph Arethusa, rises in Sicily. In keeping with the atemporal mode of pastoral, their conjunction does not discriminate a difference of priority—the pastoral river is said to flow into a body of water that is a source. Comparably, the mythos of the play links its places of pastoral so that their two kingdoms will form one undivided kingdom comprising entities of equal importance. Bohemia and Sicilia are prospectively united when Florizel and Perdita travel from north to south, their youth and generativity a sign of pastoral's two springs— seasonal and aqueous—and the common culture that binds one people to another. The agent critical to the success of their venture and to the dynastic integrity of both kingdoms is the Bohemian Shepherd who first finds and cares for Perdita. His role is emblematized in his description at the moment of recognition and reunion that concludes the play. Weeping for joy, he is said to have stood by the royal couple "like a weather-beaten conduit of many kings' reigns" (5.2.56–57). Visibly a "fountain" of tears, he has actually served as the channel connecting the two regions now to be united by marriage.

The Business of Difference

The conflict that separates Bohemia from Sicilia at the play's opening evolves from a misrepresentation of a difference that is in fact open to resolution by recourse to the measures of equity, the virtual equalization of inherently unequal entities. As the courtiers of Bohemia and Sicilia describe Polixenes' gratitude for Leontes' hospitality, it looks as if Bohemia will leave Sicilia as a friend and beneficiary. The hospitality or "entertainment" Leontes has shown Polixenes, which will not be matched when Leontes visits Polixenes, will nevertheless not cause a disgraceful debt. Bohemia will pay Sicilia by "their loves," and the "great difference" between the resources of the two kingdoms will be "justified" in a commerce of the spirit (1.1.3–9). In any case, as Camillo, Leontes' counselor notes, what Bohemia has taken from Sicilia was "given freely" and must not therefore be returned at "too dear" a rate (17–18). The origin or "root" of these kings' mutual affection is in the "kindness" of a shared childhood. The opinion of their courtiers is that it cannot but continue to flourish or "branch" in the future (21–24). But because this "branching" is also a separation, it implies the emergence of differences over and above its essential unity. Whether whatever disjunctions occur can continue to be overcome by love is partly a question of perspective. Although public duties have forced the actual separation of these monarchs, the "interchange of gifts, letters, [and] loving embassies" has allowed them "to seem to be together though absent" (27–29). As Camillo remarks, their relation can be preserved with divine assistance: "The heavens continue their loves" (31–32). The first of a series of references to the interventions of divine will in human affairs and history, Camillo's pious exclamation finds its dramatic exposition in the reunions that will follow what he has alluded to as an inevitable branching in the relations of the two kings.

The relations of hospitality that the courtiers celebrate reveal their fragility when they are challenged by opposed intentions and described not in the language of love but rather of business.[5] Polixenes hints that Leontes' "entertainment" has a price when he counts himself as a "cipher" who augments his thanks exponentially. But it is Hermione's display of hospitality and account of "Grace" that provoke Leontes' threat to the loving relations Camillo has prayed for. Summoned by Leontes to persuade Polixenes to postpone his departure, she announces that were he to swear he longs to see his son, she would send him home. Then she contradicts herself and insists that despite all the oaths in heaven, she would demand he stay in Sicilia. Throughout this dialogue she behaves as if her will were instrumental, her "verily" or woman's word as "potent as a lord's"—his or, presumably, Leontes' (1.2.34–56). Why she believes she has such a standing is suggested by her contributions to Polixenes' account of his childhood and its sequel, the separation of the two kings.

As Polixenes states, he and Leontes were "twinned lambs" in boyhood. Their exchanges then were no more material than "innocence for innocence." In time, however, the "stronger blood" of sexuality asserted itself, and after marriage, the monarchs separated and entered new unions. Hermione excuses their "slipping"—into sexuality and from innocence—by invoking "Grace" (80, 99, 105), a concept that in early modern usage connoted a concession a superior granted a subordinate either to enjoy a privilege or to be excused from a punishment. Its principal reference was to the divine forgiveness of sin, here identified as the original sin, the "hereditary imposition" of sexual knowledge (74–75). Hermione indicates the divine agency that mitigates the effects of such "slipping" when she states that "Grace" inspired her words of betrothal to Leontes;[6] she

---

[5]For the economy of the gift, see Bristol on the "ethos of gift"; "In Search of the Bear," 154. On market relations as social relations, Jean-Christophe Agnew remarks: "Exchange for the sake of exchange, which Aristotle labeled 'chrematistic exchange,' threatened to transform . . . the householder's obligation of hospitality and liberality into a narrow calculus of cost and benefit; it diverted goods from their natural uses and limits to a sphere of intermediaries, where circulation and accumulation could accelerate and expand without purpose, and more important, without limit"; Jean-Christophe Agnew, *Worlds Apart: The Market and the Theater in Anglo-American Thought, 1550–1750* (Cambridge: Cambridge University Press, 1986), 21.

[6]Leontes ignores the divine grace that absolves sexuality and in so doing exhibits a false innocence. As Michael Taylor notes, "Leontes is an innocent in the worst sense . . . [he] looks at the world and sees reflected there his own hysterical forebodings"; "Innocence in *The Winter's Tale*," *Shakespeare Studies* 15 (1982): 227–42.

implies that it also has favored her hospitable invitation to Polixenes. In all these instances, she is drawing on the power of equity. She is allowing a relation determined by difference, whether between God and man, maid and man, or host and guest, a means to resolve natural and customary distinctions of place or office in favor of a commonality of interest among them. Occupying the subordinate office of wife, her wishes and her "verilys" or professions of truth (1.2.51–52) are as "potent" as her superior's (Leontes') because marriage, although of persons of different status, makes spouses one by virtue of grace. Taking the place of host, she extends hospitality to a guest and here, too, distinctions of place are effaced; she regards her guest as if he were kin or kind and not a stranger from another country. These concessions are instances of a loving rather than a merely executive power. Too much at odds with an absolutism that refuses to recognize and therefore also to reconcile differences with love, it is a power that will drive Leontes mad. Aware of Hermione's attractive "liberty" (112), her freedom to improvise upon her offices of wife and hostess, he reads into it the pretext for an actual crime: adultery.

The mentality Leontes exhibits at this critical moment is responsible for his mistrust of his wife and his friend. To him, Hermione is not playing the hostess but engaging in a kind of business—she and Polixenes are "paddling palms and pinching fingers" as if to close a deal, "the mort of the deer [dear]" (115–18). Opposed to what he sees as her negotiations are his own pretensions to a monopolistic hold on relations that would otherwise be open to trust.[7] His madness is especially evident when he speaks to his son, Mamillius. Inevitably, Leontes disparages the

[7]Perplexed by the nature of transactions involving things "dear" or valuable, Leontes is representative of the culture of early modern commerce. The extension of credit to borrowers was especially dependent on relations of trust, not to precise calculations recorded in legal contracts; the principal instrument of lending at interest, the bill of exchange, was extended in the expectation the borrower was honorable; J. H. Baker, in *The Legal Profession and the Common Law* (London: Hambledon, 1986), 341–68. Robert Ashton stresses that in such actions, "the personal reputation of the borrower was the prime element of security"; Robert Ashton, *The Crown and the Money Market, 1603–1640* (Oxford: Clarendon Press, 1960), 2. More generally, trust was conceded to be the basis for all social as well as commercial relations. As Innocent Gentillet states: "whosoever will take away Faith and loyaltie from amongst men (as Machiavell would doe) he withall takes away all contracts, commerce, distributive and politicke justice, and all societie and frequentation with one another, none of which can stand but by the observation of Faith." Innocent Gentillet, *A discovrse vpon the means of vvel governing* (London, 1602), Z2, Z2ᵛ; STC 11743. Thus every kind of exchange was to be secured by an act of conscience, whatever its conditions.

woman's part in reproduction. He sees himself reflected in Mamillius—"they say we are/Almost alike as eggs" (1.2.129–30)—but less than completely and so less than satisfactorily: Hermione has "too much blood in him" (2.1.57–58). Leontes concludes with a pathological logic: if children are not precise clones of their father, then all mothers are bawds. Women are merely impressionable matter and a child who differs from his (legal, putative) father must be a bastard. Leontes' obsession with parthenogenic generation mirrors a corresponding willfulness of rule.[8]

How Leontes accounts for his suspicions of his wife and friend looks forward to the means by which he will be cured. Obviously responsible for his deluded accusations is what Leontes calls "Affection," which he defines as a kind of passion that is experienced initially in the imagination or as "dream," and then sometimes realized in actual relations.[9] In the first instance it is a "nothing"; when "cojoined" with what is real or external to the mind, as in marriage or friendship, it becomes "something." None of this would be exceptionable were it not that Leontes regards the actual relations "Affection" produces as expressions of passion and unaffected by love. They are to be limited by "commission," that is, regulated not free, restricted by the terms of an office not open to modification by virtue of grace.[10]

[8]Commenting on 3.2, Charles Frey observes that Leontes as king has "some reason to become trapped in divine analogy" but that "as a man, dependent upon a woman in order to play his part in creation, he cannot be self-sufficient," *Shakespeare's Vast Romance*, 131.

[9]For a useful analysis of this term, see David Ward, "Affection, Intention, and Dreams in *The Winter's Tale*," *Modern Language Review* 82, 3 (1987): 545–54. The suddenness of Leontes' change of heart has often puzzled critics; considering the play's link to the "allegorical morality drama," Darryll Grantley suggests that its motivation is less important than its emblematic value as a sign of sin: Darryll Grantley, "*The Winter's Tale* and Early Religious Drama," *Comparative Drama* 20, 1 (1986): 17–23; 20. See also Maurice Hunt, *Shakespeare's Romance of the Word* (Lewisburg: Bucknell University Press, 1990), 90–93. For an analysis of Leontes' jealousy as a feature of his "hyper-mimetic" character, see René Girard, "The Crime and Conversion of Leontes in *The Winter's Tale*," *Religion and Literature* 22, 2–3 (1990): 193–219. Maydee G. Lande, analyzing the play from a psychoanalytic view, regards Leontes as deluded in seeing the world as a projection of his own devising. The deaths of his wife and son check his fantasies of omnipotence and are reality's "final confirmation"; "*The Winter's Tale*: A Question of Motive," *American Imago* 43, 1 (1986): 51–65; 62.

[10]William R. Morse reads this passage as an expression of Leontes' investment in a self-serving rationalism that assumes the preeminence of the individual subject; "Metacriticism and Materiality: The Case of Shakespeare's *The Winter's Tale*," *ELH* 58 (1991): 283–304. Leontes' presumption that relations are to be defined entirely according to his will is, however, represented as irrational and an indictment of absolutist notions of rule.

Affection! thy intention stabs the centre:
Thou dost make possible things not so held,
Communicat'st with dreams;—how can this be?—
With what's unreal thou coactive art,
And fellow'st nothing: Then 'tis very credent
Thou mayst cojoin with something; and thou dost,
And that beyond commission.

(1.2.138–44)

Because the audience knows that there is no evidence of Hermione's infidelity, it can see that Leontes betrays a trust: passionate but unloving, he is unfaithful to the terms of his marriage contract. His condition illustrates the extraordinary power of the imagination that becomes pathological not when its constructions are "nothing" (dreams in themselves are innocuous) but when, having no basis in love, they are perceived to determine relations by "commission." Relations not so determined—atypical of the market and, in any case, not to be justified by calculation—are preeminently familial or friendly. Indicating status, they are experienced as effacements of status, and they either benefit from largesse or generate equitable arrangements. In each case, difference is observed but not made the basis of practice. In this sense it is a fact without consequences. That part of Mamillius which is like Hermione does not indicate her infidelity to Leontes, and when Paulina later declares the infant Perdita to be the "copy" of Leontes, the fact that she differs from him by being female does not mean that she is not his child (2.3.97–99). Leontes' propensity to mistrust those for whom he feels no more than "Affection" correlates with his tyrannical unwillingness to be crossed, to encounter difference in others. Neither Camillo, nor Antigonus, nor Paulina—all faithful counselors—will come close to persuading him of his errors.

Commanded by Leontes to poison Polixenes for committing adultery with Hermione, Camillo tells Leontes that he will obey because he "must believe" his master (1.2.333). But later, understanding that Leontes is "in rebellion with himself, [and] will have /All that are his, so too" (354–56), Camillo declares that he will disobey his king and leave the kingdom. His decision reflects his judgment of the case at hand and, more important, what he asserts are the lessons of the past:

> If I could find example
> Of thousands that had struck annointed kings
> And flourish'd after, I'd not do't: but since
> Nor brass, nor stone, nor parchment bears not one,
> Let villainy itself forwear't.

(1.2.357–61)

By not committing murder, Camillo obeys divine law, of course; but he takes the occasion of his disobedience to his king to assert that divine justice is demonstrable even in historical record. It does not show that villains prosper. Remarkable for its anti-Machiavellianism in one sense (villains clearly do prosper), Camillo's pious historicism is, I think, meant to affirm a providence that, like Jupiter in *Cymbeline*, works through time to just ends. Camillo's words will draw attention to Leontes' tyrannical claim that he needs no counsel—whether from a divine source or his people.

Charging Hermione with adultery, Leontes tells his courtiers that to speak for her is to be guilty. Moreover, their advice is superfluous: "Our prerogative calls not your counsels, but our natural goodness/Imparts this . . . . [T]he matter,/The loss, the gain, the ord'ring on't, is all/Properly ours" (2.1.163–70).[11] When Antigonus observes that Leontes might have "tried" the case in his "silent judgment" (170–71)—that is, by reflecting on the evidence in light of prior knowledge—he is also describing recourse to the counsel of conscience. Antigonus's faith in his own wife, Paulina, is as exemplary as was Camillo's discerning providence in history. Allowing Paulina to appear before Leontes and to disobey his "rule," Antigonus is accused by Leontes of a feeble uxoriousness (2.3.46). But Antigonus applauds Paulina's assertion of her own agency. He rules her, she states, only "[f]rom all dishonesty" (47); in this case, she determines the nature of the honesty she is to respect. Knowing Paulina's character, Antigonus declares: "When she will take the rein I let her run;/But she'll not stumble" (51–52).

---

[11]Leontes rejects counsel; by contrast, Cymbeline's Queen is too tyrannical to counsel and Antiochus makes anything but silence punishable by death. For the conception of counsel in *The Winter's Tale*, see Stuart M. Kurland, "'We need no more of your advice': Political Realism in *The Winter's Tale*," *Studies in English Literature, 1500–1900* 31, 2 (1991): 365–86.

Nothing speaks more directly to Leontes' madness and its expression in tyranny than his impious rejection of all forms of law—positive law which requires an examination of evidence; natural law which prohibits abuse of dependents, especially children (Leontes orders the infant Perdita to be left in a "remote and desert place" outside his kingdom); and divine law. He agrees to consult the oracle of Apollo at Delphi, not for enlightenment (he has already decided that Hermione is guilty) but to quiet his people (2.1.189–94). Hearing its decree—"Hermione is chaste; Polixenes blameless; Camillo a true subject; Leontes a jealous tyrant; his innocent babe truly begotten; and the king shall live without an heir, if that which is lost be not found"—he pronounces it "mere falsehood" (3.2.132–36, 141). He only recognizes divine law when he sees divine justice in the death of Mamillius: "Apollo's angry and the heavens themselves/Do strike at my injustice" (146–47). This experience converts Leontes to a faith in divine will. What it does not do is restore him to his family or allow his kingdom a secure future. The condition of its heir is uncertain, and the promotion of an alternative, another heir, is prohibited by Apollo. These deprivations of kin, kind, and future will end when Leontes' faith gains a correlative practice through love.

Equitable Unions

The liberty Leontes most feared in Hermione and continues to fear in his courtiers—a liberty closely tied to the subject's right to speak and to have agency—depends on the equitable resolution of differences created by commission. As Fleming had ruled in Bates's case, it was a function of the monarch's absolute power to rule by granting privilege; when absolutely empowered, he was not required to respect a right but to exercise wisdom.[12] Equity was originally a legal concept and featured regularly in discussions of justice that addressed the problem of applying general rules to particular cases. For English readers, St. German's treatment was representative. Grounding the application of law in "conscyence," St. German identified "equytye" as:

---

[12]See chapter 3, pp. 90–91. The subject's right to speech was claimed by the Commons in their "Apology," 1601; see chapter 2, pp. 45–47.

a ryghtwysnes that consyderyth all the partyculer cyrcumstaunces of the dede the whiche also is temperyd with the swetnes of mercye. And such an equytye must alway be observyd in euery lawe of man and in euery generall rewle therof.

For, he added, "extreme ryghtwysenes is extreme wronge . . . to folowe the words of the lawe were in some case both agaynst justyce and the common welth."[13] By specifying that equity was to be observed in all legal interpretation, St. German made it a tool of government. Conscience was a rational faculty devoted to practical ends; it had to embrace knowledge in order to promote interests beyond those of the self.[14] Preeminently the knowledge needed by monarchs and magistrates, conscience had its opposite, which was "affecyon." Misled by "syngularytie, as when a man foloweth hys owne wyt & wyll and wyll not conferme hym selfe to other, nor folowe the good common wayes," driven by "an inordynat affeccyon to hym selfe whereby he makyth conscyence to folowe his desyre & so he causyth her to go out of her ryght course" (i$_{iii}$), no ruler could govern well. Because equity recognized common interests, it established social and political harmony. James's formulation of equity follows St. German and is a model of succinctness: "Vse Iustice," he declares, "but with such moderation, as it turne not in Tyrannie: otherwaies *summum Ius*, is *summa iniuria*."[15]

A text defending James's proposed Union of the kingdoms, John Hayward's *A Treatise of Vnion of the Two Realmes of England and Scotland*, 1604, is especially clear on equity's role in politics. It was the agency that

---

[13]Christopher St. German, *The fyrste dyaloge in Englysshe (betwixt a doctour of dyvynyte and a student in the lawes of Englande)* (London, 1531), i$_{iv}$, i$_{iv}$^{v}; STC 21562. For St. German, see Glenn Burgess, *The Politics of the Ancient Constitution: An Introduction to English Political Thought, 1603–1642* (University Park: Pennsylvania State University, 1992), 29–37. The idea that extreme righteousness is unjust underlies the concept of a "modest Justice" in *Pericles*; see chapter 2, p. 66. For an early formulation of equity, see Aristotle, *Nicomachean Ethics*, 1137^{a}1–1138^{b}1. See also Edmund Plowden, *Commentaries or Reports* (London, 1761), below, p. 140.

[14]St. German analyzed the practicality of conscience by reference to etymology; it is what is achieved with or by means of knowledge, *cum scientia*. See chapter 5, p. 157.

[15]James's examples of equitable judgments—viz. the acquittal of a "man of a knowen honest life" claiming to have acted in self-defense though not in the presence of witnesses for the killing of one "knowen to bee deboshed and isolent"—are also unexceptionable. James VI and I, *Basilicon Doron*, in *Political Writings*, ed. Johann P. Sommerville (Cambridge: Cambridge University Press, 1994), 43.

determined a common interest and thus fashioned a harmonious state. Hayward, who imagined the Union as two kinds of marriage—between two kingdoms and a king and one people—derived his imagery from James's statement to Parliament that as monarch of both England and Scotland, he was the "Shepherd" to "two Flockes," and also a "husband" to two "wives." But as a "Christian King vnder the Gospel," he wished neither to be a "Polygamist" nor to have his "Flocke parted in two." But, as James himself noted, his English subjects saw his predicament in another light. They were afraid that were they and the Scots to constitute a single "flock" and one "wife," he would turn out to be two differently disposed shepherds and husbands: beneficent (to the Scots) and tyrannical (to the English ["19 March 1604," 136]).[16] Hayward attempted to allay English fears of unequal treatment by comparing the proposed Union to a marriage in which James, a loving husband, would treat all elements in his united kingdom lovingly and as one "wife."

Hayward stated that a valid union only could be rooted in "the vnion of mindes or of loue": "Without [this union], the bodily vnion is of little strength, either for present vse or for continuance." "Loue"— when England and Scotland become one people—would flow from the monarch and would fashion the bond between them.[17] Such love, said Hayward, is the spirit of "equitie"; not an "Arithmetical equalitie . . . in degree or in estate," but rather a virtual equality "in libertie and priuiledge." It "maketh friendship and is the very mother of friendship." "Inequalitie" is, by contrast, "the ground of suspition" and the "fewell of discord." Equity recognizes the differences that create inequality, but it

---

[16]Cf. James I: "There is a conceipt intertained, and a double iealosie possesseth many, wherein I am misiudged. First, that this Vnion will be the *Crisis* to the ouerthrow of England and the setting vp of Scotland . . . The second is, my profuse liberalitie to the Scottish men more then the English, and that with this Vnion all things shalbe giuen to them and you turned out of all"; "Speech to parliament, 31 March 1607," James VI and I, *Political Writings*, 164–65.
[17]Sir John Hayward, *A Treatise Of Vnion Of The Two Realmes Of England and Scotland* (London, 1604), D; STC 13011. Hayward implies that such love comes from a king whose mind is "sound" when he cites in support of the Union Seneca's dictum: "*Rege incolumi mens omnibus una*" (by virtue of a king who is sound, i.e., unimpaired, one mind, i.e., will, arises from many); *De clementia*, 1.4.1; *Treatise*, D. Seneca had cited Vergil, who speaks of the emperor as "the bond by which the commonwealth is united" (*vinculum per quod res publica cohaeret*); *Georgics* 4.212. For Hayward, see J. P. Sommerville, *Politics and Ideology in England, 1603–1640* (New York: Longman, 1986), 70–71; and Glenn Burgess, *Absolute Monarchy and the Stuart Constitution* (New Haven: Yale University Press, 1996), 72–76.

suspends or ignores them: "That the Sunne riseth and shineth to all alike, so the law should comprehend all in one equall and vnpartiall equitie ... [A]s *Tacitus* saith, [to be equitable is] *To make other mens aduantages as grieuous vnto them as their proper iniuries*" (D2, D2ᵛ). Like Bacon (who in his speech and treatise of 1606 was perhaps following Hayward), Hayward regarded a general interest as the foundation of empire: "this was one principall meane whereby the Romane state receiued both continuance and encrease; because the people did so easily impart the liberties of their citie almost unto all" (D2ᵛ). In such a case, differences become occasions to institute "conformitie and similitude" (D4ff.).

All the benefits to be derived from agreements instituting unions are jeopardized by a mind incapable of trust, the basis of love. It suffers from a pervasive and debilitating doubt, which Hayward characterizes as a kind of sickness:

> Assuredly, I feare that it is with vs [i.e., those who doubt the possibility of a Union] as with some good women who are often sick, forsooth, but in faith they cannot well tell where. Our fancies runne, that something will be amisse; but neither can it be well discerned by others, neither it is fully perhaps resolued by our selves. Things of greatest suretie breede many doubts in mindes that are determined to beleeue the contrary whereas, in matters of this nature, all points are not alwaies cast into question which may possibly happen; for that many inconueniences are in imagination onely ... much lesse are we bound to listen vnto those who confounding feare with discretion or else couering some corrupt conceit vnder the name of foresight or preuention, doe stretch their thoughts beyond probabilitie and make all doubtfull accidents as if they were certaine. .... A wit too curious in casting of doubts for the most part hurteth. (H3ᵛ, H4)

The work of the imagination is controlled, Hayward said, by prevailing assumptions and beliefs. A mind habitually fearful sees what is merely possible as a dreadful certainty. Castigating English doubters, Hayward asserted that James, as king of Great Britain, would respect the "reciproque oathes" binding monarch to all his people, for these oaths "doe altogether concerne the soule and conscience, and therefore are vnderstood and ruled onely by the lawes of religion" (Gᵛ). Subjects may establish relations by contracts enforceable in positive law, which are "stricti iuris," but the relations of princes are made "good by reason of faith," "bonae fidei." They depend on a "naturall equitie, *boni viri arbitrio*, according to a good mans conscience" (G3^v). In one sense, Hayward was merely testifying to the fact that the monarch's extraordinary powers are beyond positive law. In another, however, his apology implied, perhaps unintentionally, how terrible an affront to all law might be the rule of a monarch who chose to govern without having faith in his subjects. Hayward did not discuss the possibility that the monarch's conscience might malfunction but the topic was a usual one in political discourse.[18] Leontes' rejection of all law in the absence of any trust in his subjects indicates a negative aspect to Hayward's more specific picture of a monarch's conscience as guaranteed by bona fides.

The Monarch as "Husband"

Hermione's trial illustrates how she is harmed by the effects of an Affectionate rule that lacks a basis in love and faith. Accusing her of crimes for which there is no evidence, Leontes speaks an incomprehensible language of fantasy that she must accept as an index of reality: "My life stands in the level of your dreams,/Which I'll lay down," she says (3.2.81–82). The cause of her faint (and apparent lapse into death), a servant's report of Mamilius's death (and not Leontes' rejection of the Oracle's message), suggests that Leontes' love sustains her generativity as well as her person. Heir-less, she can no longer breathe and so she begins a lifeless kind of life, her winter of privation. Had Leontes overcome "Affection" with love, their union would have remained vital and generative. As metaphor, its reference is to a growing and fertile body politic.

In the language of medieval political thought that exploited the analogy between household and state, a king's marital duties were specified as those he should perform for his people, who were said to cohere in a material body and, in some accounts, to be figured as his wife. His

---

[18]Edward Forset, castigating the "imbecillitie of iudgement" and the "sensuall and irrationall mocions" monarchs were subject to, saw that passion, compounded by "absolutenes of sole power in law-giuing," caused monarchs to draw "supplies out of their politicall bodie to make good what wanteth in their naturall"; Edward Forset, *A Comparatiue Discovrse of the Bodies Natvral & Politique* (London, 1606), C$_{iiii}$^{v}, D.

sexuality was consonant with her fruitfulness, which was identified with that of the land and the productions of the body politic. His desire for increase was paradoxically thwarted when he was driven only by self-interest. As pseudo-Aquinas had noted, the perfect state was one like a household, directed by a notion of a "common good" (*bonum multitudinis*).[19] Commenting on Proverbs 29.4—"The king by judgment establisheth the land: but he that receiveth gifts overthroweth it"—pseudo-Aquinas described a "just king" (*rex iustus*) as one who "makes the land rich" (*erigere terram*; 16–17). His harvest was not, however, his property but his people's: their labor had to give them "a sufficiency of material goods" (*corporalium bonorum sufficientia*), and once their "wealth" (*copia*) was secure, the king had to provide for its "conservation" (80–81). Prosperity was therefore a communal phenomenon and signaled the "health of the community" (*salus consociatae multitudines*; 10–11). To illustrate this mutuality of interest, pseudo-Aquinas paraphrased Proverbs 11.24—"There is that scattereth, and yet increaseth; and there is that withholdeth more than is meet, but it tendeth to poverty"—and clarified its apparent paradox by specific reference to tyranny: "some—that is, monarchs—divide their own goods to benefit their subjects, and they themselves become richer. Others—that is, tyrants—take what is not theirs, and they are always in want" (60–61). In short, the monarch who failed to attend to justice or "what is meet," deprived the body politic of its well-being.

Literature describing commercial activity during the early years of James's reign emphasized the importance of monarchic husbandry, now increasingly regarded as a factor in empire-building. Treatises on commerce promoted the idea that the king was supposed to support trade within the kingdom and, more important, between kingdoms. William Fulbecke, in his *Pandectes of the Law of Nations*, 1602, saw that "Princes . . . maintayne their realmes and their estate royall by importing and bringing in such things as be of value or price"; their interest is to be for the "publike good" (T2^v, T3^v, T4). A few years later, Edward Forset pictured the king as "nourishing" his kingdom: he is to "amplifie the dominions thereof for profit and dignitie, to spread abroad the encrease of the people by Colonies in the nature of generating or propagating" (*Comparatiue Discovrse*, C$_{iii}$, C$_{iii}$^{v}). Royal duties of this kind had already

---

[19]St. Thomas Aquinas, *De regimine principum ad regem cypri*, in *Selected Political Writings*, ed. A. P. D'Entrèves, trans. J. G. Dawson (Oxford: Oxford University Press, 1959), 4–5, 8–9.

been reconceived along lines that responded to the exigencies of a mercantile economy rather than one based on patronage. The move was marked by uncertainty; the monarch was both a dispenser of largesse, taking for himself only what he needed to govern, and a trader in merchandise, profiting from the common wealth. In 1601, John Wheeler had defined "commerce" as the activities undertaken in all kinds of relations: "the Prince with his subiects, the Maister with his seruants, one freend and acquaintaunce with another, the Captaine with his souldiers, the Husband with his wife, Women with and among the selues, and in a woord all the world choppeth and chaungeth ... so that all things come into Commerce."[20] The anonymous author of *The Merchants New-royall Exchaunge*, 1604, returned to the Thomistic notion of a generative economy, but altered to fit the mercantile activities of foreign exchange which could be represented as benign. To engage in trade was certainly to enjoy a profit over and above the necessities motivating the exchange, but these profits were distributed over the whole economy: "the benefit [of commerce is] double, for both the forreign & the freeborne are crowned with wealth by it; the black Indian & the white English-man fill their purses by one & the same bargaine." In this economy, the care the medieval monarch was to have taken to increase his kingdom's resources became the acuity with which his descendent promoted its trade: "Kings haue bin, & at this day are of the Societie [of merchants]"; their trade or "propagation," transpiring throughout the kingdom, creates "a Tree of Entercourse," whose fruits are not the Hesperides' sterile "golden Apples" but "politique experience."[21] In short, a monarch's husbandry must support a commerce of and by the people and for their common prosperity.

To identify the monarch as a merchant in this period was also to refer to actual practices by which he was allowed to raise revenue, in theory to support the costs of government. Practices involving commerce were the levying of customs duties on imports and exports, and the granting of exclusive patents of manufacture or monopolies in return for a fee. Both practices, customarily legitimate exercises of the prerogative, provided royal revenue. Bate's case, decided in 1606, had designated as

[20]John Wheeler, *A Treatise of Commerce* (London, 1601), B2; STC 25330.
[21]*The Merchants New-royall Exchaunge* (London, 1604), A2, A2ᵛ; STC 16784.

absolute the monarch's power to regulate trade by customs duties. Like other of his extraordinary powers, this was a matter for his wisdom and not to be referred to the subjects' rights (see chapter 3, pp. 90–91).

The history of monopolies was more contentious. A lucrative kind of monarchic husbandry, monopolies affected the entire economy of the nation not just its foreign trade. It therefore engaged issues customarily within the purview of the common law and touching on the liberties of the subject. Elizabeth I had responded to protest against monopolies by agreeing to limits.[22] Appearing before Parliament, she declared that some of the most offensive "should be presently repealed, some suspended, and none put into execution but such as should first have a trial according to the law for the good of her people." The last provision was especially telling. It meant that no monopoly should violate the common law of property. She issued a proclamation to this effect in 1601. As impressive as its law were her words to her grateful subjects, speaking, as she did subsequently, of the reasons for her action:

> I do assure you there is no prince that loves his subjects better, or whose love can countervail our love. There is no jewel, be it of never so rich a price, which I set before this jewel: I mean your love. For I do esteem it more than any treasure or riches; for that we know how to prize, but love and thanks count unvaluable. And though God hath raised me high, yet this I count the glory of my crown, that I have reigned with your loves.

Elizabeth's language describes a relation of incommensurable benefits, of values that have worth but cannot be priced. Her "esteem" or trust in her subjects does not devolve from her knowledge of their

---

[22]Parliamentary agitation against monopolies focussed on their damage to subjects and their consequent unlawfulness; those protesting the practice had to prove that to restrict monopolies was not to compromise the queen's prerogative. Henry Montague, commenting in 1601 on a bill introduced by Lawrence Hyde that asked for clarification of the common law in relation to "certain cases of Letters Patent," simply stated that the "law and prerogative are one and the same thing. A grant to the hurt of the subject is void." Quoted in J. E. Neale, *Elizabeth I and Her Parliaments: 1584–1601* (London: Jonathan Cape, 1957), 382. For the importance of the struggle over monopolies in relation to notions of liberty, see David Harris Sacks, "Parliament, Liberty, and the Commonwealth," *Parliament and Liberty from the Reign of Elizabeth to the English Civil War*, ed. J. H. Hexter (Stanford: Stanford University Press, 1992), 85–121; for Elizabeth on monopolies and her "Golden Speech," see Sacks, "The Countervailing of Benefits: Monopoly, Liberty, and Benevolence in Elizabethan England," in *Tudor Political Culture*, ed. Dale Hoak (Cambridge: Cambridge University Press, 1995), 272–91.

"treasure," but rather from her experience of their "love," the basis for their intangible exchanges of goodwill. Unquestionably idealistic in its profession of mutual faith, her speech also placed her rule under a providential direction by linking her power to love her subjects with God's grace in directing her wishes:

> I have cause to wish nothing more than to content the subject.... [A]s I am that person that still yet under God hath delivered you, so I trust, by the almighty power of God, that I shall be His instrument to preserve you from every peril, dishonour, shame, tyranny and oppression.... What you bestow on me, I will not hoard it up, but receive it to bestow on you again. Yea mine own properties I account yours, to be expended for your good; and your eyes shall see the bestowing of all for your good.[23]

The queen's willingness to limit her prerogative in favor of the people's interest out of deference to their mutual "loves," found definite corroboration the following year in a decision against a monopolist. Edward Darcy, to whom the queen had given a grant for the exclusive manufacture of playing cards, sued Thomas Allein, a haberdasher, for violating his patent. Chief Justice Popham decided for the defendant. The importance of the case lay in its formulation of a principle restricting monarchic power, as expressed in monopolies, over the material and physical lives of subjects. As reported by Sir Edward Coke, a monopoly was "against the common law" because it impinged on the liberties of the subject—that is, it threatened his livelihood and therefore his life. To prohibit it was to conform to "the equity of the law of God, as appears in Deut. cap xxiv ver. 6; ... [Y]ou shall not take in pledge the nether and upper millstone, for that is his life [i.e., of the working subject]; by which it appears, that every man's trade maintains his life, and therefore he ought not to be deprived or dispossessed of it, no more than of his life."[24] Coke later commented on the equation between a

---

[23]Neale, *Elizabeth* I, 389. This is the version of the so-called "Golden Speech" that is supposed to have been the one actually delivered. A much altered version, in which the Queen's concessions to the subject are not recorded, was published in London in 1601 as *Her Maiesties most Princelie answere, deliuered by her selfe at the Court at White-hall on the last day of Nouember 1601;* STC 7578.

[24]Sir Edward Coke, The Case of Monopolies, *Reports* (London, 1776–77), the eleventh part, vol. 6: ff. 86, 86ᵛ, 87. Coke discussed the case at some length with the following reasons.

monopolist and a murderer: "the monopolist that taketh away a man's trade, taketh away his life . . . . [H]e is *vir sanguinis* [a man of blood]. Against these Inventers and Propounders of euill things, the holy ghost hath spoken, *Inventores malorum, &, digni sunt morte*" (inventors of evil things, they are worthy of death).[25] The fact that the monopoly in question governed a relatively unimportant manufacture—playing cards—only increased the significance of Popham's ruling. Some trades were not to get more protection from murderous practices than others; all trades that limited manufacture "murdered" prospective manufacturers in that trade. When Richard Martin, speaking to Parliament in 1601, identified monopolists as "Bloodsuckers of the Common Wealth," he described their deadly effect on the whole body politic.[26]

Like the politics of the Union (as framed by Hayward), the politics of royal monopoly in the last years of Tudor rule distinguished a monarch's loving relations with her people as equitable and implied that without such love, the body politic would lose its generativity. As the practice of granting monopolies grew more usual, as it did under James I, it drew attention to ways in which the duty of the monarch to husband the people's wealth could be perverted.[27] An economy governed entirely

"Trades," he declared, "are profitable for the commonwealth"; to grant a unique manufacture is against "the benefit and the liberty of the subject": monopolies generally damage "all other subjects, for the end of all these monopolies is for the private gain of the patentees." Were monopolies to be allowed, "artificers . . . who before, by the labour of their hands in their art or trade had maintained themselves and their families . . . now will be constrained to live in idleness and beggary"; 86, 86ᵛ. On Darcy, see Sacks, "The Paradox of Taxation," in *Fiscal Crises, Liberty, and Representative Government, 1450–1789*, ed. Philip T. Hoffman and Kathryn Norberg (Stanford: Stanford University Press, 1994), 61–63.

[25]Sir Edward Coke, "Against Monopolists, Propounders, and Projectors," *The Third Part of the Institutes of the Laws of England*, ed. Sir Edward Coke (London, 1644), 181. For the figure of *vir sanguinis*, see Psalms 5.6 in the Geneva Bible.

[26]Quoted in David George Hale, *The Body Politic: A Political Metaphor in Renaissance English Literature* (The Hague: Mouton, 1971), 74. Cf. the action of the viperous Daughter in *Pericles*; see chapter 2, p. 43.

[27]On the difference between Tudor and Stuart economies, Clive Holmes writes: "Under Elizabeth the subsidy acts emphasized that taxation was related, not as a formal obligation but as a matter of gratitude [on the part of subjects], to the queen's beneficent government. . . . James's financial embarassment was manifestly a product of mismanagement and extravagance, and as a consequence taxation was discussed not in an atmosphere of loyal gratitude for generalized benefits but in terms of the calculation of the value of concessions the king might be obliged to yield in order to secure the necessary subsidies." "Parliament, Liberty, Taxation, and Property," in *Parliament and Liberty*, ed. Hexter, 122–54; 152, 154.

by the monarch's will was, in effect, an extension of the monarch's will, a sterile replication of his wishes and desires. An affront to equity and conscience, its effects are figured in the Bohemian desert in which Antigonus is killed and Perdita is abandoned.

Antigonus, unlike Camillo who leaves Sicilia and therefore does not cross Leontes face to face, is left the task of mitigating whatever sentence against the infant Perdita the king might substitute for the "fire" he had originally decreed. To Antigonus's declaration that he would do "anything possible" to save the child (2.3.165–66), Leontes devises a possibility literally so "remote"—that a "desert" might be a place of prosperity—as to appear impossible without the intervention of "chance" (175–82). How unlikely it is that the Bohemian desert (to which Antigonus's ship arrives [3.3.2]), will prove prosperous is suggested by the shipwreck of the Sicilian boat. It is more forcefully depicted by contemporary events, especially Antigonus's own manner of death: his famous exit "pursued by a bear" by whom he is later reported to be eaten (3.3.56–58). Proverbs describes "a wicked ruler over the poor people" as a "roaring lion" or a "raging bear" (28.15); pseudo-Aquinas, commenting on the verse, identified such a ruler as a "faithless" (*impius*) tyrant (*De regimine principum*, 18–19). The Shepherd, listening to the Clown's account of the disaster remarks that a bear is only "curst" when it is hungry (3.3.128–30), and so conflates the cannibalistic practices of a tyrant with those of his poor subject, a "bare" (as "poor Tom" is "bare" on King Lear's heath) who has no choice but to eat when he is starving. The infant Perdita makes a third such equivocal figure when the Shepherd declares he has found "A very pretty barne," a princely child and also a naked human being, a "bare 'un" (69–70). The misgovernment of Leontes (always *leo* and now also *ursus*) is thus inscribed in Bohemia's desert. His subject, Antigonus, dies and his heir, Perdita, is abandoned to chance. Bohemia is a desert only in a Sicilian perspective, however; it will be illustrated by the pastoral economy of the Shepherd's household, the site of an extraordinary prosperity and renewal. The Shepherd's "barne" is not a "thing dying" but "new-born" (112–13); possessing Perdita's gold, he can forget his two lost sheep (3.2.124) in view of more substantial investments in what will become an "unspeakable estate" (4.2.39–41). The disjunction between points of view and experience at the close of 3 corresponds to the larger play of meanings that characterizes the action to take place in 4. Signaled by paradox, the Sicilian desert of Bohemia is also a place of "deserts" or equitable recompense. The principles of a graceful rule, inspired by love and faith, are revealed in its artful representation and its representation of art.

The Nature of Art

Paulina puts on the play's most important show and her intention in doing so is to obey the divine will that "the king shall live without an heir, if that which is lost be not found." Her faith is comparable to Camillo's, who had earlier seen providence in history. Paulina must believe that Perdita, literally "that which is lost," is the only heir Leontes can have and hope that she will be found. She must also have accepted the fact that if Perdita is not found, Apollo has decreed that the king must remain childless. Paulina is therefore obligated to encourage Leontes to hope for Perdita's reappearance, but also to tolerate celibacy: were Hermione to be restored to him before she was "wrinkled" or he to marry another woman, he could expect another child. He does so hope, apparently, because he has already experienced conversion. He chooses Apollo's authority over reasons of state, which would permit a second marriage for the sake of an heir as his courtiers desire (5.1.24–34). But to live in physical and sensuous privation as a consequence of obeying divine law is a task of another order. Leontes' celibacy must find a purpose compatible with a pious and, more precisely, a sane life. The moral health he seeks will have to controvert the pathology of "Affection" that has allowed him to live in a world of dream, as he himself has acknowledged (3.2.82). If his faith is not to be merely another kind of dream, it must find sensuous correlation in human love. As Paulina's art will establish, Leontes cannot know that sensuousness without feeling first its absence, without consciously experiencing the sensory vacuity of fantasy.

Following Hermione's "death," Paulina at first testifies to what seems to be a character so evil that it cannot be regenerated, telling Leontes: "Do not repent these things, for they are heavier/Than all thy woes can stir: therefore betake thee/To nothing but despair" (3.2.208–10). On second thought, after being reprimanded for her "boldness," she advises Leontes to have "Patience" (231–32). Her counsel here is unexceptional, almost, indeed, banal. Like the cardinal virtue of *fortitudo* or *constantia*, patience was a topic usual in moral discourse, much celebrated as the suffering conducive to Christian humility and sometimes deserved as a punishment for sin. In such contexts, its end was in forgiveness, what Leontes must hope for through the agency of divine grace. But patience also had a place in epistemology. Bacon's *Advancement of Learning*, particularly "The Second Book" on applied knowledge, speaks to the formative role of patience as "trial" in the perfection of an active life. Telling his readers to tolerate contradiction and frustration, the ambiguities in historical record and the disappointments of "trials" in natural philosophy, Bacon equates the virtue these processes require with self-discipline and finally self-knowledge:

> like as a man's disposition is never well known till he be crossed, nor Proteus ever changed shapes till he was straitened and held fast; so the passages and variations of nature cannot appear so fully in the liberty of nature as in the trials and vexations of art.[28]

The art Bacon refers to here is "Mechanical," that is, practical rather than speculative. The artist as natural philosopher does not contemplate objects in nature, but subjects them to testing. The process resembles the shaping of the self. The crossings the philosopher gets in life are traced in his character and, like experiments on natural objects, refine what they thwart.

Paulina's art—her deception in hiding Hermione, her language persuading Leontes to obey divine will—creates and sustains a desperate kind of crossing that Leontes must and does endure for sixteen years. The faculties that her art affects are not spiritual—these have already been touched by Apollo's justice at the moment of Mamillius's death—but rather moral. Leontes will be moved over a longer period by the effects of real, that is, physical and sensuous, experience; and in ways that reform his character. Paulina's cure is painful. Trying Leontes' senses, it draws him from fantasy, a habit of mind the more dangerous in that, as a king, his will is so readily realized.

[28]Sir Francis Bacon, *The Advancement of Learning*, in *The Works of Francis Bacon*, ed. James Spedding, Robert Leslie Ellis, and Douglas Denon Heath, 15 vols. (Boston, 1860), 6: 188.

This treatment of Leontes is supported by Bacon's claim that belief is an insufficient guarantee of virtue. Without a reference in materiality, the intellectual qualities of piety are inert and as if lifeless. Merely to contemplate "the good" is not to "husband" its productions:

> without which [husbandry] the former [the good] seemeth to be no better than a fair image or statua which is beautiful to contemplate, but is without life and motion: whereunto Aristotle himself subscribeth in these words: '. . . *Inutile enim fere fuerti virtutem quidem nosse, acquirendae autem ejus modos et vias ignorare. Non enim de virtute tantum, qua specie sit, quaerendum est, sed et quomodo sui copiam faciat: utrumque enim volumus, et rem ipsam nosse, et ejus compotes fieri'* [it is useless to know Virtue and remain ignorant of the means and ways of acquiring it. For virtue as an entity is not to be sought but rather the ways it is made productive; for we want to know the thing itself and to become its companions].

To give life and motion to the beautiful "statua" of the good—worshipped in the belief that it is good—we must become sharers (*compotes*) in its interests. The "thing itself" is known by its expressions outside the self.

> [We] need medicine, not only to assuage the disease, but to awake the sense. And if it be said, that the cure of men's minds belongeth to sacred Divinity, it is most true: but yet Moral Philosophy may be preferred unto her as a wise servant and humble handmaid. For as the Psalm saith, *That the eyes of the handmaid look perpetually towards the mistress*, and yet no doubt many things are left to the discretion to the handmaid, to discern of the mistress' will.

(329–30)

The procedure Bacon describes is deliberate not casual: "We do not speak of a dull and neglected suffering but of a wise and industrious suffering, which draweth and contriveth use and advantage out of that which seemeth adverse and contrary . . . which we call Accommodating or Applying" (331). Paulina's art realizes Baconian theory to the extent that it accommodates what appears to be adversity—the absence of wife and child—to a therapeutic end. It is dramatized in Hermione's return to Leontes in 5; its techniques are represented earlier, in the pastoral scenes in 4.

Images of crisis conclude the play's third act and open its fourth. The death of Antigonus and the discovery of Perdita signal the romantic turn from tragedy to comedy, and the Chorus, "Time," presides over the aftermath of that transition, represented as a term of sixteen years.[29] "Time" here is both an agent and a principle of cognition. Stating "I that please some, try all: both joy and terror/Of good and bad, that makes and unfolds error" (4.1.1–2), "Time" identifies himself as the truth of history, a *magister vitae*.[30] As one whose "power" can "o'erthrow law," "plant and o'erwhelm custom," while being himself a constant— "Let me pass/The same I am, ere ancient's order was,/Or what is now receiv'd" (9–11)—"Time" is also a principle, double and paradoxical, in what it governs. As perennial change, it transforms and reforms difference. As that which is perennial, it is without change and the "same," and it constitutes a difference which is beyond accommodation. As the occasion of "trial" and the condition of temporality, "Time" provides Paulina's art with its rationale and justification. It inscribes the conditions of human life—change and continuity—in the "statua" Paulina brings to life, not in fact but *for* Leontes. The play in 5 confirms the power of art to transform an object of knowledge into a subject that is understood. It provides Leontes a means to recover what he lost although not in the condition or form in which he lost it.

The display of social disorder that begins in 4 puts the concept of difference into immediate play. Florizel, whose "removedness" has caused his father, Polixenes, to send spies to keep track of him, has betrayed his rank by visiting "a most homely shepherd," whose property has exceeded what his rank would require: "from very nothing, and beyond the imagination of his neighbours, is grown into an unspeakable estate" (4.2.35–41). The Shepherd's daughter, who only the

---

[29]Andrew Gurr has shown that the Shepherd's words to the Clown, "thou met'st with things dying, I with things new-born," echo the grammar school identification of tragedy and comedy: "in tragoedia fugienda vita, in comedia capessanda exprimitur" (In tragedy, the ending of life is expressed, in comedy, the beginning) and signal the abrupt transition that is about to occur from 3 to 4. "The Bear, the Statue, and Hysteria in *The Winter's Tale*," *Shakespeare Quarterly* 34, 4 (1983): 420–25; 421.

[30]Inga-Stina Ewbank, noting that both Truth and Justice are traditionally daughters of Time, compares "Time's" words with Rosalind's: "Time is the old justice that examines all such offenders [those late for a lovers' meeting], and let Time try" (*AYLI*, 4.1.210–11); "The Triumph of Time," 88.

audience knows is Perdita, symbolizes this apparently anarchic shifting of place. To Polixenes, Perdita is an "angle," the means by which Florizel has been hooked and becomes her prey (46–47). Her angling also reflects the fact that she is the site at which two social parameters meet. Royal by blood, she is common by education.

Although born a princess, Perdita is known and knows herself as a shepherdess. She also assumes a playful yet nondeceptive persona—dressed for a feast, she looks like "Flora" and the "queen" in a gathering of "petty gods." But she is troubled by Florizel's disguise as a shepherd, assumed in order to visit her without being known:

> To me the difference forges dread (your greatness
> Hath not been us'd to fear): even now I tremble
> To think your father, by some accident
> Should pass this way, as you did: O the Fates!
> How would he look to see his work, so noble,
> Vilely bound up?

> (4.4.17–22)

Her distinction between her own "vile" being and his, which is "noble," suggests that she may see the difference of rank within human kind as a difference in kind; that is, she may equate social with ontological difference and regard a marriage crossing ranks as a conjunction of two kinds, a monstrous union. Her subsequent argument from nature against hybrids follows a similar line of thought.

Perdita assumes that the combinatorial art of the gardener corresponds to the gestures of the magus who claims a divine power to create things which have no prior being. She rejects the practice that breeds "carnations and streak'd gillivors." Although they are "the fairest flowers o' th' season," they are created by "an art which, in their piedness, shares/With great creating nature" (81–88). Her mistake is to think that horticulture can do the impossible; it illustrates the difference between art and what is claimed to be magic although known as deception. In fact, the scope of art is much more modest than Perdita's fears suggest. In Polixenes' sophisticated response to her rejection of hybrids—"over that art,/Which you say adds to nature, is an art/That nature makes" (90–92)—the gardener or artist merely promotes the resources in nature to make it generative. His reformation of nature alters its definitions but does not disturb its original finitude. Nature keeps the being the gods gave it; art builds upon but does not add to or diminish that being.[31] "Time" is similarly the shaping of artistic creation; art can re-present the past in the present but it cannot efface the difference between the two.

For all its conceptual lucidity, however, Polixenes' theoretical endorsement of hybrids proves subject to contradiction and to irony. He has implied that hybrids should be fostered because they result in "conceptions" that are desirable:

> we marry
> A gentler scion to the wildest stock,
> And make conceive a bark of baser kind
> By bud of nobler race.

(92–95)

But he acts as if the opposite were true. When Florizel proposes to "contract" a marriage to Perdita before witnesses—including his father in disguise—Polixenes objects, effectively "divorcing" the couple. Perdita, a wild stock, may not be married to his son, a gentle scion, he states; she, who is "base," has already affected him with that quality.[32] Having deceived his father and consorted with shepherds, Florizel has become "too base/To be acknowledg'd" as a prince (418–20). Perdita would not be improved by Florizel, he would be corrupted by her. Here contradiction marks not Polixenes' representation of art—he does not question his dictum—but his neglect of the question of intention. His denial in practice of a principle he has professed in theory invites debate on the role of culture, education, and the influence of discipline

---

[31] For a study of the image and function of art in *The Winter's Tale*, considered in iconographic and psychoanalytic perspectives, see B. J. Sokol, *Art and Illusion in The Winter's Tale* (Manchester: Manchester University Press, 1994).

[32] Polixenes' protest might not have made social sense, however much it also reflected diplomatic prudence. Fortescue had imagined a marriage that linked persons of different rank as relatively innocuous: "And what then if he [a husband] haue graffed a slyppe of a swete nature in a stock of a sower tree: So that the tre be his owne, shall not the fruites, thoughe they euer sauer of the stocke, be his owne fruites?" *A learned commendation of the politique lawes of Englande* (London, 1567) , N$_{vii}$^{v}. Polixenes' argument against rank-mixing is comparable to Leontes' madness. Leontes had expected Mamillius to be his precise copy; Polixenes expects his descendents to be of his blood; he speaks of Florizel as his "parasite"; 1.2.166.

in achieving the goals of art. In practice, all "graftings" take shape around designs intended to promote particular outcomes and to prevent others. These are not the work of "excellent witchcraft," as Polixenes suggests when he damns what he sees as Perdita's debilitating influence on Florizel (424), but rather of artists who, like gardeners, cultivate nature in order to produce good effects. Polixenes' protest against pastoral culture has the effect of emphasizing what his theory overlooks: the role of the artist in creating beneficial "conceptions."

There is also an irony in Polixenes' denunciation of Florizel's choice of a society. Bohemia condemns his son for associating with shepherds: "Thou, a sceptre's heir,/That thus affects a sheep-hook!" (420–21). By condemning Florizel's affection for Perdita and his affectation of pastoral, Polixenes gives critical discrimination to the pathology exhibited earlier by Leontes. It is true that Florizel is in love and therefore affectionate; more specifically, like Leontes, he is given to fantasy. He imagines his union with Perdita in hyperbolic terms involving monstrous transformations comparable to those performed by Ovidian gods, and he terms its prospect a "jollity." But prompted by a "beauty rarer" than the crude objects of their desire, his union has remained lawfully chaste (24–34). When he names Perdita as the factor that gives a value to all the elements of his world, even the "most imperial" monarchy that he stands to inherit (373–79), he epitomizes the ideal monarch of political theory who promotes the interests of his subjects before his own. Like his affection, his affectation is also an approach to the propriety of rule. It calls up the figure of the shepherd-king, the model by which monarchic practice and policy was traditionally measured.

The exemplarity of Bohemia's pastoral draws on the ancient comparison between shepherd and king that, in its scriptural formulations, speaks especially to the distress of a flock that lacks a shepherd. Pseudo-Aquinas's reference to the shepherd-king of Ezekiel is representative of subsequent theory on the duties of rulers:

> If . . . the community is directed in the particular interest of the ruler and not for the common good, this will be an unjust and perverse government (*regimen iniustum atque perversum*). Such rulers were warned by God, speaking through Ezechiel (34.2), when he said: "Woe to those shepherds [that do feed themselves! should not the shepherds feed the flocks?]" Shepherds must care for the

good of the flock, and all who are in authority for the good of those entrusted to them. (*De regimine principum*, 18–19)

An ideal image in Plato, the shepherd-king in More's *Utopia* is represented as a model governor, but one that is, sadly, almost bound to remain unrealized. Hythloday invokes pastoral to point out its irrelevance to politics. No king, he claims, can avoid putting his interest before those of his flock. No counselor would be heeded should he:

> declare that the communaltie chooseth theyr King for their owne sake and nor for his sake . . . and that therefore the King ought to take more care for the wealth of his people, then for his owne wealth, euen as the officc and dutie of a shepheard is . . . to feede his sheepe rather then himselfe.[33]

In general a positive exemplum but often represented in negative or monitory settings, the figure of the shepherd-king stood for a perfectly conscientious ruler. Disaster followed his indolence or indifference; typically they caused a dispersal of his flock. An image of the separation of Judah and Israel in Scripture, the divided flock pictured by the prophet was the object of divine solicitude: "I wil gather the remnant of my shepe out of all countreys . . . I wil set vp shepherdes ouer them, which shal fede them" (Jeremiah 23.3–4). The prophet could chastize a king or a people by indicating how far they had departed from a pastoral ideal: "I [i.e., God] am against the shepherds . . . I will deliver my flock from their mouth that they may not be meat for them" (Ezekiel 34.10). So contextualized, the figure of a prince who assumed the attributes of the shepherd, even in play, ventured symbolically into the sphere of government. If he did so chastely, tempering his own desires for the sake of a customary propriety—as does Florizel—he indicated a disposition to wise government. Polixenes among the shepherds exemplifies a ruler who fails to respect the traditions of pastoral rule. He honors the precepts of art in nature, which approve the grafting and growth of a kingdom's "stock," but he neglects to recognize its skills.

[33]Syr Thomas More, *A Most pleasant, fruitfull, and wittie worke, of the best state of a publique weale, and of the new Yle called Vtopia*, trans. Raphe Robinson (London, 1597), G^v. See also Thomas More, *Utopia*, ed. George M. Logan and Robert M. Adams (Cambridge: Cambridge University Press, 1989); these editors refer to Aristotle, *Politics* 5.11, for statements similar to Hythloday's characterizing tyranny; p. 33, note 63.

The Discipline in Art

Art that engages outcomes seriously and cultivates artistry to good purpose is discriminated from trickery or what may be taken for magic by the actions of the courtier turned peddler, Autolycus, who admits that his commerce is a kind of theft.[34] His "sheets" (of "lesser linen" and broadside ballads) are his "revenue" and "a silly cheat," each item a stolen property that then is sold to gullible customers (4.3.23, 28). His art appears in impersonations (he acts the part of a traveler who has been robbed), and impositions (he sells his ballads as true to fact), that are sufficiently convincing to naive and artless shepherds—shearers who, he hopes, will prove to be sheep he can fleece (115–17)—so that he ends by getting something for almost nothing. He is less reprehensible as a trickster than as a kind of sophist, in this case one who exploits differences of place and office to gain rhetorical power. His art has two ends: pleasure and profit. The first is justified, the second is made equivocal.

When Autolycus enters extolling the universal joys of spring, "the red blood" that "reigns in the winter's pale" (4.3.4), he illustrates the ethos of pastoral, the common subjection of all men to nature and its generative powers. His song is a comic version of Imogen's dark observations on the beneficial rigors of nature (*Cymbeline*, 3.6.19–22). His claim that "A merry heart goes all the day" excuses art devoted solely to pleasure, an art subsequently exemplified by Mopsa and Dorcas's singing his ballads, and, incidentally, also by the dances of the "Saltiers" to which Polixenes gives permission over the objections of the more censorious Shepherd. Even the crude fables in Autolycus's "ballads in print," though the shepherds take them for "truth," may count as allowable fun. Yet the profit of this art is almost entirely monetary and it goes

[34]Barbara Mowat identifies Autolycus as both a trickster, a moral category of person whose most obvious prototype is Mercury; and a rogue, a social category of person whose character is sketched in contemporary documents dealing with the problem of the "thriftless poor" or "counterfeit distressed." As a rogue, Autolycus represents the potential for "frightening social conflicts." Barbara Mowat, "Rogues, Shepherds, and the Counterfeit Distressed: Text and Infracontexts of *The Winter's Tale* 4.3," *Shakespeare Studies*, 22, ed. Leeds Barroll (Cranbury, N.J.: Associated University Presses, 1994): 58–76. For Autolycus as artist, see Mary Ellen Lamb, "Ovid and *The Winter's Tale*: Conflicting Views toward Art," in *Shakespeare and the Dramatic Tradition*, ed. W. R. Elton (Newark: University of Delaware Press, 1989), 69–87.

to Autolycus not his audience. In this sense, Autolycus, who turns the differences between court and country cultures to his own account, is the negative double of his master, Florizel, who seeks to transcend and to unify them. By "haunting" the gatherings of common folk only to rob them (98), Autolycus represents a ghostly presence of rule—in effect, its ironic absence. His cheating sheets that make something out of nothing give a certain credibility to Perdita's (now not so innocent) fear of art as illicit creation.

How art goes beyond deception to achieve a liberal profitability is brilliantly suggested by Perdita's statement at the moment Polixenes unmasks Florizel and denounces his courtship. Her words establish the function of art—to persuade and move its audience to generally beneficial conceptions (as Polixenes had stated)—while they also exemplify its means: fictions that draw on but do not supplant nature. She recalls Polixenes' words on the nature of art, as if to remind the shep herds and Camillo how heedlessly their significance has been overlooked. "Even here, undone" she exclaims, but then she adds:

> I was not much afeard: for once or twice
> I was about to speak, and tell him [Polixenes] plainly
> The self-same sun that shines upon his court
> Hides not his visage from our cottage, but
> Looks on alike.

(4.4.442–46)

Perdita's figure of the equalizing sun has a history as popular metaphor. More important, her appeal to the sun's universal benefit has meaning in various contexts—moral, political, social, and epistemological—all of which give weight to her conviction that shepherd and king can be considered equals in the eye of heaven.[35] In short, her words defying Polixenes convey a lesson. Had he stayed to hear her, he would have learned both the means and the end of the art he had earlier professed to support.

---

[35] Walter Cohen regards the relations between persons of high and low rank in 4 as an extensive representation of the possibilities of social change: court and country are not "irreconcileably antagonistic," Perdita is the "embodiment of . . . synthesis," and the shepherds turned courtiers its "ratification. . . . To a considerable extent, then, Shakespeare's hopes of national unity depend on the rural lower classes." Walter Cohen, *Public Theater in Renaissance England and Spain* (Ithaca: Cornell University Press, 1985), 392, 395.

Her imagery has an obviously ancient source in Scripture, notably in Matthew 5, who asked that "love" efface *moral* difference: "Loue your enemies ... That ye may be the children of your Father that is in heauen: for he maketh his sunne to arise on the euil, and the good and sendeth raine on the iuste & vniuste" (44–45). Seneca, stating that benefits originate with the gods, called the sun and the rain their universal blessings, enjoyed by good and bad alike.[36] The rhetoric of these dicta is persuasive and ethical: the reader is to appreciate and be like the sun. When translated to the literature of *politics*, the image of a beneficial sun conveys the conditions in which social harmony is achieved. Hayward, in his treatise on the Union, had described the law in a united Britain by analogy: "the Sunne riseth and shineth to all alike so the law should comprehend all in one equall and vnpartiall equitie."[37] He went on to characterize the agent achieving political union, equity, in *social* terms. He defined it as a practice that equalizes by granting to persons of different "degrees and estates" a common "libertie and privilege." Guaranteed by the graceful actions of a superior, it dispenses privileges that make irrelevant conditions imposed by the terms of office or what Leontes had referred to as commission. Finally, the image of a fair sun had a place in *epistemology*. For Bacon, its function was also its justification—to give light to all was to express a divine charity.

Discussing "sacred and inspired Divinity" in *The Advancement of Learning*, Bacon invoked the "prerogative of God" which he saw authorizing an obedience beyond the grasp of "sense" or "reason." He saw that the "light of nature" as it "springeth from reason, sense, induction, argument," was guaranteed only by the "light imprinted upon the spirit of man by an inward instinct, according to the law of conscience." The two "lights" had to be consonant. "*Coeli enarrant gloriam Dei* [the heav-

---

[36]Seneca, "De beneficiis," 4. 28; in *Moral Essays*, ed. G. P. Goold, trans. John W. Basore, 3 vols. (Cambridge: Harvard University Press, 1989), 3: 261.

[37]Hayward understood equity as a universal principle of empire building. It was the "principall meane whereby the Roman state receiued both continuance and encrease; because the people did so easily impart the liberties of their citie almost unto all"; *A Treatise*, D2^v. This argument, associating the condition of the "libertie" of a city with imperial expansion, recalls Bacon's "Of the True Greatnesse of the Kingdom of Britain," and also, by implication, the aspirations of the last years of Elizabeth in which her subjects both pressed for their liberties and expected to extend their mercantile empire into the New World.

ens declare the glory of God]" not "*voluntatem Dei* [the will of God],"
he observed; God left human beings to shape their destiny. But their
society, their government, their way of life, their positive law had to
conform to the "word and oracle of God," not only in "points of faith"
but specifically in those that concerned "the law moral truly inter-
preted," that is: *"Love your enemies: do good to them that hate you: be like
to your heavenly Father, that suffereth his rain to fall upon the just and unjust"*
(*Works*, ed. cit., 6: 393–95). In short, divine law is realized in moral law,
and moral law is exemplified by equitable judgments. To invoke
Matthew to support the idea that a rule is validated by a conscientious
rather than strictly literal jurisprudence was to foreground equity as a
principle of government. Bacon generally supported absolutist rule and
stated that the monarch should be independent of positive law. In this
instance, by insisting that authority and power respond to equity, he
indicated how absolutism should in practice be limited. If the monarch
was in James's words *lex loquens* or the law speaking,[38] he should be
ruled by the principles of divine law—such as a natural equity—which
were also those legitimating the moral dimension of positive law.

The fact that Bacon illustrated the action of equity, whose rationale he found not in "reason" but in the supra-sensory faculty of "conscience," by a version of what would have been recognized as a divine
"legal fiction"—an equitable and equalizing sun—drew his epistemology further into the sphere of art. It underscored how much art
entered into the practice of government once law was understood as
rendering justice by works of the imagination as well as by "reason,
sense, induction, and argument." Earlier in *The Advancement of Learning*,
Bacon had noted that the rhetorical function of art was to win "the
Imagination from the Affection's part," and to contract "a confeder-
acy between the Reason and Imagination against the Affections." For,
citing Plato, he explained,

> Virtue, if she could be seen, would move great love and affection;
> [but] seeing that she cannot be shewed to the Sense by corporal
> shape, the next degree is to shew her to the Imagination in lively
> representation: for to shew her to Reason only in subtilty of argu-
> ment [will not affect] the will of man. (298–99)

[38]James VI and I, "Speech to parliament, 31 March 1607," in *Political Writings*, 161.

He was pursuing a familiar argument. Imagination had a place in discussions of morals and politics because equitable judgments, critical to conceptualizing a common good, invariably entailed fictions. Edmund Plowden had implied a role for the imagination when he considered how the "letter" of the law might not convey its sense; to represent that sense writ required the construction of hypothetical situations.[39] Thomas Ridley approved of fictions in more precise terms.

> A fiction . . . [is] an assumption of the Law upon an untruth for a truth in a certaine thing possible to be done and yet not done. . . . [I]f that which is in controversie may be obtained by any other meanes than by a fiction, a fiction is not to be afforded: but if ordinarie means cannot be had, then fictions may be entertained to supply the defect of the ordinarie meanes, that thereby, although the truth bee otherwise, yet the effect of the Law may be all one.

In other words, the law ventures into art to be more true to itself. Yet, as Ridley went on to say, its deliberate fictionalizing is removed from fantasy—it has its grounding in "Nature":

> And as the Law cannot proceed to a fiction without equitie, so neither can it faine any thing that is impossible, for Art euermore followeth Nature, and therefore if a man would faine disproportionable things, such as the Painter did in Horace who made Boares wallow in the waues of the Sea and Dolphins wander in the woods, these fictions in no sence can be admitted for that they are such as neither nature or reason can brooke.[40]

By alluding to the universally beneficial sun to convey her sense of justice, Perdita illustrates the generally profitable ends of a poetic art or the language of metaphor, and the rhetorical techniques by which such art is achieved. Neither divine nor magical, this art eschews the ontological absolutes that she feared as elements in the unwarranted power of tyrant and magus. It will be realized by Paulina, whose art communicates an otherwise incommunicable truth—that Hermione has lived as if dead but is now as if reborn. Its terms are strictly temporal.

---

[39]Edmund Plowden, "Eyston v. Studd," *The Commentaries or Reports*, 465–67.
[40]Thomas Ridley, *A View of the Civile and Ecclesiasticall Law* (London, 1607), Q2–Q3; STC 21054.

Hermione's return is not miraculous but artfully human and marked by the passage of time. It coincides with other returns: Leontes to love from despair, his kingdom to dynastic life from an heirless death, the scene of pastoral to a "spring" in the west from its origin in the east, and Bohemia to Sicilia.

The Trial of "Affection"

Paulina's art is directed by a stratagem and realized in a performance. It is intended to try Leontes' "Affection" so that he rejects passion and accepts love sustained by faith. Her authority is oracular; her subject is an epitome of *the* subject: the monarch's wife, the kingdom, its people. Her means are fictions in which deception and disguise are deployed to re-present elements of reality in fictional modes and settings. They effect changes in perspective, alter terms of definition, shift conceptions of place, but they do not add to or subtract from the being comprised in nature. Her play follows a sequence of deceptions that further define the nature of art.

Camillo, acknowledging that Florizel is "heir" to his "affection" and "irremoveable,/Resolv'd for flight" (4.4.509–10), directs him to Sicilia and so averts anarchy, the couple's "wild dedication of [themselves]/To unpath'd waters, undream'd shores, most certain/To miseries enough" (566–69). His plan involves deception, in that he intends to betray Florizel's whereabouts to Polixenes who, he believes, will pursue Florizel and be reconciled to him by the intervention of Leontes. It furthers two interests: his own, as he will accompany Polixenes and thus return to Sicilia; and Florizel's, who will remain within a sphere of friends. Autolycus (who, under Camillo's direction, exchanges clothes with Florizel to disguise his boarding ship), initiates a second deception. Meeting the Shepherd and the Clown who intend to reveal to Polixenes the contents of the "fardel" and "box" they found with the infant Perdita, Autolycus (apparently a courtier and assumed by the shepherds to be in the know), directs them not to the king (who, he says, has ordered their punishment), but to Florizel. Like Camillo, Autolycus acts in his own as well as Florizel's behalf: "I am courted now with a double occasion—gold, and a means to do the prince my master good"

(833–35). Both plans conceal a mystery quite fundamental to the dramatization of "Time's" agency, that is, why Perdita's identity remains unknown until she returns to Sicilia and is in Leontes' presence.

The Shepherd appears to have deduced from the gold and the "bearing-cloth" contained in Perdita's box and fardel that her birth is gentle. He has hinted that matched with Perdita, "Doricles" (Florizel's pastoral self) will receive "that/Which he dreams not of" (4.4.180–82; see also 386–87). Antigonus had deposited her on the Bohemian shore with her "character" (3.3.47), the written account of her lineage, later specified as "letters" (5.2.35); and the Clown, who could read (4.3.36 ff.), might have deciphered at least some of that script. If the shepherds know who Perdita is, they have kept it a secret. If they do not know, they have been content to not to make sense of the contents of the box and fardel. What the audience knows is that they seek to disclose (or to know) the truth only at a time when the effects of an earlier chance (Florizel's "good falcon" flying over the Shepherd's ground) have jeopardized their own lives and make necessary a disclosure of the "strange sights" in the Perdita's baggage (4.4.820–22). A second if less imposing mystery, again depending on chance, attends Florizel's journey to Sicilia. Despite Autolycus's report of the shepherds' "fardel and I know not what," Florizel does not examine this evidence in which he has considerable interest, apparently because he is seasick (5.2.114–21). These instances of human inaction, exemplifying a strange lack of curiosity, suggest a counterpoise to the deliberate actions of Camillo and Autolycus, which are characterized by a high degree of self-interest. Like the chancy plans of Pisanio in *Cymbeline*, they create the indeterminate space, a kind of chaos of intentionality, onto which the providential hand of the Oracle, identified with Paulina's agency, can inscribe a history. At the end of the play, timing is almost everything.

Leontes' "Affection" undergoes the first of its final trials when he meets Florizel and Perdita. His temperance must be thoroughly tested without reference to incest. Leontes cannot be certain of this virtue if he knows Perdita is his daughter; thus at this point, he must not know the shepherds or what they are bringing him. Greeting Florizel, Leontes seems to have retained his obsession with monopolistic control. He notes that Florizel has "printed" his father off; he sees Florizel as Polixenes' brother. Florizel replies by emphasizing temporal difference; he reports that Polixenes is full of age and infirmity. Leontes picks up the cue. Now he registers generational difference: Perdita and Florizel seem like the "spring," the son and daughter he would have had. When, however, Florizel receives news that Polixenes has arrived and begs Leontes to be his "advocate," Leontes slips back into his passionate ways. He thinks he himself may marry Perdita. Paulina must force him to respect temporal difference: "your eye hath too much youth in it" (5.1.123–224). Her warning controls his intentions and he renounces his desire—presumably as he has renounced his desire for sixteen years. His "Affection" is to be shaped by the measures of time.

Paulina's play of Hermione's return to life represents the second and last of Leontes' trials, critical in that it makes manifest the conditions in which passion is transformed into love. They depend on a faith that relations need not be determined by mechanisms of the market but can exist by virtue of an understanding guaranteed by trust. In markets, agents strive for monopoly, the more absolute the better; everywhere else, relations rest on confidences that are not subject to negotiation. Love is linked to faith in that without faith there is only passion. Faith in kin and kind, and ultimately in a divinity beyond the self is revealed to be sanity almost by default, in that its contradiction, the divinity of the self, is made illusory by the experience of time.

Temporal difference is profoundly inscribed in Paulina's "Hermione," who in Baconian terms is the "statua" which elicits contemplative veneration but may be made vital by and in a material work. To Leontes, who expects to see Hermione's image as it would be were it only an object for contemplation, Paulina's statue is disappointing: "Hermione was not so much wrinkled, nothing/So aged as this seems" (5.3.28–29). Paulina answers by praising the "carver" who made his work truer to time: Hermione's statue is "As she liv'd now" (32). The possibility that Hermione might in fact live—that "Hermione" might soften into living and breathing flesh—intensifies Leontes' frustration to a point at which he recognizes that the conditions of time promise a gratification they had earlier appeared to deny. True to time, the person represented by the statue might have been a "comfort"; immune from time, she signifies privation (32–38).

Paulina transforms Leontes' wish for a youthful Hermione into a love of Hermione, a mortal and therefore a subject of time, by insisting that he experience her sensuously and not merely as a projection of his desire. His "Affection" had triumphed in the absence of such experience; Paulina must revitalize his senses. Leontes identifies Hermione's statue with his own lifelessness; he states he is "more stone" than her statue (37–38). When Paulina orders "Hermione" to "bequeath to death" her "numbness," her words reflexively affect Leontes. The vitality they invoke, and the music or air by which it is invoked (98), each as much an acknowledgment of death as of life, are predicated on an act of faith.[41] To Leontes as he moves to touch "Hermione," Paulina declares: "It is required you do awake your faith" (94–95). Leonard Barkan, commenting on the shaping influence of the Ovidian subtext in this scene, has noted that the figure of Leontes here is indebted to the stories of Pygmalion as well as, though less obviously, Deucalion. Pygmalion illustrates a condition in which human beings know the living being from its lifeless representation. Aided by Venus, he vivifies his statue, Paphos, by touching her: "temptat pectora," "temptatum mollescit ebur" (he touched her breast, having been touched, the stone softened; 10.282–83).[42] *Temptare* is not only to touch but to try, to render, to attempt; its operations are on matter that comes alive through

[41]Cf. the music or "air" that revives Thaisa in *Pericles*; chapter 2, p. 60.

[42]Ovid, *Metamorphosis* 10.282–83; quoted in Leonard Barkan, "'Living Sculptures': Ovid, Michelangelo, and *The Winter's Tale*," *ELH* 48 (1981): 639–67. Martin Mueller has pointed out a further reference to the Ovidian subtext: Pygmalion's wish for a wife that is "similar to the statue" (*similis . . . eburnae*; 10.276) is echoed later by his great-grandaughter, Myrrha, who wishes for a husband "similar" to her father (10.364). Mueller asks: "Is it accidental that the motif of the hidden wish [Pygmalion's], expressed in the displaced form of desire for a 'similar' object recurs in this story of incest, or that an incestuous union is the consequence in the third generation of the artist's passion for his own creation?" Martin Mueller, "Hermione's Wrinkles, or Ovid Transformed: An Essay on *The Winter's Tale*," *Comparative Drama* 5 (1971): 226–39. The link between a desire for a spouse who is a clone of oneself and incest is also established in Shakespeare's romances, where it makes obvious the fact that generation always implies difference and hence also temporality and mortality. Jonathan Scott Bentley has noted that Aquinas condemned Hermetic statues because they falsely claimed to have the power of life. Such statues cannot reproduce themselves, however; "hence it is clear that statues of this kind do not have the principle of life, nor are they moved by virtue of a heavenly body" (*Manifestum est igitur quod huiusmodi statuae non habent principium vitae, neque moventur virtute caelestis corpore*). "The Hermetic Tradition in Three Shakespeare Romances: *Pericles, The Winter's Tale,* and *The Tempest*" (Ph.D. diss., University of Oregon, 1986, p. 194), quoting *Summa Contra Gentiles*, 3.civ.11.

a sensuous or touching love. By contrast, Deucalion illustrates that such experience is circumscribed by the limits of mortal powers. Despite wishing that—like his father, Prometheus—he could "restore the nations with the arts of the father" (*populus reparare paternis/artibus* [363–64]), that is, bring a people into being miraculously, he follows oracular guidance. This, not the promptings of his own wit, allows success. His stones become men and women because he has faith in the gods, not because he is a god.

Paulina's art requires the senses and faith for its appreciation precisely because it is neither divine miracle or illusionistic magic. Paulina must insist that she has no "wicked powers" (5.3.89–91). Leontes asks that her art be a "magic . . . Lawful as eating" (110–11)—that is, be a recombination of existing elements to produce new conceptions of nature (as Polixenes had suggested). Leontes' courtiers had characterized Hermione's statue as the work of high illusionism (5.2.94–101), and Paulina had described it as excelling "whatever . . . [the] hand of man hath done" (5.3.15–17), both independently true but misleading descriptions. Were Leontes not to have touched Hermione with faith, he would have risked experiencing her only in fantasy or mechanically, as a mere object, a wizard's toy. In neither case could he have husbanded her generativity, a virtue now clearly to be qualified by time.

Perdita's future is made possible by the conventions of pastoral. She is preserved and educated by its spirit, embodied in characters who are shepherds. At the play's conclusion, that spirit is registered in a comic mode by a pastoral conception of rank. As Perdita's foster family, the Shepherd and the Clown believe they have become "gentlemen born" within "four hours" (5.2.129–37). Their solecism may be intended ironically (indicating an actual market in coats of arms) and is certainly a sign of the equitable practice Perdita announced from her place at the sheep-shearing feast: difference of blood or rank is not a difference of kind or being, but of kin or relation within a family however large. The Clown's claim that he is now "brother" to two kings, a prince, and a princess, recognizes facetiously the social and political reference in his foster sister's earlier allusion to Matthew 5: it was a tenet of constitutionalist theory that a monarch's relation to his people was fraternal. The idea that all human beings are of one kind mitigates, but does not efface distinctions among kin. The shepherds' figurative kinship to royalty realizes in metaphor the beneficial effects of a graceful monarchy, one that rules in the general interest, with equitable recompense for all subjects but without anarchic indifference to the place and office of each subject. Leontes' recovery of his wife and daughter occurs in a moment of grace in which such differences are both recognized and set aside for the sake of atonement. Paulina's "poor house" is "graced" by Leontes (5.3.7; see also 5.2.110–11); "awake," Hermione calls on the gods to "grace" her heir (122). Perdita's career is also shaped by the mythos of pastoral. It provides her and her mother with their experience of spring, not as an illusory rebirth, but as a return consistent with expectations of historical time. The generationally appropriate union of Florizel and Perdita prefaces the transfer of political power from old to new, from parents to children. Renaissance poets saw pastoral as the genre in which filiation or the right of a poetic son to his father's place was most directly acknowledged. Shakespeare made use of pastoral convention to remind his audience both of generation and the passing on of political authority, and of the conditions in which a monarch and his people might best cohere in one body politic and make its commonwealth productive.

CHAPTER 5

The Tempest, i

I N ROMANCE NARRATIVE THE TRIALS OF THE HERO'S RETURN TO HIS place of origin validate his claim to a superior virtue. Even so, it is no more than a human virtue, limited by the condition of mortality. Knowing that he lacks divine power, Odysseus rejected the goddess Kalypso's offer of immortality and continued his journey back to Ithaka and his wife of many years, Penelope. In the story of its hero Prospero's return to Milan, *The Tempest* dramatizes a version of romance homecoming, but adds a second dimension to the portrait of heroic self-consciousness. Prospero, the legitimate yet deposed Duke of Milan, faces a challenge typically political. He has not only to recognize his mortality, but also to refuse to practice deceptions that mask his human condition. At the end of the play, Prospero manifests a virtue that allows him to deploy his prodigious art to benefit his subjects rather than to coerce their obedience by illusionistic display.

The plot of the play is driven by a concern with dynasty. In this respect it resembles all the earlier romances. Prospero's heir Miranda is exiled with him on a remote island. His dukedom in Milan, usurped by his brother Antonio with the assistance of Alonso, king of Naples, is now a tributary of Naples and denied its original liberty. Alonso's heir Ferdinand, separated from his father by the wreck of their ship on the shores of Prospero's island, appears to have drowned. Alonso spends most of his time on stage searching for his son, but without much hope of finding him. The future of both dukedom and kingdom is at last secured by the marriage of the two heirs Miranda and Ferdinand; the romance of *The Tempest* concludes in a political union. These outcomes—the recovery of a dynasty and a rule—are achieved through Prospero's own agency.

Banished from Milan to an island of indeterminate place, Prospero is ruling a ghostly state; its subjects are his daughter and two "servants," one indentured for a term, the other apparently enslaved for life. Whether they constitute a people is doubtful. Caliban tells Prospero that he is the duke's only subject.[1] Inasmuch as Caliban is "earth," an exponent of man's flesh and therefore of Prospero's own body, Caliban implies that on his island, Prospero rules only himself. Ariel is a spirit or air, and Miranda is also an heir. Once populated by Alonso's subjects, Prospero's island does become the site of a kind of rule, however obscure. His government is mysterious, its effects are unaccountable, and its means verge on the sinister. Without a court, he lacks counselors, at least of a usual kind. He is advised instead by his own history and its mistakes. Rescuing what he has learned of the art of government from its theoretical representation in books, he vests his knowledge in Ariel who, realizing the unreal, gives a momentary and apparent presence to his master's insubstantial but strategic projects. As Ariel performs it, Prospero's art is devoted to creating representations of reality on a scale that dwarfs Paulina's modest play. Its purpose is not like Paulina's, simply to educate and inspire a single viewer, but to control and coerce the actions of many persons of different rank, some of whom (Alonso's captain and crew), are not in any obvious need of correction or direction.[2] Its rep-

---

[1] William Shakespeare, *The Tempest*, ed. Frank Kermode (New York: Routledge, 1990), 1.2.343.

[2] Commenting on Prospero's art and magic, Stephen Orgel observes that "what the play's action presents is not experiments and empiric studies but a fantasy about controlling other people's minds" and that its intention, "to bring about reconciliation . . . works only indifferently well" in that Antonio remains unrepentant; "Prospero's Wife," in *Representing the English Renaissance,* ed. Stephen Greenblatt (Berkeley: University of California Press, 1988), 217–29; 225. Margreta De Grazia has shown that Prospero's art forces subjects to do what they would otherwise not do; "*The Tempest*: Gratuitous Movement or Action Without Kibes and Pinches," *Shakespeare Studies* 14 (1981): 249–65, esp. 250–52. Paul Brown, who sees Prospero's art as designed to control the sexuality of his subjects, identifies the power of the "royal gaze" generally as one that can "transmute hitherto recalcitrant elements of

resentations are fearful not comforting—and worse—give no indication that they are artificial and not real. Deception was an allowable resource of government, but it always raised questions of motive.

The tempest that opens the play by wrecking Alonso's ship is revealed to be an illusion, a *lusus pseudo-naturae*. When Miranda begs Prospero to calm the "wild waters" of the storm, he tells her they are inoffensive, no more than play ("There's no harm done" [1.2.14]), and he then takes off his "magic garment" (24) as if to indicate that for the time being he will play no more. He appears to be in complete control of his art. One could argue, however, that by practicing deception Prospero risks deceiving himself. In one sense, the victims of his tempest are what he wants them to be—in his power. In another sense, their obedience is a poor thing. Prospero has created an illusion of reality so pervasively convincing that they, now effectively his subjects, are no longer capable of true agency. They live as figures in a dream of his, as Hermione did when Leontes fantasied her adultery. More helpless than she, who was conscious of the wrong done her, they, and particularly the court party, are unconscious of everything except their fear. A duping of this magnitude has to be justified by a cause of great consequence.

Prospero himself seems to have no illusions about the power he gives Ariel. He terms it a "magic" and thereby invites comparison of himself with a magus. As a practitioner of so-called white magic, Prospero could have been considered a benign philosopher. A magus was revered in esoteric tradition. He was supposed to be able to draw on cosmic forces in order to enhance his human agency. But for most

the body politic, engendering in the place of disorderly passion desire for service that is akin to an erotic courtship"; " 'This thing of darkness I acknowledge mine,' *The Tempest* and the Discourse of Colonialism," in *Political Shakespeare*, ed. Jonathan Dollimore and Alan Sinfield (Ithaca: Cornell University Press, 1985), 48–71; 53. This too closely limits the sphere in which such royal transformative power is supposed to work. The question to ask of the play is whether such power, magical or like magic, is legitimate and what end does it purpose. Criticism on the idea of magic in the play, some of which I consider in detail below, is extensive and varied; see, among others, Cosmo Corfield, "Why Does Prospero Abjure His 'Rough Magic'," *Shakespeare Quarterly* 36, 1 (1985): 31–48; Anthony Harris, *Night's Black Agents: Witchcraft and Magic in Seventeenth-Century English Drama* (Manchester: Manchester University Press, 1980), 129–48. Frances Yates appears to be alone in considering Prospero's magic as wholly benign; Frances Yates, *Shakespeare's Last Plays: A New Approach* (London: Routledge and Kegan Paul, 1975), esp. 93–96. See also, Frank Kermode, "Prospero's Art," in "Introduction," *The Tempest*, ed. Kermode, xlvii–li.

students of natural philosophy, the distinction between white and black magic was finally unclear, and to appeal to spirits to do the world's work was generally regarded as suspect. In his *Daemonologie*, 1597, James had condemned the practice of all kinds of magic, no matter what the end,[3] and the new English translation of Augustine's *De civitate dei*, 1610, described in detail the theological basis for rejecting contact of any sort with a spirit world.[4] Scripture simply stated that "wizards" were to be stoned to death (Leviticus 20.27).

Verses in Acts describing Paul's shipwreck on Malta, the terms of which parallel the wreck of Prospero's "ship of state," provide a comparative view of the Duke's art and distinguish it from the saint's miraculous power. Paul's history is graced by continuous divine concern. A prisoner of the Romans (Acts 27.1) and on his way by sea to Rome, he is caught in a "tempest." Assured by an angel of God that he "must be brought before Caesar," he tells those on board to "be of good cheer": "there shall be no loss of any man's life among you," "there shall not an hair fall from the head of any of you" (22–25; 33–34; cf. 1.2.26–32). Once ashore on Melita [Malta], an island of barbarous people, Paul is miraculously healed and therefore thought to be "a god"; he also performs miracles of healing (Acts 28. 4–6). But his power, although clearly from God, has no political effect or end. Throughout Acts, Paul remains subject to the civil power of Rome: a prisoner and thus radically unfree. His domain is wholly spiritual. Prospero echoes Paul in attributing his arrival on his island to "Providence divine" (1.2.159), by describing Miranda's "cherubin" smile, and Gonzalo's "charity" (153, 162), and as an event occasioned by an "accident of Fortune" (178).[5] But unlike the

---

[3]For a study of the play and its relation to James's *Daemonologie*, see Jacquline E. M. Latham, "'The Tempest' and King James's 'Daemonologie,'" *Shakespeare Survey* 28 (1975): 117–23; and my comments, chapter 6, pp. 204–206.

[4]Augustine declared that men must not seek to control their fates by manipulating spirits but instead seek salvation by praying to God to overcome such spirits: "Godly men doe expell the aereall powers opposing them [and] from their possession [i.e., possessing them] by exorcismes not by pacification; and [they] brake their Temptations by prayer not vnto them but vnto God against them. For they conquer nor chayne no man but by the fellowship of sinne." *Of the citie of God: with the learned comments of Io. Lod. Vives, Englished by J. H. [Healey]* (London, 1610), Book 10, Chapter 22, Ll$_3$; STC 916.

[5]Philip Brockbank comments on many of the sources of 1 including Acts; "'The Tempest': Conventions of Art and Empire" in *Later Shakespeare* by Philip Brockbank (New York: St. Martin's Press, 1967), 183–201, esp. 188–89.

divine science of Paul, Prospero's art is chiefly a device and tool of civil government. He is certainly not engaged in what Perdita had termed a diabolical rivalry with the art of "great creating nature." He is merely being theatrical, magnificently so of course, but nevertheless restricted by conditions of time and history. His belief that providence protects Milan does not confer divine power on him, nor does it follow from his piety that his art accord with divine law. The extent to which Prospero will assume a Pauline character—as Paulina did—will be indicated by the effects of his art over the course of his play, in essence Shakespeare's play and the play the audience sees.[6] As critics have noted, it reforms some, it leaves others as they were. Like Paulina's play, the manifestations of Prospero's art asks for a discrimination between works of a magus, who claims to affect being, and those of an artist that change the character of particular human beings.

Self-Rule: Ariel

Prospero's career as an artist is part of the play's prehistory. It begins in Milan and its formative moments are consistent with his conduct as a ruler. Its frustration in Milan is emblematized by Prospero's virtual isolation on an island presumably near the "Bermoothes," and on a route between Tunis and Naples—in short, of no fixed geographic location.[7] The history of his exile, told to Miranda as a prelude explaining the action to follow, clarifies what he intends his "art" to do.

"A prince of power" in Milan, Prospero had referred his rule to his brother, Antonio, and made "the liberal Arts" rather than his dukedom "all [his] study" (73–74):

[6]Barbara A. Mowat indicates that aspect of Prospero's art that has affinities with not only the magus but the "streetcorner 'art-Magician' or 'Jugler'" so popular at fairs and markets, and indeed in London theaters; they had the skill "'to stretche out imaginations even unto apperaunce, of which there shall afterwarde no signe appeare'"; "Prospero, Agrippa, and Hocus Pocus," *English Literary Renaissance* 11, 3 (1981): 281–303. For an account of the "mechanics" of magic perceived as a manifestation of the supernatural, see Vaughan Hart, *Art and Magic in the Court of the Stuarts* (New York: Routledge, 1994), 84–87.

[7]For an analysis of the play's action in relation to mythographic coordinates of place, see John Gillies, *Shakespeare and the Geography of Difference* (Cambridge: Cambridge University Press, 1994), esp. 140–55.

> The government I cast upon my brother,
> And to my state grew stranger, being transported
> And rapt in secret studies.

(75–77)

"Neglecting all worldly ends" in the manner of a contemplative, he dedicated himself to "the bettering of [his] mind." Unwilling to question motives and with a "confidence sans bounds" in his security, he had "[a]wak'd an evil nature" in his brother Antonio. "Transported" or carried off into a purely mental world, Prospero became a "trunk" on which his brother, a parasitic ivy, became entwined in order to "suck" his "verdure" out (85–97). Antonio's rule as a pseudo-"Absolute Milan" was itself the consequence of another kind of self-deception. By a "telling" of his status as the Duke of Milan, Antonio came to believe that he actually and justifiably held that office. Language here created an illusion that substituted for the reality it masked (99–104). Antonio executed "th'outward face of royalty,/With all prerogative," although he lacked the integrity expected from a legitimate ruler. Once formally deposed, Prospero was put to sea in "A rotten carcass of a butt," his ship of state now also a moribund body politic (146). He carried with him the objects that had caused his downfall: the "volumes" that he prized "above [his] dukedom" (167–68). The contribution of charitable Gonzalo, these books will prove critical to his return to Milan. Having induced his isolation when he held office, they will help him recover his office while in isolation. By the time Ariel performs the tempest, Prospero has converted their knowledge or science to his own "prescience," an awareness of time that makes acting—not thinking—an immediate imperative:[8]

> by my prescience
> I find my zenith doth depend upon

[8]David G. Brailow identifies Prospero's art as "Knowing the right time and using it precisely"; "Prospero's 'Old Brain': The Old Man as Metaphor in *The Tempest*," *Shakespeare Studies* 14 (1981): 285–303. Prospero's sense of time suggests that he controls the tempest (an image of his intemperance retrospectively relived) by the virtue of temperance. Stephen Orgel has specified what I take to be the play's restorative memorializations: Prospero "will go on to restage his usurpation through the conspiracy of Antonio and Sebastian, to see in Caliban's attempt to kill him a version of his brother's murderous intentions, to find Caliban in Ferdinand and Antonio in Caliban"; "Introduction," *The Tempest*, ed. Stephen Orgel (Oxford: Clarendon Press, 1987), 15.

A most auspicious star, whose influence
If now I court not, but omit, my fortunes
Will ever after droop.

(180–84)

Prospero's art is therefore a function of his exile.[9] Having neglected to exercise it while in office, he deploys it to regain office. He grasps his fortune in a place to be visited only in the imagination and at a moment in which past and future, cohering in an fleeting present, allow him to test and secure a government that will, presumably, be proof against future misgovernment.[10]

In the language of contemporary political thought, magic sometimes described the monarch's extraordinary power—a power that was absolute, that had to answer only to the monarch's wisdom, and from which the only appeal was for grace. Ben Jonson's masques allegorized royal directives as preternaturally effective. In *Oberon, the Faery Prince*, 1611, Jonson called the king's "sole power" a "magic" that sustains the subject "in form, fame, and felicity,/From rage of fortune or the fear to die."[11] Edward

---

[9]Kurt Tetzeli von Rosador observes that the Prospero's power has two historical referents: the magician's art and also "royal magic," chiefly exemplified by "the touching for the evil." Prospero attempts "to appropriate both charismas," but the play "very carefully and quite rigidly separates them again sequentially" so that at last Prospero is left with the limited power of the touch and the protection of Providence; "The Power of Magic: From *Endimion* to *The Tempest*," *Shakespeare Survey* 43 (1990): 1–13. For a history of the monarch's "thaumaturgical power," see Donald Hanson, *From Kingdom to Commonwealth: The Development of Civic Consciousness in English Political Thought* (Cambridge: Harvard University Press, 1980), 80–91. Historians have frequently noted that James's interest in science caused him to be laudibly represented as a Hermes: "Your Majesty standeth invested of that triplicity which in great veneration was ascribed to ancient Hermes, the power and fortune of a King, the knowledge and illumination of a Priest, and the learning and universality of a Philosopher", Francis Bacon, the dedication to *The Second Book of the Advancement of Learning*, quoted in Graham Parry, *The Golden Age Restor'd: The Culture of the Stuart Court, 1603–42* (New York: St. Martin's Press, 1981), 30. See also Stephen Orgel, "Introduction," *The Tempest*, 20. When considered as justification for kinds of political power, such hyperbole could elicit criticism.

[10]For an analysis of Prospero's magic as illusionary and the play's representation of introspective states of mind, see D. G. James, *The Dream of Prospero* (Oxford: Clarendon Press, 1967).

[11]Ben Jonson, "Oberon" in *The Complete Masques*, ed. Stephen Orgel (New Haven: Yale University Press, 1969), 11: 248–52. Orgel states further that in the masques generally "[T]he glories of the transformation scene [i.e., the heroic dead revive, the golden age returns] express the power of princes, bringing order to human and elemental nature, partaking thereby of the divine.... [T]he King ... is abstracted—to Pan the universal god, to the lifegiving sun, to Hesperus the evening star, or even, in an extraordinary example, to a

Forset was more specific. He described the "force" of the monarch's command, inhering in "certaine prerogatiue rights . . . of most free exemptions whereof true reuerence . . . admitteth no questioning disputes," as that which "dazleth the eyes of all beholders . . . [so] as to transforme sauageness into ciuilitie"—in short, as a magically transformative power.[12] But because it admitted no disputes it did not transform the characters of the beholders. Their wills remained untouched. Such, too, is the effect of Prospero's art. The fact that he abjures his art after regaining his dukedom reveals that he sees its deployment in a settled and secure state as suspect or even illegitimate. The fact that it provides for his return to Milan also suggests that on occasion it may be acceptable.

James's *Basilicon Doron*, 1603, a treatise on monarchic government addressed to Prince Henry, had warned against bookishness. By his own admission, the king had learned "the theoricke and the practike" of kingdoms, and was not a "simple schoole-man that onely knowes matters of kingdomes by contemplation."[13] "[S]tudie not for knowledge nakedly," he advised:

> but that your principall ende be, to make you able thereby to vse
> your office; practising according to your knowledge in the points
> of your calling: not like these vaine Astrologians, that studie night

physical principle, pure potential, through whom the ultimate scientific mysteries of perpetual motion and infinite power are finally solved." Stephen Orgel and Royal Strong, *Inigo Jones: The Theatre of the Stuart Court*, 2 vols. (Berkeley: University of California Press, 1973), 1: 13. Orgel later characterizes the "absolute power" of the monarch, as Jonson saw it, as "pure energy, a principle of physics, through whom the ultimate mysteries of infinite power and perpetual motion are finally solved"; Stephen Orgel, *The Illusion of Power: Political Theater in the English Renaissance* (Berkeley: University of California Press, 1975), 57.

[12]Edward Forster, *A Comparatiue Discovrse of the Bodies Natvral & Politique* (London, 1606), D_{iii}, F^v. In his study of the figure of the magician king, Douglas Brooks-Davies comments on Prospero's magic: he is "the magician ruler who has to learn to drown his book and break his wand in order that he may return to his kingdom. The play does not say that magic and monarchy are incompatible, merely that total preoccupation with 'secret studies' . . . prohibits the just exercise of kingly power. The true magician monarch holds a sceptre, not a wand. But the sceptre subsumes the powers of the wand." Douglas Brooks-Davies, *The Mercurian Monarch: Magical Politics from Spenser to Pope* (Manchester: Manchester University Press, 1983), 191–92. I suggest that Prospero rejects "secret studies" in favor of political action; he also dismisses a certain kind of action—the dangerous effects of studies in the secrets of magic—on the body politic.

[13]James VI and I, *Basilicon Doron*, in *Political Writings*, ed. Johann P. Sommerville (Cambridge: Cambridge University Press, 1994), 10.

and day on the course of the starres, onely that they may, for sat-
isfying their curiositie, know their course. (44)

On the "liberall artes and sciences" other than "authentick histories,"
James would require only a reasonable acquaintance, "but not preassing
to bee a passe-master in any of them: for that cannot but distract you [i.e.,
Henry] from the points of your calling" (46). These dicta were unexceptionable. Indebted to Aristotle's division of the mental faculties in the
Nicomachean Ethics, the necessity of applied over pure knowledge in government was a critical commonplace from the time of Cicero's *De officiis*.

Aristotle had distinguished a virtue of the mind (*virtus intellectiva*)
that develops from a study of doctrine (*ex doctrina*) and a virtue in action
(*virtus moralis*) that arises from practice (*ex consuetudine*).[14] Intellectual
virtue promotes "wisdom" (*sapientia*) and "intelligence" (*intellectus*); virtue
in action is promoted by "art" (*ars*) and "knowledge" (*scientia*) as well
as "wisdom," but it is actually brought into being as a result of "applied
knowledge" (*prudentia*; VI.3, f. 104^v; [1139b], and VI.5, f. 107^v; [1140b]).
Although "art" itself is practical, in that it "effects" a creation or makes
an object, it does not actually "act upon" anything (VI.4, f. 106; [1140a]).
The best artists have wisdom (*sapientia*; VI.7, f. 110^v; [1141a]); but wisdom in itself is essentially "impractical" (*inutilia*); "[wise men] do not
seek human goods" (*non quaerunt bona humana*; VI.7, f. 111; [1141b]). It is
only "applied knowledge" (*prudentia*) which actually does things—
guided by wisdom, prudence deploys the artefacts of art fashioned by
knowledge in the interest of performing a good action. Prudence is
directed at good action, which is its own end: "A good action is its own
end" (*est enim ipsa bona actio finis*; VI.5, f. 107^v; [1141b]). To the extent that
"art" participates in prudential action, it can be thought of as a tool of
government. A ruler's "applied knowledge" (*prudentia*) is not intensely
intellectual (*studiossima*) or wedded to doctrine, because it is directed to
the various interests of human beings (VI.7, f. 111; [1141b]).[15] Inasmuch

---

[14]*Aristotelis Stagiritae Peripateticorum principis, ethicorum ad nichomachum libri decem* (Paris, 1555),
II. 1; f. 25^v; (1103a). The translation is by Johannes Argyropylus, i.e., Argyropoulos. For an
English translation, I have consulted Aristotle, *Nicomachean Ethics*, trans. H. Rackham (Cam-
bridge: Harvard University Press, 1972).

[15]Richard Tuck points out that this view separates those philosophers who, following Aristotle, privilege contemplation above civic action, from others who endorse a Ciceronian
preference for the state as the principal object of human endeavor; Richard Tuck, *Philosophy*

as "applied knowledge" is what is realized in a practice, it is not really "knowledge," strictly speaking; it depends to some extent on "sense perception" (*sensus*; VI.8, f. 113, 113^v; [1142a]). It is tied to what the body can tell it; without the body, it loses its essential character, its end in the actual, the worldly, the material. A feature of political science (*civil facultas*; VI.8. f. 113), "applied knowledge" is directed to the welfare of the state (*civitas*) and is legislative (*facultas ferendarum legum*; ibid.).

In Nicholas Grimald's translation of *De officiis*, 1556, Cicero argues the political case more directly. He begins by remarking that the "noblest philosophers," who "neither could abide the maners of the people nor of the rulers" and have "liued in desert places . . . , shoote at the same marke that kinges doo: that is, to haue neede of nothing, to obey noman, and to vse their own libertie whose propertie is to liue as ye list."[16] But such recluses are generally censured. "We are borne not for ourselves alone" but also for others, declares Cicero. Our knowledge is therefore to find a practical end:

> For the knowledge and consideration of naturall causes should after a certein sorte been maimed and vnperfite if no performaunce of deedes should followe. . . . [B]efore the studies & duties of knowledge, the duties of iustice ar to bee preferred which doo belonge to the profit of men, than the which a man ought to holde nothing derer. (H$_{iiii}$^{v}, H$_v$)

and Government, 1572–1651 (Cambridge: Cambridge University Press, 1993). It is, nevertheless, the case that for Aristotle as for other political philosophers, knowledge and wisdom are manifest in language and the rhetorical strategies designed to make arguments persuasive; they are therefore linked to prudence or applied knowledge through participating in oratory. For comments on Aristotle and Cicero, see Victoria Kahn, *Rhetoric, Prudence, and Skepticism in the Renaissance* (Ithaca: Cornell University Press, 1985), esp. 29–36.
[16]*Marcus Tullius Ciceroes thre bokes of duties*, trans. Nicholas Grimald (London, 1556), D$_{iii}$, D$_{iiii}$; STC 5281. This is a fairly faithful translation of the original text, which I quote in the Loeb edition, 1975. Grimald's translation was reissued in 1596 with the Latin in facing columns. Cf. Augustine: "[O]ne may not bee so giuen to contemplation that hee neglect the good of his neighbour: nor so farre in loue with action that hee forget diuine speculation. In contemplation one may not seeke for idlenesse, but for truth: to benefite himselfe by the knowledge thereof, and not to grudge to impart it vnto others. In action one may not ayme at highnesse or honor, because *all under the sunne is meere vanitie*, but to performe the worke of a superiour vnto the true end, that is, vnto the benefite and saluation of the subiect." *Of the citie of God*, Book 19, Chapter 19; Vvv4^v, Vvv5. For the importance of Cicero's *De officiis* in English political thought, see Markku Peltonen, *Classical Humanism and Republicanism in English Political Thought, 1570–1640* (Cambridge: Cambridge University Press, 1995), 18–45.

To give up such "performaunce" is to possess only "a verie bare and alonewandering knowledge"; more important, this knowledge will eventually debilitate the knower's "vertue" (*magnitudo animi*; literally "courage"): "severed from common feloushippe and neybourhod of men, [it] muste needes bee a certein sauagenesse and beastly crueltie" (*feritas et immanitas*). So horrible would such a solitude be, reasons Cicero, that even if a man could acquire all his wants by waving a "divine wand" (*divina virgula*; Grimald translated this phrase "by the grace of God [as they saie]"), and "settle himself holly in knowledge and science," he would rather elect to "flee solitarinesse and choose a companion of studie, both teache & lerne: both heare & speake." Thus, Cicero concludes: "all duetie which auaileth to mainteine neybourhod, & felowship of men is to be preferred aboue the dutie which consisteth in knowledge & science" (H_{vii}^{v}).[17] Christopher St. German's *Fyrste dyaloge in Englysshe (betwixt a doctoure of dyuynyte and a student in the lawes of Englande)*, 1531, represents a Christianized version of Ciceronian norms. St. German could not appear to value applied knowledge more than its pure form, which he derived from the "hygher parte of reason [that] hedyth heuenly thynges & eternall," but he could specify the importance of reason's "lower parte," which governs temporal things: "she groundeth her reasons moche vpon lawes of man and vpon reason of man wherby she concludyth that that is to be done that is honest and expedyent to the common welth and not to be done for it is not expedyent to the common welth." Reason's "lower parte" affected the common wealth through the intervention of "conscyence," "the actuell applyenge of any cunnynge or knowlege to . . . any partyculer acte of man" (h_{iiii}^{v}–i).[18]

---

[17]Grimald's translation does not note the distinction between pure and applied knowledge (or the higher and lower reason in St. German's scheme) that serves to emphasize the obligation to translate contemplation to action in the Latin text. Cicero's terms reflect those in Aristotle's *Ethics*: pure knowledge is *sapientia* (or *sophia*); applied knowledge is *prudentia* (or *phronesis*).

[18]For another Christianized Ciceronian, see Pierre de La Place, *Discours politiques sur la voye d'entrer deüement aux estats*, 1574. La Place (like St. German) values the contemplative part of the understanding as "the noblest and most excellent . . . hauing, as it were, no neede of worldly thinges," and the active as "exercised by the lesser and inferiour parte of man hauing neede of al things created." But (like Cicero) he also sees that the active understanding is what makes government possible: for "what is most decente, naturall, and meete for the weale, profite and continuance of humane societie, we shall not finde anything so conu-

The strong preference for civic action over private contemplation registered by political philosophers was seconded by James's insistence that a king in particular was born to *onus* not *honos*. To avoid the burden of rule was to be tyrannical:

> A good King, thinking his highest honour to consist in the due discharge of his calling, emploieth all his studie and paines, to procure and maintaine ... the well-fare and peace of his people ... by the contrarie, an vsurping Tyran, will ... (by inuerting all good Lawes to serve onely for his vnrulie priuate affections) frame the common-weale euer to aduance his particular: building his suretie vpon his peoples miserie: and in the end (as a step-father and an vncouth hireling) make vp his owne hand vpon the ruines of the Republicke. (20)

Here the paradox of the contemplative—his thought may become thoughtlessness—illustrates the dangers of a "King's studie" when it is not devoted to the interests of his subjects. Exemplified by Prospero, the reclusive Duke of Milan, this paradox allows us to see in his bookishness the shadow of tyranny and to identify him with his usurping brother, each dangerous as "Absolute Milan."[19] It also provides grounds to link the art revealed in his books and expressed in his wand-waving with efforts to contend with his isolation on his island, where he puts artful devices into play to secure his fortunes and, presumably, the lib-

enient as the actiue life." To avoid it is "against nature": "There is nothing so monstruous ... as the abandoning of this commonalitie by neglecting the action." I quote from the English translation by Egremont Radcliffe, entitled *Politiqve Discovrses, treating of the differences and inequalities of vocations, as well publiqve, as priuate* (London, 1587), K_{iii}, N_{iii}^v, N_{iiii}, N_{iiii}^v; STC 15230.5. Lodowick Bryskett distinguishes a "contemplatiue felicitie" from an "actiue or practike felicitie" by saying that the former is available only in heaven, although some "haply draw neare vnto but cannot perfectly attaine [it] in this life." "Practike felicitie" is attained by moral action; it follows the subordination of passion. Lodowick Bryskett, *A Discovrse of Civill Life* (London, 1606), $D3^v$; STC 3959.

[19]Unlike other rulers in the romances who in various ways lose the good offices of their wives, Prospero is a widower for the term of the play: he does not throw his wife overboard (Pericles), or decree her execution (Leontes); and he does not effeminately submit to the rule of a virago (Cymbeline). As Stephen Orgel observes, however, "The absent presence of the wife and other in the play constitutes a space that is filled by Prospero's creation of surrogates and a ghostly family ... [and by] a whole structure of wifely allusion and reference"; "Prospero's Wife," 218. Prospero does, however, provide for a uxorial presence in the future of his state. He leaves the island having secured his daughter's marriage, her inheritance, and the dynastic integrity of the Milanese dukedom.

erty of the Milanese people from the rule of the usurper, Antonio. Speaking of the monarch's authority and power in relation to positive law, James had described it repeatedly as interpretive; the monarch is *lex loquens*, the spoken law—that is, its application in a particular case.[20] As I have suggested, whether Ariel's performances legitimately express the art of government by this and other contemporary standards is debatable. It was generally agreed that some fictions permitted a revelation of the truth, and that deceit and deception were sometimes justified by reasons of state. But when Prospero jettisons his wand and books as a condition of return to society, he implicitly rejects art dedicated to creating illusion. He will govern Milan without its devices— if he governs at all.

Certainly Prospero's "spirit," the former servant of Sycorax, carries with him the stigma of tyrannical rule. As Harry Berger Jr. has observed, Ariel's imprisonment in the witch's cloven pine is "an emblem of Prospero's Milanese experience."[21] Ariel's release from that pine gives him no more than a limited freedom, however; by granting it at all, Prospero seems to recognize as legitimate Ariel's disobedience of the witch's "earthy and abhorr'd commands" (1.2.273), and expects to make Ariel obedient by giving him commands that are just and inoffensive. Of course, Ariel may abhor Prospero's service as much as he did that of Sycorax; it is Prospero who describes Sycorax, and Ariel obeys Prospero only because Prospero threatens to return him to the cloven pine.[22] Prospero's isolation was originally the state of Sycorax,

---

[20]"Speech to parliament, 31 March 1607" and "21 March 1610," *Political Writings*, 161, 171, 183.
[21]Berger sees Ariel's service on the island as simply artful and hence unworthy of a Duke of Milan, who must reject it before returning to govern. "Miraculous Harp: A Reading of Shakespeare's *Tempest*," *Shakespeare Studies* 5 (1969): 253–83.
[22]Paul Brown, noting correctly the "apparent voluntarism" of Ariel's service, sees it as deceptive in that Prospero is actually coercive and exemplifies the first consequences of colonialism; "This thing of darkness," 61. Contracts of the kind Ariel's appears to have been modeled on—the indenture—were of course coercive in that they required of the parties a "specific performance" and provided "criminal penalties" as "legal remedies for breach"; Robert J. Steinfeld, *The Invention of Free Labor: The Employment Relation in English and American Law and Culture, 1350–1870* (Chapel Hill: University of North Carolina Press, 1991), 5. But they were not unique to colonial economies. Most "unfree" labor—that is, paid labor— was contractual in this period. For a study of labor in the first years of the Virginia colony, see Sigmund Diamond, "From Organization to Society: Virginia in the Seventeenth Century," in *Colonial America: Essays in Politics and Social Development*, ed. Stanley N. Katz (Boston: Little Brown and Co., 1976), 3–30.

and his control of Ariel is like the dominion of Sycorax—through terror of incarceration.

Self-Rule: Caliban

Prospero's second servant, Caliban, is an even more enigmatic figure than Ariel. He has been seen as postlapsarian man, a New World native, and the English "slave" of the monarch's absolutist practices.[23] There is a case, too, for seeing him as a figure in which all of these identities cohere, a figure both containing and revealing oppositions.

Like Ariel, Caliban longs for freedom from servitude. His history is also linked to Sycorax. She was his mother and by her he claims the island as his kingdom. Unlike Ariel, who can be made to obey by verbal threats, Caliban is "earth" (316) and responds to physical punishment. He is almost all body: he wants food, he feels lust, he succumbs to drink as to a god. Ugly and incapable of a "kind" answer (311), he is described as a "slave" whose menial service cannot be missed (310): as Prospero explains to Miranda, "he serves in offices/That profit us" (1.2.314–15). Yet as Sycorax' heir, he claims he should be "King" of the island (344). He was dispossessed by trickery, he tells Prospero: "When thou cam'st first,/Thou strok'st me, and made much of me . . . then I lov'd thee,/And show'd thee all the qualities o' the isle" (334–38). Prospero states that Caliban was treacherous and after "human care," attempted to "violate" Miranda (348–49). He is, moreover, unregenerate. "Stripes" (his punishment [347]) have not caused him to repent his attempted rape:

> O ho, O ho, would't been done!
> Thou didst prevent me; I had peopled else
> This isle with Calibans.

> (351–53)

Here, questionable act appears to have followed questionable act: attempted rape follows a conquest of doubtful legitimacy. Who is

---

[23]For an extended study of Caliban, see Alden T. Vaughan and Virginia Mason Vaughan, *Shakespeare's Caliban: A Cultural History* (Cambridge: Cambridge University Press, 1991).

blameworthy, who exonerated? If Caliban is Prospero's only subject, he must represent some aspect of the Duke's self, whoever else he also is. Illegitimate or tyrannical rule was often understood to originate in a failure of the ruler's *self-government*; in its simplest manifestation, a misgovernment of the self succeeds a failure of reason to control passion, or the bodily self. The matter is addressed briefly in *Basilicon Doron*.

In keeping with the principle expressed in the opening sonnet of his treatise—"and as their subiects ought them to obey,/So Kings shold feare and serue their God againe"—James asserts that Prince Henry's rule will actually be guaranteed by temperance. This virtue is to control "affections" and "appetite," both expressions of the physical body. Here moral qualities supersede dynastic integrity in determining legitimacy:

> As he cannot be thought worthy to rule and commmand others, that cannot rule and dantone his owne proper affections and vnreasonable appetites, so can hee not be thought worthie to gouerne a Christian people, knowing and fearing God, that in his owne person and heart, feareth not and loueth not the Diuine Maiestie. (12)

"Temperance," said James, is a "wise moderation, that . . . shall as a Queene, command all the affections and passions of [the] minde" (43). This dictum, a political commonplace, recalled what Fortescue and others had indicated was the monarch's servitude. Unfree in that he served his people, he was also commanded by temperance in order that he be able to serve his people. Affections and passions inhibiting such service were linked to the humors of the body, that part of human nature commonly considered bestial. Temperance found its original challenge in fleshly wants and desires.

Christian doctrine represented man's "communities with beasts" (as Augustine termed his bodily appetites) as a consequence of the fall and defined the man whose bestiality dominates his reasonable soul as a "seruant of sinne" and the subject of the "extreame tirany" of lust.[24]

---

[24]St. Augustine, *Of the citie of God*, Book 19, chapters 14, 15 (entitled "Nature's freedome, and bondage caused by sinne: in which man is a slaue to his owne affects though he be not bondman to anyone besides"), 771. Vives glosses the concept of sin's servant in this edition by citing John 8. 34. Augustine makes explicit what Aristotle implies: no man is *naturally* servile. For an analysis of Augustine's idea of the body in postlapsarian man, see Peter Brown, *The Body and Society: Men, Women, and Sexual Renunciation in Early Christianity* (New York: Columbia University Press, 1988), esp. 416–19.

Although the body itself was not the origin of this bestiality or sin, Augustine declared, the corruption of the body was occasioned by "the first sin"; after the fall, "the workes of the flesh" were categorically sinful.[25] To counter (proleptically) the influence of the corrupted flesh of postlapsarian man, God made man "vpright": it follows that the man who is unregenerate grovels or walks on all fours (*Of the citie of God*, 14, 3–4; Vv4, Vv4ᵛ). The most cogent example of the corrupted body's willfulness was "the vncleane motion of the generatiue parts," because over that "motion" the rational mind is notoriously powerless (14, 16, Yyᵛ, Yy2). Pseudo-Aquinas, arguing a similar case, stated that man's spirit (*anima*) governs his body, while reason (*ratio*) orders his passions and appetites (*partes irascibilis et concupiscibilis*).[26] When such government fails, man becomes a "beast": "for a man divorced from reason and following desire is no different than a beast" (*quia homo absque ratione secundum animae suae libidinem praesidens nihil differt a bestia*, 18–19). Paradoxically, this is the condition of both the tyrant and those who live under him: a tyrant who "is a slave to avarice, steals from his subjects" (16–17), and his rapacity drives his subjects to an animalistic servitude: "it is natural that men living in fear and servitude deny their souls and become fearful of all manly and strenuous work." Such "men fly from tyrants as from cruel beasts" (18–19).[27]

In his *Enchiridion militis christiani*, Erasmus described the body of the Christian in general terms. It was not only to be governed by reason but "chastized" because it was continually tending to sin:

> A man is than a certain monstruous beast compact togyther of partes, two or thre of great diuersitie, of a soul, as of a certain goodly thing, and of a body as it were a brute or dombe beast . . . . [N]ow [i.e., after the fall] they neither can be seperate without very great turment & payne, neyther lyue ioyned togyther without continual

[25]Richard Hooker would later note that the state was a consequence of the Fall. For Hooker "nature as such can have played no part in founding civilized societies. . . . [P]olitical societies have conventional and not natural bases and are artificial structures"; Frederick John Shirley, *Richard Hooker and Contemporary Political Ideas* (London: S.P.C.K., 1949), 94–95.
[26]St. Thomas Aquinas, *De regime principum ad regem cypri*, in *Selected Political Writings*, ed. A. P. D'Entrèves, trans. J. G. Dawson (Oxford: Oxford University Press, 1959), 6–7.
[27]"Naturale etiam est, ut homines, sub timore nutriti, in servilem degenerent animum, et pusillanimes fiant ad omne virile opus et strenuum: quod experimento patet in provinciis, quae diu sub tyrannis fuerunt." For a restatement of the idea that men under tyranny are enfeebled, see my analysis of *Le Reveille Matin*, chapter 6, pp. 186–187.

war . . . . Paule writeth . . . I chastyce my body and bring him into seruitude . . . . Plato put two soules to be in one man. Paul in one man maketh two men so coupled togither that neyther without other can be eyther in heaven or hel, and agayne so seperate that the death of the one, must be lyfe of the other.

Man as soul is Christlike; man as body is the old (and fallen) Adam: "as was the man of the erth suche are terrestyall and earthlye persons."[28] Constructing a Christian psyche, Erasmus conflated the Augustinian notion of postlapsarian man, bestial to the extent that he is desirous, with the Platonic image of man divided between heaven and earth, and introduced his composite figure into a scheme consistent with salvation history. Transposing these figures to suit political situations in the *Institutio principis christiani*, Erasmus took a harsher view of the body of a man who is also a ruler: unless he controls his desires, he bestializes his subjects as well as himself. A worthy king is only the image of a god (*simulacrum dei*, i.e., not godlike in the sense of being a surrogate; 150); his "servitude" is actually the most burdensome there is (152). A tyrant denies his servitude; he is a "master" (*dominus*, 152) whose subjects are "treated like beasts" (*equii, asinii*; 153), and he himself is like an animal.[29] He even eats his subjects, as Homer's Achilles had noted when he described a tyrant as *demoboros basileus* (160). Like pseudo-Aquinas, Erasmus insisted that the rule of a bestial tyrant bestialized its subjects. A tyrant deploys an *ars Circes* which, while it appears to enhance the tyrant's power, actually reduces it.[30] Treatises written later in the century and especially after the accession of James, made comparable distinctions. Henry Crosse's *Schoole of pollicie: or The araignement of State-abuses*, 1605, distinguished between "Vice" and "Vertue" as two kinds of "Animalia" or living creatures: "in respect of *Vertue* a man is said to be a man, which is the *Etymologie* of the word, and in respect of *Vice* to be a beast."[31] The animalium which is bestial must answer to his higher half, the virtuous man.

[28]Desiderius Erasmus, *Enchiridion militis christiani, which maybe called in englyshe the hansome weapon of a Chrysten knyght* (London, 1548), ch. 4, E_{iii}^v, E_{iiii}; ch. 6, F_{ii}^v; STC 10485.
[29]"si tyrannis quaeris imaginem, leonem, ursum, lupum aut aquilam cogita" [if you seek an image of a tyrant, think of a lion, a bear, a wolf or an eagle], 157.
[30]"Proinde deterius fecerit imperium, qui liberos cives verterit in mancipia" [He who turns free citizens into slaves makes his rule the worse as a result; 166].
[31]H[enry] Crosse, *The Schoole of pollicie: or The araignement of State-abuses* (London, 1605), B, B^v; STC 6071. Crosse later describes how virtue is cultivated: "Vertue is diuided into two

If Caliban is understood to figure his master's flesh, his old Adam, Prospero's harsh treatment of him makes sense. As a Christian and particularly a head of state, Prospero's body must be ruled by his spirit and so affected by his art that it does nothing but work. Miranda testifies to Caliban's essential corruption—he is an "Abhorred slave,/Which any print of goodness wilt not take,/Being capable of all ill!" (353–55). Caliban's labor is therefore endless: to his "There's wood enough within," Prospero replies: "Come forth, I say! there's other business for thee" (316–17). Inasmuch as a sequestered life in Milan had left Prospero prone to the bestial and bestializing self of a tyrant, as contemporary doctrine on prudence would suggest, his control of Caliban is not only necessary but also an indication that he is reforming that self, earlier incarnate in the witch and malevolent artist, Sycorax, and her god, Setebos.[32] As Caliban declares: "I must obey: his Art is of such pow'r,/ It would control my dam's god, Setebos" (374–75).

There is a Caliban or "earth" in virtually all of Prospero's subjects, however, and Ariel tempers those who are members of the political body of Naples. His influence, consistently frustrating, governs the sensuous side of Ferdinand (whose discipline mirrors Caliban's), the drunken riot of Trinculo and Stephano, and the seditious lust of Antonio and Sebastian, itself predicated on the earlier sedition of Antonio and Alonso. This extension of rule (whether of the monarch or any other officeholder) from the self as its own subject to its actual subjects was often imagined analogically. James had noted that self-rule was the basis of

parts, the *Intellective*, and the *Morrall*, the former is begotten and nourished by good tutors, reading good Bookes, and exercise; from this floweth wisedome, science, prudence, memorie. The latter commeth by custome and vse, for these two are so forcible, as by it a man may get him a second nature and this worketh this thing called *Actus* (i.e., performance) . . . and is the mother of Liberalitie, Fortitude, and of all good manners (B").

[32]In a structural sense, Sycorax occupies the place of Cymbeline's Queen; the difference between them is that Sycorax's influence over Prospero has vanished by the time the play begins. Her legacy to him is Caliban, the son she bore and the creature Prospero adopted: as a single character, Caliban epitomizes the flesh of the tyrant's body. Orgel notes the absence of wives and mothers in the play and argues that their place is filled by the ghostly Sycorax and the nubile Miranda, with Prospero assuming the role of spiritual mother in a family drama understood in largely psychological terms; "Introduction," 18–20. For a comprehensive study of mothers in Shakespeare, see Mary Beth Rose, "Where Are the Mothers in Shakespeare? Options for Gender Representation in the English Renaissance," *Shakespeare Quarterly* 42, 3 (1991): 291–314.

all rule, and Erasmus thought that to rule the self was like ruling a "communaltye." There, reason must be absolute king and "vyle appetytes"—"lechery, ryot, enuye, and such lyke diseases," "the most rascal and vyle sort of the commune people"—"without exception must be kept under with prison and punishment [so that] as vyle and bond seruauntes that they may rendre to their maister their taske." When "concupiscence rageth" and the appetites rebel against reason, there "tyrannye reygneth" (*Enchiridion*, ch.4; $E_v{}^v$, $E_{vi}{}^v$). But a temperate monarch will reflexively infuse his subjects with his own virtue. Henry Crosse, for example, saw "Temperance" as "a sad and sober Matron" (*School of Pollicie*, C2), who radiated powers of self-restraint:

> What a diuine glory is heere? that striketh the beholder in admiration, dazeleth his sight, and forceth the very abiect to reuerence him in whom it dooth appeare, for shee is so beautifull a Lady as she maketh many gaze at her a farre off, that haue no power to come nigh heer but striketh into wonderment at her incomparable maiestie, are metamorphosed, as it were by *Medusa*. (D2)

A year later, Forset identified the power controlling the "body" of the body politic as the monarch's prerogative or "absolute power" (*Comparatiue Discovrse*, $¶_{iii}$). Like Crosse's Temperance (a virtue Forset may have wanted to link to the prerogative), this "absolute power" is a "dazzling" force that works "vnlimitably . . . yet vndiscerned . . . hidden and concealed from the eyes of men," in order to "seeme to stand more with maiestie" (D^v, $D_{ii}{}^v$, E). It is registered "in so admirable effects as to transforme sauageness into ciuilitie, repugnances into concords, vices into vertues, procuring loue yet implying feare, compelling obedience, yet with yeeld of highest honour" (F). Yet it also requires restraint: it can be misguided if it assumes "sole power in law-giuing" ($C_{iiii}{}^v$) or succumbs to "Appetites" (D_{ii}). Finally, it is characterized by "holding towards all the proportion of iustice yet extending withall the remorse of mercie" (F^v).

Figured in his wand and made irresistible by Ariel, Prospero's temperance is first deployed against the lust of Caliban and then governs Ferdinand's passion for Miranda. Ariel draws Ferdinand to Miranda by music; without a will and therefore as if disembodied, heir meets heir by virtue of air (1.2.394–97). Ferdinand first sees Miranda as divine, and the Vergilian lines he cites, "Most sure the goddess/On whom these airs attend!" (424–25), allude to the mixed character, Venerian and Dianesque, that she will continue to have for him. Prospero, "lest too light winning/Make the prize light," makes the lovers' "business uneasy" (452–54). He accuses Ferdinand (Naples's heir) of treachery (463), and he orders him to do servile work. In the terms of romance, Ferdinand's is a Petrarchan desire, licit as long as it is thwarted. His virtue counters the bestiality Prospero must control in Caliban.

The contractual and generative aspects of the match between Ferdinand and Miranda contribute to its image as the basis of dynastic integrity. Ferdinand sees Miranda as "that which quickens what's dead" (3.1.6), and Prospero asks the heavens to grace their loves and "that which breeds between 'em" (75–76). Miranda speaks for herself in a way that recalls Thaisa's declaration of love for Pericles (3.1.48–58, 77–86), and Prospero insists only on a "contract" at betrothal that observes temporal proprieties (4.1.19). Like Simonides, Prospero rejoices at his daughter's match; like Leontes, he recognizes that he is excluded from its pleasures (3.1.92–96; see also 5.1.307–11). The pastoral masque that celebrates their prospective marriage features Juno, the queen of heaven, but excludes Venus, who must wait for Hymen (4.1.91–101), in favor of Ceres, whose "sunburn'd sicklemen" dance together with country nymphs (134)—a sign of rural work and its productions.

Ariel's enchanting music acting on the court party is designed to force illegitimate desires to manifest themselves, if only that they may be thwarted. Putting the intended victims of Antonio's conspiracy to sleep, his music creates a false sense of security for the conspirators who seek to exploit the moment. Antonio ridicules "conscience" as the faculty that could prevent his regicide (2.1.270–73), but he is stopped by Prospero's conscience, the application of his art *cum scientia*, that, as Ariel, infuses a palpable temperance into the scene. Music regularly evoked images of social concord. William Fulbecke, citing Cicero, likened "concent . . . as in musicall instruments," to "the principall meane and inferior sorts of men agreeing amongest themselues"; this brings about the "good estate of a Citie," "concord" in the "commonweale," and can "neuer be without iustice." Ariel's song here is instrumental in preventing a further disruption of an already illegitimate state. It revives Alonso's counselor, Gonzalo, and prevents Antonio and Sebastian's murder of Alonso, itself a proximate imitation of Antonio and

Alonso's deposition of Prospero. To unreceptive ears, unsympathetic to any kind of harmony, however, music could sound cacophonous. Without justice (or presumably to unjust men), Fulbecke declares, music "offends human eares," and sounds like "an unpleasant iarring."[33] Sebastian describes Ariel's music, which the audience and Gonzalo have heard as the spirit's song, "While you here do snoring lie," as the "hollow burst of bellowing/Like bulls, or rather lions" (2.1.295, 306–7). To hear music as harmony is itself an indication of a temperate soul.

Ariel also controls a second group of conspirators—Caliban, Stephano, and Trinculo—who threaten anarchy by aspiring to rule yet are themselves incapable of self-restraint and without knowledge or science (their book is a bottle of liquor).[34] His ventriloquism marks their capacity for dissension among themselves (3.2.40 ff.), and his music, which rectifies their erroneous notes without identifying the musician (124–25), testifies to their inability to agree among themselves, their inharmoniousness. They sing of "[t]hought [that] is free"—a statement contradicted by Ariel's image as Prospero's servant as well as by their own predicament. In this sense Ariel is prudence (unfree or applied thought) controlling license (free and ungoverned thought).[35] None in the group can resist following his better harmony, a "catch" that enchants them all.

In Ariel's most impressive performance—his playing Harpy at Prospero's mock banquet—Prospero's art works against the long-standing and habitual treachery of his enemies. It creates what they experience as a frustration of a fundamental bodily need, food (implying a comparison of their nature with Caliban's), and explains this discipline

[33]William Fulbecke, *A Parallele or Conference of the Civill Law, the Canon Law, and the Common Law of this Realme of England* (London, 1601), §₍ᵢᵢᵢᵢᵢ₎ᵛ; STC 11415. For a study of music in relation to the play's political philosophy, see Robin Headlam Wells, "Prospero, King James, and the myth of the musician-king," in *Elizabethan Mythologies: Studies in Poetry, Drama, and Music* (Cambridge: Cambridge University Press, 1994), 63–80.

[34]Curt Breight suggests that *The Tempest* can "be viewed within a sphere of oppositional discourse" because it stages a "demystification of various official strategies within the discourse of treason," and "the audience is allowed to see that conspiracy is often a fiction"; "'Treason doth never prosper': *The Tempest* and the Discourse of Treason," *Shakespeare Quarterly* 41, 1 (1990): 1–28; 1. Such a reading oversimplifies the play's many representations of treason and, by suggesting that Shakespeare merely exposes the monarch's use of deception, overlooks the play's references to a rule neither tyrannical nor absolute.

[35]For a discussion of surveillance of the subject in relation to this scene, see Annabel Patterson, *Shakespeare and the Popular Voice* (Oxford: Basil Blackwell, 1989), 160–62.

by a speaking picture of their moral condition. Untrue as history (Ferdinand is not dead; 3.3.75–76), Prospero's banquet works as a legal fiction, as did Paulina's statue. Seen by the audience as an illusion although comprising real (in the sense of factual) elements, the banquet provides the setting for Ariel's prophecy: he explains the misfortunes of the court party as punishment for their crimes and warns of retribution unless they reform their ways (76–82). His warning awakes the consciences of the guilty. But it also goes further than any representation of a human justice by invoking divine justice (60–61). This puts the guilty in "fits" and "distractions," the result of Prospero's "charms" and "power" (88–91). Ariel does not mention mercy and at the moment the banquet is destroyed, it is not yet clear whether and to what extent Prospero's three enemies can or will lead a "clear life" (83), or whether his temperance will be magnified by mercy if they fail to reform.[36]

Natural Man

Caliban is not simply a figure of unregenerate flesh, however; he is also one who works and as such he cannot be missed (1.2.313). Moreover, his history suggests that his appetitiveness was preceded by an earlier and primordial state in which he was ignorant of possession. Lust in any form other than desire for satisfaction of bodily needs appears to have been unknown to him. An innocent and essentially *pre*lapsarian Caliban is shadowed in his own account of Prospero's arrival. At first, he "lov'd" the man who later would become his master: unaware of meum and tuum, Caliban did not understand that the island (and presumably even Miranda) could not be shared between them. "[I] show'd thee all the qualities o' th'isle,/The fresh springs, brine-pits, barren place and fertile" (1.2.339–40). The assumption behind his willingness to reveal the island's wealth—that "th'isle" is common and not contestable property—is made explicit later in Gonzalo's speech on his ideal and

---

[36]To show mercy a governor did not necessarily require that the guilty be remorseful or ready to reform; in theory, it was a function of the monarch's "body natural" and could be extended to a deranged person incapable of knowing right from wrong. In any case, it brought attention to the governor in question: Forset had claimed that the monarch's "justice" when extended with "mercie" gave him "a more admired glory and a more deere esteeme." *Comparatiue Discovrse*, F.

patently unrealizable "plantation." Just as this "plantation" without "land, tilth or vineyard" is a contradiction in terms, so is the commonwealth without property or any of its political or legal guarantees that Gonzalo would construct upon it (2.1.143–60). Prospero's aged counselor and his slave are clearly linked by their shared vision of a Golden Age, a recollection of a primordial "childhood" of the human race and of a fundamental human character that has no sense of itself as a possessor or a possession. It is a character vulnerable to the intelligence of others (Caliban is actually dispossessed, Gonzalo's vision is mocked).[37] More important, it is a pre-moral and pre-political character that cannot participate in a civil society as it is imagined in the play. Controlled by the most benign expressions of Prospero's art, the soporific harmonies of Ariel, the innocent Caliban can only dream of a wealth (perhaps the wealth he believes he once had and now has lost) that is stored in heaven: "The clouds methought would open, and show riches/Ready to drop upon me" (3.2.139–40). This Caliban seems incapable of vice. Waking to the knowledge of his poverty, he plans no kind of resistance but only cries "to dream again" (141).[38]

Pre-Christian and especially Aristotelian treatments of temperance provide a context for an innocent Caliban. Such accounts of human nature represented sensuous life as inherently amoral, unaffected by reason and rational choice. They conceived of natural man, the human being as mere body, as innocent of virtue and vice. For Aristotle in

[37]In other respects, the two characters are quite different; Caliban is essentially innocent as well as morally and politically undisciplined, Gonzalo is capable of great sophistication. As John Gillies points out, Gonzalo's portrait of a Platonic commonwealth is intentionally ironic; Gonzalo presents it to "minister occasion" to Antonio and Sebastian who are used to laughing at "nothing" (2.1.176–70); John Gillies, "Shakespeare's Virginian Masque," *ELH* 53, 4 (1986): 673–707. It would have reminded the audience that to rule "with perfection" as Gonzalo says he would (2.1.163–64), is possible only in a fiction of the Golden Age.

[38]Paul Brown suggests that Caliban's dream locates "a site beyond colonial appropriation"; "this is to say, the colonialist project's investment in the processes of euphemisation of what are really powerful relations here has produced a utopian moment where powerlessness represents a *desire for powerlessness*"; "This thing of darkness," 66. The extent to which Caliban desires freedom is indeed problematic; there is a sense in which he represents the most abject kind of subject (see chapter 6, p. 186). The relations of power in which he figures are not, however, colonialist—too narrow a frame to contain them—but rather those created by tyranny. For a reading comparably restricted to a consideration of colonialist terms and issues, see Richard Halpern, "'The Picture of Nobody': White Cannibalism in *The Tempest*" in *The Production of English Renaissance Culture*, ed. David Lee Miller, Sharon O'Dair, and Harold Weber (Ithaca: Cornell University Press, 1994), 262–92.

particular, sensuous life in its pure form was epitomized in a creature he called the "naturally bestial" man.

As he is represented in the *Nicomachean Ethics*, this creature is, I would argue, a kind of fiction, important for the sake of argument but vacuous in any real or objective sense. The "naturally bestial" creature appears in a moral context in which he who is "bestial" (*feralis*) "by nature" (*natura*) and entirely sensuous is essentially amoral; and a political context, in which he who is naturally bestial and hence incapable of civil behavior is essentially apolitical (literally: he does not live in a city). In each setting, the life of the naturally bestial man is neither virtuous nor vicious. To describe his activities as morally or politically culpable is misleading in that they are not the result of rational choices. He can be considered to have moral or political failings only "by analogy" (*per similitudinem*; *[E]thicorum ad nichomacum libri*, VII.5, 133ᵛ; [1148b, 1149a]). "Bestiality," insofar as it is represented by his behavior, is not a term denoting a moral or political condition but rather signifies the absence of a rational consciousness. In a discussion of government or civil order, the "naturally bestial" man stands in theoretical contrast to the man who is in control of his body, his flesh (even for selfish reasons), and who is therefore not naturally bestial but rather both moral and political.

Aristotle's idea of man as a beast, sensuous and uncivil, is central to his ethics, chiefly because it allows him to discuss virtue and vice as the consequence of rational as opposed to sensuous behavior. In distinction to the naturally bestial man, who is unrestrained "by nature" but not vicious because acting under compulsion he has not chosen a course of action, a man who has intellectual faculties, knows the meaning of virtue and vice, and yet habitually behaves without "self-restraint" (*continentia*) or, worse, without "temperance" (*temperantia*; VII.4, f. 131ᵛ–132ᵛ; VII.5, f. 133ᵛ; VII.6, f. 135 [1147b–1150a]), is morally and politically culpable. Men in the first category, the naturally bestial, are rare: those "who by nature lack reason and live entirely by the senses are monstrous" (*qui natura quidam ratione carent sensumque tantummodo vivunt, immanes sunt*). And they do not live in cities: "such are the nations of barbarians who live in distant regions" (*quales nunnullae nationes sunt longe habitantium Barbarorum*" (VII.5, f. 133ᵛ [1149a]). Unlike these "barbarians," men in the second category, the morally and politically culpable, are open to various criticisms. *Incontinence* is chiefly instinctual; it responds to sense perception and not true knowledge

(VII.3, f. 129 [1147a], and it does not involve "choice" (*electio*; VII.4, f. 132 [1148a]). A man who acts incontinently or without restraint is like one who is asleep or drunk (VII.3, f. 129). He is blameworthy but cannot be called vicious because his behavior does not fully engage "reason" (*ratio*; VII.5, f. 133ᵛ [1149a]), and he can be reformed (VII.8, f. 138 [1150b]), presumably through a consciousness of well- or ill-being. By contrast, "*profligacy*" reflects rational choice. The actions of someone who is capable of both self-restraint and temperance can be driven by strong feelings and show the lesser of unethical behaviors—a "lack of restraint" or incontinence. Worse, he can be intemperate and profligate. In this case, his behavior is categorically vicious in that it is chosen and entirely without "principle" or any sort of moral consideration (VII.8, f. 137ᵛ–138 [1150b]). In sum, Aristotle placed the naturally bestial man outside moral and political frames of reference. He considered degrees of culpability only in relation to the capacity to be moved, through conscious reflection or rational choice, in social or civil settings.

Seen in light of Aristotelian norms, Caliban acquires that quality of the marvelous associated with paradox.[39] To the extent that he represents pure body, natural man, the natural beast in man, he cannot be regarded as culpable. A figure of the sensuous body, he represents an innocent and pre-political entity, a fiction derived from the memory of an uncivilized past, a time when human beings knew only themselves, each a barbarian in the Aristotelian sense of that term. But Caliban must also be understood in light of his behavior after Prospero and Miranda arrive on his island and he becomes one of their society: he assaults Miranda and conspires against Prospero. To the extent that this behavior is seen as blameworthy or vicious, Caliban must be regarded as capable of a moral and political life and cannot be dismissed as a beast (as Prospero repeatedly calls him). The question to ask is why he, Caliban, turns out so badly after experiencing Prospero's rule. Two answers appear plausible. On the

[39]No character in the play has received greater attention. In general, two views predominate—Caliban is a version of the fictional "wild man" of European legend; Caliban is an amalgam of varieties of New World native. As "wild man," he is often seen as an aspect of Prospero's own character. Donna B. Hamilton argues that Caliban is a political subject but not necessarily one restricted to the New World; he is preeminently the subject of absolute rule whether in or out of England; Donna B. Hamilton, *Virgil and The Tempest: The Politics of Imitation* (Columbus: Ohio State University Press, 1990), 44–66. Richard Halpern describes him as a figure of the "mestizo," "The Picture of Nobody," 297; Gillies, as an Amerindian, "Shakespeare's Virginian Masque," 151.

one hand, Caliban's defiance of Prospero may be understood in terms of a Christian morality, as the failure of the Duke's spirit to govern the flesh, its "thing of darkness"; on the other hand, it may instance a form of resistance to a superior. In these perspectives, to blame or to attribute viciousness to Caliban is to call into question the nature of Prospero's rule, both of himself and of his subject. This rule can be understood in practice if Prospero is regarded as a tyrant who is "bestial" in the Aristotelian sense of that term, and who therefore governs "beasts" in the language of Christian political doctrine. These conditions of rule are not literal but figurative and speak to the need for reform.

Whatever the discipline Prospero justifiably imposes on Caliban, there is some evidence that he cares for the "body" of his body politic. Accounting for his history to Miranda, he states that Antonio did not "destroy" them because his "people" held him "so dear" (1.2.139–41). More important, his first work of art, the tempest that opens the play, provides an apt illustration of the common humanity of ruler and subject as well as the material dependence of ruler upon subject. As an author, Prospero presumably knows the meaning of the play he is producing. His *Tempest* (as it were) reveals a ruler's indebtedness to his subjects and implies his servitude to the people. On Alonso's sinking ship, the court party must rely on the ship's master, who is helpless without his mariners, who in turn contend with the forces in nature. While the mariners respond to the Shipmaster's commands, they also acknowledge an altogether different superior—the storm itself, which cares for no human authority, not even a king's. "If you can command these elements to silence, and work the peace of the presence, we will not hand a rope more; use your authority" (1.1.21–23), the Boatswain tells Gonzalo. This inversion of the usual hierarchy of government reveals the crux at the heart of absolutist theory. If an authority has no concomitant power necessary to enforce itself, then its claims to absolute freedom to rule are either entirely false or credible only to the extent that they engage illusion. The *power* of authority is thus in a sense an illusion. In reality, a ruler has no power apart from what his subjects give him. What transforms his commands from words to deeds is only a borrowed power—one susceptible to revocation.[40] Repre-

---

[40]Wage-earners, day laborers, and indentured servants were not of course the people and therefore had no liberties of the kind constitutionalists claimed. The mariners of *The Tempest*, like other characters who are represented chiefly as workers or artisans, would have been

senting the subject and worker in the body politic, who "serves in offices/That profit us," in the words of Prospero (1.2.314–15), the "villain," bondman, or wage-earner is not the "villain" or scoundrel Miranda does "not love to look on" (1.2.311–12). He is, rather, one who produces the wealth of the commonwealth. As *prudentia* works through *sensus*, the ruler cannot function without his body politic.

As pure "body," the merely sensuous Caliban assumes some of the play's most degraded positions; he also has some of its best lines. But as a man capable of moral and political life, he is a much more complicated character and fully revealed only by reference to contemporary political discourse. A civil Caliban could legitimately rebel against an unwarranted appropriation of his property—his own body (as he has not sold his labor) and the island (whether located somewhere in the vastness of the New World or the Mediterranean or metaphorically representing England itself) of which he is a native. Assuming that Caliban *is* the island's rightful lord, his resistance to Prospero can be seen as a retaliatory response to Prospero's earlier seizure of him and his "kingdom."[41] But as I have mentioned, Caliban's resistance also involves illicit behavior. Like Belarius's abduction of Cymbeline's sons, Caliban's attempted rape of Miranda and his treasonous plotting against Prospero are criminal acts. On what grounds, if any, can they be justified? The question is answerable only provisionally and in relation to different perspectives.

recognized as members of the whole body politic and hence as the beneficiaries of liberties if not actually possessing them in their own right. This scene recapitulates some of the elements of the sixth book of the *De republica*, which as I have suggested, are answered by the *Politicus* and represented allusively in the storm scene in *Pericles*; see chapter 1, pp. 57–60.

[41] Stephen Orgel, arguing that Caliban's claim to the island is designed to be suspect inasmuch as he derives it from his mother, who, as Prospero claims, was unmarried; "He [Caliban] need not do this; the claim could derive from the mere fact of prior possession: he was there first," points out how ambiguous is the play's apparent legalism; "Introduction," 25. Much of the commentary on the play's dramatization of "colonialism" represents Shakespeare as an apologist for European power appropriating territory in the New World. See especially Peter Hulme, "Hurricanes in the Caribbees: The Constitution of the Discourse of English Colonialism," in *1642: Literature and Power in the Seventeenth Century*, ed. Francis Barker et al. (Essex: University of Essex, 1981), 55–83; and Paul Brown, "This Thing of Darkness." For a critique of this scholarship—based on its neglect of historical record—see Meredith Anne Skura, "Discourse and the Individual: The Case of Colonialism in *The Tempest*," *Shakespeare Quarterly* 40, 1 (1989): 42–69. I suggest that the play incorporates elements of colonialist discourse, but in the interest of representing a comprehensive picture of tyranny, its means of domination, the measures by which it may be reformed, and the conditions in which it is perpetuated.

CHAPTER 6

The Tempest, ii

PROSPERO WILL SUCCEED IN PREVENTING TWO CONSPIRACIES—
the first against Naples, the second against his own island government. He will also reverse the effects of the action by which his brother Antonio, with the aid of Alonso, king of Naples, deposed and forced him into exile. His art will dominate his desirous subjects (the innocent Caliban, the loving Ferdinand), and his political enemies (the seditious Antonio and Sebastian). If the deceptions Prospero practices on these antagonists lead to a renewed moral and political order, they may fall into the Baconian category of a creative vexation; as Bacon suggested, to "try" in this sense is to change and to refine. If, however, they are merely coercive, they may prove more dangerous than constructive. Government requires a sentient body politic. To lull it into a stupefied obedience is to inhibit its vitality, its capacity to respond to contingencies not foreseen by any legislator. It must remain alert. When Ariel intervenes to stop Antonio and Sebastian's murder of Alonso, an event that were Prospero simply committed to revenge he would relish, Ariel prefaces his monitory action (waking Gonzalo) by stating the reason for his mission:

My master through his Art foresees the danger
That you, his friend [Gonzalo] are in; and sends me forth,—
For else his project dies,—to keep them living.

(2.1.292–94)

Here at least, Prospero's art is designed to vivify not to deaden. Its "project," like Paulina's experimental play, will entail not only rousing his old counselor, but also pricking the consciences of those who will eventually constitute the body politic of a unified Milan and Naples.

Ariel's report of his having performed the tempest according to Prospero's command illustrates the debilitating consequences of art that is merely illusionistic. Boarding Alonso's ship, Ariel says he "flam'd amazement," burning "in many places: on the topmast,/The yards and boresprit . . . ,/Jove's lightnings . . . more momentary/And sight-out-running were not" (1.2.198–203). This caused havoc: "Not a soul/But felt a fever of the mad" (208–9), became desperate, and leapt overboard. Presented as a theatrical performance, a show of lights, Prospero's spirit describes what was known as St. Elmo's fire, a natural phenomenon that, while subject to all kinds of "construction" by "superstitious seamen," was "usual in storms," as William Strachey noted in his *A True Reportory of the Wreck and Redemption of Sir Thomas Gates*, 1610. Strachey, accounting for his own shipwreck, had stated that his men were deluded by a "little, round light like a faint star . . . shooting sometimes from shroud to shroud . . . [that] did not light us any whit the more to our known way, who [as a result] ran now (as do hoodwinked men) at all adventures."[1] The two wrecks differ in that what Ariel describes as events in Prospero's tempest are not recognized as constructions upon natural phenomena, but rather experienced as a kind of enchantment, destroying sense and reason, while onboard Gates's ship, at least Strachey knew he was watching a *lusus naturae*. Prospero's art will become truly constructive when he, like Paulina educating Leontes, allows his audience to become sentient, to feel and to know

---

[1] William Strachey, *A True Reportory of the Wreck and Redemption of Sir Thomas Gates, Knight, upon and from the Islands of the Bermudas . . .* , ed. Louis B. Wright (Charlottesville: University Press of Virginia, 1964), 12, 13. For another account of St. Elmo's fire known to readers of New World travel, see *A Briefe Declaration of the Vyage or Navigation Made Abowte the Worlde*, in Richard Eden, *The Decades of the newe worlde or west India*, in *The First Three English Books on America, 1511–1555*, ed. Edward Arber (Birmingham, 1885), 250.

who they are and what they are doing. This he partly accomplishes by his monitory masque of Harpies (3.3.18–103). But his last act as an artist is the culmination of this didactic process: to free those who have done him "high wrongs," but are now "penitent" from the delusory and incapacitating charms induced by that masque (5.1.11–19; 28–30):

> Go, release them Ariel:
> My charms I'll break, their senses I'll restore,
> And they shall be themselves.

> (5.1.30–32; see also 21–24)

By making this move, Prospero obviously unifies what have been two distinct impulses sustaining the continuous manifestations of his art: the first is to regain his dukedom; the second is to rule well. The first impulse derives from self-interest, the second reflects a commitment to the interests of subjects. Prospero's spirit has paralyzed resistance to his rule; Prospero's grace will allow his (and prospectively Miranda's) subjects both freedom and a conscious (hence also conscientious) life.

His restorative actions imply a commitment to some kind of contractualism with respect to rule within the body politic, a commitment that further implies support, however qualified, for the subjects' liberties and liberty. *The Trew Law* had implied that the king's "Coronation Oath" required him to "procure the weale and flourishing of his people . . . knowing himselfe to be ordained for them, and they not for him." Furthermore, his fatherly "kindness" would rule out the possibility that he could legitimately deny subjects their "ancient Priuiledges and Liberties"[2]—that is, in the language of contemporary political debate, he could not "enslave" his subjects. Admittedly vague, the notion that a monarchy, even an absolute monarchy, had to stop short of instituting a servitude of the people provided opponents of tyranny with terms of resistance.

[2]James VI and I, *The Trew Law of Free Monarchies*, in *Political Writings,* ed. Johann P. Summerville (Cambridge: Cambridge University Press, 1994), 65. James rejects any idea of a strictly conceived contract between monarch and people; see 81–82. But James also believed that the monarch's oath required him to observe as well as to execute the laws of his kingdom. See "Speech to parliament, 21 March 1610," *Political Writings,* 183–84.

The Servile by Nature and the Political "Slave"

The subject Prospero will not free is, of course, Caliban, and while that "monster" can signify the ruler's "flesh" and be called a "thing of darkness," the passion and lust of the body, he also claims to have been dispossessed of property he rightfully inherited. In a figurative sense, he therefore dwells in two bodies, the body natural of the deposed Duke, and the body politic of the state the Duke once ruled and intends to rule again. It is as this latter figure that Caliban, a subject and worker who receives only his livelihood, is what Prospero repeatedly calls him: a "slave." He is, moreover, a slave of a particular kind. While Prospero also calls Ariel a "slave," his condition is known to be a temporary one defined by the terms of a contract and hence artificial. Caliban's status is never revoked and seems to be irrevocable. His is therefore a servitude that raises the question of categorizing human beings as less than free by nature, a question common to traditional political argument and central to the defense of colonialism and colonial government.

The topic had been broached initially by Aristotle in his *Politics*, a work available in English translation in 1598. I have argued that the *Ethics*, distinguishing what it refers to as the naturally bestial man from the rational man, represents naturally bestial man as a philosophical fiction, useful for discriminating purely sensuous life from one involving conscious choice. His theoretical possibility is sustained by a language of analogy in which the vice of rational man is termed "bestial" and the sensuous life of the bestial man is termed "vicious." The *Politics* represents the naturally servile man in much the way the *Ethics* represents the naturally bestial man: as a philosophical fiction.

The *Politics* assumes that "man is naturally a sociable and ciuill creature." Moreover, "he which naturally and not by accident or chaunce is cittilesse and unsociable is to be esteemed either a wicked wretch or *more then a man*"—that is, the asocial man is either bad or godlike.[3] When Aristotle illustrated his concept of the naturally asocial, however, he

[3] Aristotle, *Aristotles Politiqves, or Discovrses of Government,* trans. J. D. Dickenson (London, 1598), I, 2; D$_{iiii}$, D$_{iiii}$^{v}; STC 760. This edition is Dickenson's translation of Louis Le Roy's translation of the original Greek text, and is accompanied by Le Roy's commentary. Aristotle's premise is problematic in that it fails to discriminate between the generic nature at work in the man who is *naturally* social and the idiosyncratic nature driving the one who is *naturally* asocial or without a society or city (*Politics*, 1.1.1253a).

avoided the literature of philosophy and chose to cite Homer's description of the Cyclops as "tribelesse, lawlesse, and houselesse." A creature both primitive and mythic, Homer's Cyclops figures in Aristotle's idea of politics not as a fact of experience, but as a hypothesis necessary to establishing a case: the natural sociability and civility of all men and of man as a species. The civil society of man is categorically distinguished from the random grouping of animals by man's ability to communicate with his kind. His speech is devoted not to expressing feelings, which animal sounds can do, but rather distinctions of worth. These may be commensurable, between "the profitable and the unprofitable," or indices of value, marking "what is iust and what is uniust" (I, 2; D^v).

The category of the natural also figures in Aristotle's discourse on the social and civil in relation to the physical or bodily work of servants or slaves. Among such workers, Aristotle defines a type as *naturally* servile. This type is similar both to the asocial or Cyclopean man in that he is incapable of civil behavior, and to the naturally bestial man or "barbarian" in that he is irrational, sensuous, and typically apolitical or living outside a city. He has the use of his body and only mind or "reason" enough to know that he lacks reason: "whosoeuer is able by the strength of his body to put those commandements [of the master] in execution, is a subiect and seruant by nature (I, 1; D^v); [he] so farre partaketh of reason, that hee understandeth it and yet hath it not in himselfe" (I, 3; F^v). The "worke [of such natural slaves] consisteth in the bare vse of their bodie, [and they] have bodies strong for necessarie vses" (ibid.). By contrast, "he that is able by reason and the forecasting of his mind to foresee and provide aptly in affaires, commandeth by nature, and beareth the maistership by nature" (I, 1; D^v). Correspondingly, his body is "straight and vnprofitable for [servile] workes howbeit fitte and behoouefull for the ciuill life which is deuided into affaires of peace and warre" (I, 3; F^v). Aristotle goes on to define the natural slave by his work and the manner in which he does it—that is, uncritically and without resistance. A slave "by nature" is all body and has no mind to speak of: he is "a certaine part of his master, as a living part of a bodie, and yet separated not conjoyned." Their relations are intimate and harmonious: "there is a kinde of mutuall utilitie and friendshippe betweene that servant and his master, which are by nature disposed to those places." Understanding his master's reason, he himself lacks the reason that could direct him to his own "affaires" and thus to rebel against his employment. A legally constituted bondman or legal slave, who is likely to be a man captured in war, differs from a natural slave in that his relation to his master is unnatural and determined only by "lawe and compulsion" (I, 4; F_{ii}, F_{ii}^{v}).

The question to ask of this exposition of the naturally servile is the same as that asked of Aristotle's account of the naturally bestial. The reason the legal slave possesses and the slave by nature lacks is, presumably, the same reason that the moral man possessed and the bestial man lacked in the *Ethics*. In both texts, reason is an unexceptionable element of the human being, however much it is also possible analogically to characterize human behavior as bestial or servile in some instances or circumstances. Both texts characterize the *natural* as a nonverifiable distinction of being and its reference is only to those creatures who in theory are physically—as opposed to mentally or spiritually—constituted. Like the "barbarians" of the *Ethics* who mark the limits of the known as opposed to an imagined world, Aristotle's natural slave signifies how speculative a human being is who has no sense of his own affairs and no consciousness of property, if only as something that he does not possess.[4]

---

[4]Commenting further on conceptions of the "natural," Aristotle renders his categories even more theoretical by observing that "some [freeman] haue only the bodies of free men" and "others [i.e., slaves by law] are indued with wit and understanding." This suggests that servility is an attitude that is variable within a particular person rather than the status of a class of persons and conferred by immutable physical characteristics; I, 3; F_{v}. True, numbers of readers of both the *Ethics* and the *Politics* have understood Aristotle's categories of the natural as valid indicators of actual human differences. Louis Le Roy, glossing Aristotle's text, identifies the "natural slave" as, among other things, a "monster" who "ought to be reputed . . . a most bloody and cruell tyrant" (D_{iiii}^{v}). But insofar as the "natural slave" was recognized as theoretical, as a creature of pure *sensus* devoid of *ratio*, he clearly could not be made an authority for a colonialism based on an assessment of the Indians as natural slaves because they exhibited reason and a civil order—a view held by a number of political philosophers some of whom I consider below. Others, such as John Mair, did invoke Aristotle to support the contention that the Indians were natural slaves, but as reported by de Vitoria and others, all the evidence (as well as common sense) went against Mair and his colleagues. For associations between Aristotle's concept of the natural slave and European colonialism, see Anthony Pagden, *The Fall of Natural Man: The American Indian and the Origins of Comparative Ethnology* (Cambridge: Cambridge University Press, 1982). Pagden differentiates the concept of a natural slave from that of a civil or legally constituted slave. To these two categories of servitude I have added a third whose status is metaphorical: the political slave or dispossessed subject of constitutionalist argument in Jacobean England as well as the dispossessed native of anticolonialist argument in Thomist Spain.

Given these parameters, Caliban again occupies an anomalous position. There is a sense in which he is said to have exhibited a purely sensuous character: his native expression (according to Miranda) was a "brutish gabble," his sense of property was virtually nonexistent, and he regarded his island as something to be shared. Once ruled by Prospero, however, he clearly resists servitude, acquires a strong sense of his own interests, longs for his freedom (although he has no explicit notion of what it might entail), and names his master a "tyrant" (2.2.162; 3.2.40–52). "Nature" cannot account for these reactions. Prospero claims that "nurture" will not stick on his Caliban's "nature" (4.1.188–89), but what Caliban has learned from Milan strangely mirrors a principal index of civilized life, the practice of linking language with possession and a desire to measure, to acquire, and to possess. His first knowledge of natural light is of the "bigger" and "less," and he calls cursing his teachers the "profit" he has gotten from language, much as if words and notions of quantity, the meum and tuum of property, were one and the same. In short, language has taught him to know that he has been cheated of what he once possessed.[5] In knowing this, his condition corresponds to what early modern philosophy defined as political "servitude."

Political "servitude" was the unjust oppression of the subject under tyranny. Defined in terms of constitutionalist notions of the liberties of the subject, a political "slave" was the subject dispossessed of his property by a monarch who abused the prerogative. Much of the literature protesting such abuse imagines a body politic in which the body, or people, play a decisive role. Fortescue's *De laudibus legum anglie*, 1468–70, locates the power of the whole body politic in its blood or

[5]Critics commenting on Caliban's language as an effect of his education have seen in it a connection with European efforts to tyrannize the native American by language; see especially Stephen Greenblatt, "Learning to Curse: Aspects of Linguistic Colonialism in the Sixteenth Century," in *First Images of America*, ed. Fredi Chiappelli, 2 vols. (Berkeley: University of California Press, 1976), 2: 561–80. What precisely Caliban reports about his language, that it teaches him to see the world in terms of commensurables, suggests that this tyranny has an economic focus. Having come to understand relative *quantity*, greater and less, Caliban realizes that to have regarded all property as common was a self-destructive illusion. For a comprehensive study of the play's language and its relation to political models, see David Norbrook, "'What Care these Roarers for the Name of King,': Language and Utopia in *The Tempest*," in *The Politics of Tragicomedy: Shakespeare and After*, ed. Gordon McMullan and Jonathan Hope (New York: Routledge, 1992), 21–54.

heart, which is the "intent of the people" and "the first liuely thi[n]g," and claims that it is exercised by the nerves, which is the law. The king or head cannot deny the body's individual members the "nourishments of bloud" or alter its nervous system, that is, their property or their laws (*A learned commendation*, D_{viii}, D_{viii}^v). The figure of the body politic reappeared with important changes in meaning and context more than half a century later, when Robert Cecil, Earl of Salisbury represented the king's case for "supply" and "support" to Parliament in 1610. According to Salisbury, the king's "good" came from rather than went to the "body of parliament." It is what the "heart" or people gives to the "brain" or monarch and without it the whole body suffers a "dead palsy"; this is despite the fact that the "good" required—money—is itself a "base creature, whereof no wise man speaks without contempt."[6] George More, who appears to be refuting Salibury, restated Fortescue's meaning when he wrote that no more than "the head of a Physicall body [could] change the ueynes and sinewes thereof nor deny the members of their proper strength or necessary nurriture," could a monarch "change the laws of that body" or take "goods" and "substance" from the people.[7] In short, the body of the body politic was predominate. By the end of the sixteenth and the first decade of the seventeenth centuries, constitutionalists emphasized the claims of the people. They characterized a tyrant as a "master" who claimed to own the commonwealth and used his subjects as "slaves."[8] In so doing, they resumed an old argument and resorted to established imagery.

---

[6]"Salisbury, February 15, 1610," *Proceedings in Parliament, 1610,* ed. Elizabeth Read Foster, 2 vols. (New Haven: Yale University Press, 1966), 2: 10–11, 25.

[7]George More, *Principles for yong Princes* (London, 1611), A6^v; STC 18068.

[8]George Buchanan, for example, modifies Aristotle's categories by stating that a kingdom is a "principality of a Free Man over Free Men"; and a tyranny is a "principality of a Master over his Slaves": George Buchanan, *De iure regni apud Scotos or, a dialogue concerning the Due Priviledge of Government in the Kingdom of Scotland* (London, 1689), 34. In general, the term "slave" had a very wide range of reference, some of which was figurative. Karen Ordahl Kupperman notes that "[t]he word slavery appears again and again in Virginia records" and refers to the "treatment of servants by masters and treatment of the whole body of colonists by their governments." In many instances it meant "base": "the colonists seem to be saying that the problem was not that some colonists were made to labor as slaves, but that men of good estate were obliged to labor as if they had been base," i.e., with their hands or in an ungentlemanly way. Karen Ordahl Kupperman, *Settling with the Indians: The Meeting of English and American Cultures in America, 1580–1640* (Totowa: Rowman and Littlefield, 1980), 137–40. In the context of Parliamentary debates on the monarch's prerogative,

In his *Institutio principis christiani,* Erasmus had claimed that a monarch who robbed his subjects of their goods reduced them to bondmen or beasts (see above, chapter 6, p. 163). Opposing absolutism in his *Conference Abovt the Next Svccession,* 1594, Robert Parsons dealt with both "slavery" and "decapitation." Stating that "the whole body is of more authority then the only head and may cure the head if it be out of tune," he concluded that "the weal publique [may] cure or *cutt of their heades* [i.e., of magistrates] if they infest the rest."⁹ The need for such a "cure" occurs particularly when a monarch sees the commonwealth as his property: this "overthroweth the whole nature of a common wealth itselfe and maketh al subiects to be but very slaues." For, Parsons added:

> slaues and bondmen as Aristotle sayeth in this do differ from freemen [in] that slaues have only the vse of things without property or interest. . . ; what soever they do gett, it accreweth to their master. . . . [T]he condition of an oxe or an asse is the very same . . . , for that the oxe or asse getteth nothing to himselfe but only to his master and can be lord of nothing of that for which he laboreth. (F7ᵛ)

In the Commons' debate on revenue taking place during the first decade of the seventeenth century, a "slave" was the subject racked by impositions on trade, impoverished by feudal tenures, thwarted by monopolies, and tormented by demands from the king's purveyors.¹⁰ Certainly free subjects continued to own property, but they objected to the king's claim

especially after 1610, a "slave" was a dispossessed subject metaphorically understood, one who had only his labor to sell. For a summary of this debate see Donna B. Hamilton, *Virgil and The Tempest: The Politics of Imitation* (Columbus: Ohio State University Press, 1990), 44–55, and below, pp. 183–84.

⁹Robert Parsons, *A Conference Abovt the Next Svccession to the Crowne of England* (London, 1594), D8ᵛ. The words are actually voiced by his "civill lawyer," who defends a monarchy under law, in contrast to his "common lawyer" who holds to an absolutist line. See also: "the whole body though it be gouerned by the Prince as by the head yet is in [i.e., it] not inferior but superior to the Prince, neither so giueth the commonwealth her authority and power vp to any Prince that she depriueth herselfe utterly of the same when need shall require to vse it for her defence for which she gaue it"; Gᵛ, G2. On what I take to be a dramatization of political decapitation, see chapter 3, pp. 94–95.

¹⁰Of course, the opposition took a different view of political servitude: John Hayward, for example, claimed that the king could not be denied absolute authority and that if he were, the consequences would be disastrous: "the libertie whereof you speak will fetter vs [i.e., his subjects] in bondage." John Hayward, *An Answere to the first part of a certaine Conference concerning succession published since under the name of R. Dolman* (London, 1603), G_{iii}ᵛ, Hᵛ; STC 12988.

that they did not own it absolutely, that is, free from any kind of appropriation they had not approved. They even feared they could lose the status of free subject if they failed to object to an appropriation they had not approved.[11] Their political "servitude" approached true slavery in only one sense: if the monarch was above the law and divinely ordained by God to be his minister, his subjects could not legally thwart or remove him, any more than a slave could disobey or change his master.[12]

In 1610 a crisis was reached. Salisbury asked Parliament for money; James insisted that he, a monarch, was godlike. Kings, he declared, are "gods on earth," and "it is treason for subjects to dispute of a king's power" ("King James, March 21, 1610," *Proceedings*, 2: 59–60). Historians have pointed out that in this and similar speeches James gave much to the law—a king was to "protect" the "Lawes of his Kingdome" and must himself observe its "fundamental laws." Yet his concessions could be equivocal: Parliament "must not set such laws as make them shadows of kings and dukes of Venice" ("King James, May 21, 1610," 103);[13] and his language was often frightening. In any case, constitutionalists responded. Mr. Wentworth asked:

> Is not the king's prerogative disputable? Do not our books in 20 cases argue what the king may do and what not do by his prerogative. . . . Nay if we shall once say that we may not dispute the prerogative [i.e., the king's absolute power], let us be sold for slaves. ("Wentworth, May 11, 1610," 82, 83)

[11]They could turn into "bondmen by allowing themselves to be treated as bondmen without objection. Once they had been treated as bondmen in one area they could be treated that way in all, since they had arguably lost their free status"; David Harris Sacks, letter to author.
[12]By true slavery I mean the condition in which one's person was owned entirely and without term by another person. Such slavery was not the same thing as being "unfree" which was simply a contractual condition relating to a term of service that was enforced by law. Free labor was "labor undertaken under legal rules that did not give employers either the right to invoke criminal penalities for departure or the right to specific performance"; Robert J. Steinfeld, *The Invention of Free Labor: The Employment Relation in English and American Law and Culture, 1350–1870* (Chapel Hill: University of North Carolina Press, 1991), 4.
[13]For a study of James's developing thought on the prerogative in this period, see Paul A. Christianson, "Royal and Parliamentary Voices on the Ancient Constitution c. 1604–1621," in *The Mental World of the Jacobean Court*, ed. Linda Levy Peck (Cambridge: Cambridge University Press, 1991), 71–95. The constitutionalist objections cited below disturb the premises of Fleming's decision in Bate's case because they concern impositions levied against property, not items traded on international markets.

James Whitelocke denied that the king had "a right of imposition": "we are masters of our own and can have nothing taken from us without our consents . . . laws cannot be made without our consents . . . the parliament is the storehouse of our liberties" ("Whitelocke, May 22, 1610," 109). The following month Nicholas Fuller also argued for the "freedom of the subject" in terms recalling his argument in "the case of Monopolies": "by the laws of England the subjects have such property in their lands and goods as that without their consent the king can take no part thereof from them lawfully" ("Fuller, June 23, 1610," 152). Thomas Hedley, citing Magna Carta, then took up the argument from conquest that had been the basis for James's claim to his "absolute and free" monarchy in Scotland. He insisted that once a people had secured from their monarch a pledge to protect their liberties, they remained entitled to these liberties in the future. And he described the "*liber homo*" by contrast to one who is unfree:

> for the king may by commission at his pleasure seize the lands or goods of his *villani*,[14] but so can he not of his free subjects. . . . [T]ake away the liberty of the subject in his profit or property and you make a promiscuous confusion of a freeman and a bound slave, which slavery is . . . repugnant to the nature of an Englishman. ("Hedley, June 28, 1610," 192)

Mr. Martin recast the figure of the subject as slave when he threatened to make those who sought to sell "the liberty of the people . . . villeins so that they and their posterity might feel that bondage which they would lay upon others" ("Martin, November 11, 1610," 328). Central to all these formulations of what might be termed the political slave was the distinction between men who had property or a property in

[14]There were two kinds of villeins, only one of which was strictly a bondman. John Cowell distinguishes between "a Villein in grosse, which is immediately bound to the persons of his Lord and his heires" and "a villein regardant to a maner, whome the Ciuilians terme (*Glebae ascriptitium*; bound to the soil)." What is distinctive is the nature of the bond, which may be by "tenure" or by "blood and tenure"; in the latter case, which is effectively restricted to villeins in the "Ancient Demesne of the Crowne," villeins "may be cast out of their tenement and depriued of their chatels at the pleasure of the Lord," in the former case not. Cowell concludes that a villein by tenure is "after a sort seruile"; John Cowell, *The Interpreter* (Cambridge, 1607), Yyy4, Yyy4ᵛ. Hedley, speaking figuratively of the effects of the monarch's prerogative, imagines a villein by "blood and tenure," although it would appear that in fact this category of servant was very small.

their bodies and what they produced, and those who had sold that property or had it taken from them.

Caliban conforms to the Commons' image of a tyrant's slave in a restricted but important sense: he is *the realization of the subject they fear they will become*. Unlike Wentworth and his colleagues who saw themselves as threatened with political slavery, Caliban, as utterly dispossessed (even of his own person), is a political slave whose degree of subjection exceeds that of an indentured servant and even that of a captive (who could buy his freedom). He resents his servitude and desires freedom, yet he has no consistent appreciation for the state he thinks he has lost and is unable to plan to regain it in a plausible way. His idea of freedom is distinctly uncivil, although it is induced by and dependent on access to drink. Thoroughly soused with the contents of Stephano's bottle (attempting to elude Prospero's spirits, he finds their material and equally compelling substitute), Caliban declares that "Cacaliban/Has a new master" (2.2.184–85). He does not protest when Stephano proposes that he himself will be king (3.2.105; see also 4.1.215–19); nor does he resent that his new masters, Stephano and Trinculo, call him "monster," "servant-monster," "man-monster," "moon-calf," "half a fish and half a monster" and so forth (3.2.3–28). Although Caliban identifies the clothing Ariel has placed on a linden tree to distract Stephano and Trinculo as "trash," understanding it as a trick, he has no use for clothing of any kind (4.1.224–31). If he has any place in the discourse of tyranny as it was then carried on in the Commons, it is as its end product: a subject dispossessed so utterly that he becomes less than fully human. He loses the ability to resist except by contemplating forms of violence.

A character of this kind had been imagined by pseudo-Aquinas and Erasmus who had both asserted that the bestial tyrant (waving his charming Circean wand) bestializes his subjects: hence an uncivil people is the inevitable product of an uncivil governor and, it would seem, not entirely responsible for their condition. But at least one monarchomach took a harsh view of subjects who—ruled by a tyrant—must in some sense be complicit in their servitude. Etienne de La Boétie, in his "De la servitude volontaire," a portion of which appeared without attribution in the anonymous *Le Reveille Matin Des François et De Levrs Voisins* and was published in 1574, attempted to revive a sense of agency in a people threatened with tyranny by specifying occasions for legitimate resistance. He supposed "that the people of a country have found some great man who has proved that he has great concern to serve and courage to defend them and that they have sworn always to obey him," and he concluded that there was no doubt that they would fear no evil from him. "But," he goes on to protest, "what a misfortune (*mal heur*) this is": "Consider an infinite number of persons, who do not obey but serve, who are not governed but tyrannized over":

> if one sees, not a hundred, not a thousand men, but a hundred countries, a thousand towns, a million men not challenging one alone, among whose subjects the best treated has the misfortune of being a serf and a slave: What can we call this? Is not this cowardice? What a monster of vice is this, which does not even deserve the name of cowardice, for which there is no name villanous enough, which nature denies having made and the passage of time refuses to name.[15]

The monster La Boétie depicted here is the servile and cowardly subject who accepts tyrannical government. The resistance La Boétie recommended stops short of rebellion or revolution: "it is unnecessary to rise up against [this tyrant], it is unnecessary to undo him, he is undone by himself: but let the country not consent to its servitude: one must not take anything away from him, but [also] one must not give him anything. . . . What ought a man to hold dearer than to retrieve his natural right (*droit naturel*) and, as it were, having been a beast return to being a man" (m5ᵛ). By refusing to support tyranny materially, the people avoid their own degeneration. Without such resistance, a people cannot help but be turned collectively into "a serf," "a slave," a "monster of vice." A comparable kind of political slave emerges in the pages of English colonial history.[16]

[15][Barnaud, Nicolas], "Dialogue II," *Le Reveille Matin Des François et De Levrs Voisins* (Edinburgh [Basle, Geneva?], 1574), m3ᵛ, m4, m4ᵛ; STC 10577+ STC 1464; my translation.

[16]By pursuing this argument I make a contestable inference: that Caliban reflects some aspects of the native of the New World as he appeared in contemporary literature. His character is also indebted to representations of English indentured servants who made up the bulk of the labor force in the Virginia Colony before 1620. By 1609, the Company was advertising for such labor. As Reverend William Crashaw said, it might consist of "the basest and worst men . . . very excrements," but, "wanting pleasures, and subject to some pinching miseries," they would become "good and worthie instruments"; Reverend William Crashaw, *A Sermon*

A New World

Attempts at legitimating the colonialization of the American continent elicited references to two concepts: dominion and possession. Dominion defined rule over a vassal state; possession typically followed conquest and resulted in the confiscation of all conquered property. Dominion was essentially a legislative matter and could be instituted by acts of fealty or tribute. Possession was more difficult to establish in that it was usually a consequence of war, which had in theory to be just to result in a legitimate rule. Possession did not, in any case, follow rights that were thought to inhere in discovery. As John T. Juricek has pointed out, possession meant "effective occupation" as instanced by plantations, trading posts, and military encampments. It often included accepting "tribute or other forms of recognition from the natives," which might testify to a sale of property or to an action professing fealty to a European or English monarch.[17] But such "occupation" was not universally recognized as conferring dominion or possession by those versed in principles of natural law or the law of nations. As Patricia Seed has shown, English colonists, following English custom, regularly disregarded natural law rights and claimed possession after constructing houses, building fences, and planting crops; in short, for English colonists, possession followed de facto occupation and was a matter of squatter's rights.[18] Protest against colonization in

Preached in London before the Right Honourable Lord le warre, Lord governor and Captaine General of Virginia (London, 1610), quoted in Sigmund Diamond, "From Organization to Society," in *Colonial America: Essays in Politics and Social Development*, ed. Stanley N. Katz (Boston: Little Brown and Co., 1976), 14–15; see his entire discussion, 3–30. These laborers, clearly dispossessed in the ordinary sense of that term, were at the very lowest end of the economic spectrum. Constitutionalists, pointing to what might become of propertied subjects, might well have instanced the experience of these laborers. Before 1622, the Virginia colonists regarded Indians as a civilized people and not as inherently servile; see Kupperman, *Settling with the Indians*, 33–63. See also Meredith Anne Skura, "Discourse and the Individual: The Case of Colonialism in *The Tempest*," *Shakespeare Quarterly* 40, 1 (1989): 42–69, esp. 52–57.

[17] Two different legal codes determined European claims for possession in the New World, the "preemptive" which depended on discovery, and the "dominative" which depended on de facto possession. Spanish claims (which initially rested on the Bull of Alexander VI in 1493) were preemptive by the 1540s; English claims came to be progressively more dominative. Neither of these claims went unchallenged in theory. "English Territorial Claims in North America Under Elizabeth and the Early Stuarts," *Terrae Incognitae* 7 (1976): 7–22, esp. 8–9.

[18] Patricia Seed, *Ceremonies of Possession in Europe's Conquest of the New World: 1492–1640* (Cambridge: Cambridge University Press, 1995), 18–19.

general was registered early in some philosophical literature that drew on natural law principles.

An important point of departure was the Thomist philosophy of Francisco de Vitoria's *De Indiis et de Iure Belli Relectiones*, 1557, a work insisting that the Spanish crown could not dispossess the Indians of their property despite their lack of belief in Christianity. As Anthony Pagden has noted, de Vitoria did not reject the European claim to sovereignty over the Indians, comprehended in a *dominium jurisdictionis* or possession of the law and legislative power. But that *dominium* did not include the possession of property or *dominium rerum*. De Vitoria insisted that the Indians were free even if they had become vassals of the Spanish crown. This meant that insofar as they were under Spanish law, their properties were to be protected by that law. No more than Christianity was absence of mortal sin, even if that sin involved cannibalism or human sacrifice, or "the use of reason . . . a prerequisite for ownership." In any case, de Vitoria wrote, these "aborigines" are of sound mind ("there is a certain method in their affairs, for they have polities which are orderly arranged") and "were true owners alike in public and in private law before the advent of the Spaniards among them."[19] They are not therefore to be regarded as natural slaves by

[19]Francisco de Vitoria, *De Indiis et de Iure Belli Relectiones*, ed. Ernest Nys (Washington, D.C.: Carnegie Institution, 1917), 115, 125. This is a translation of de Vitoria's Latin text. De Vitoria focuses on Spanish colonization but inasmuch as his arguments are based on the law of nature, what he says about Spanish rights in the New World apply also to English rights. Cf. Anthony Pagden, "The conquest of America could only be made legitimate by demonstrating that the native populations had forfeited . . . [property] rights by their own actions." "Dispossessing the barbarian: the language of Spanish Thomism and the debate over the property rights of the American Indians," in *The Languages of Political Theory in Early-Modern Europe*, ed. Anthony Pagden (Cambridge: Cambridge University Press, 1987), 79–98; 81. Stephen Greenblatt, discussing the terms on which Columbus took possession of the New World, describes the ritual formulas by which Columbus made his first claim to "possession." Although Greenblatt does not make the legal nature of these acts altogether clear, they appear to be a way of establishing sovereignty and, in their insistence that the party of the sovereign not be "contradicted" by his prospective subjects, evocative both of feudal contract and a republican notion of consent. Stephen Greenblatt, *Marvelous Possessions: The Wonder of the New World* (Chicago: University of Chicago Press, 1991), 55–81. In this and subsequent instances in which Europeans took "possession" of the New World, claims to sovereignty may have been thought to imply claims to property or *dominium rerum*—an implication that de Vitoria, working from natural law, rejected. The Spanish had to have known that clearing and building on Indian land were proprietary rather than sovereign acts and it must be assumed that they thought they could ignore natural law and law of

virtue of their supposed bestiality or political slaves by virtue of the fact that they have no property; their society exhibits a morality and a politics.[20] Indians were occupying the territory the Spanish claim and under the law of nations the Spanish have no rights of discovery (139). Nor can Indians be the objects of a just war (and therefore legal slaves): they have not wronged the Spanish. Failure to accept Christianity is not a wrong (143); moreover, the Spanish have not even preached the faith with "propriety" (144).

To de Vitoria's legal arguments, a treatise by Bartholome de Las Casas, translated into English as *The Spanish Colonie* in 1583, added the testimony of history and a further conclusion: the Indians are "free subjects & vassals" of the Spanish crown and as such have the same civil standing as its other vassals, for instance, the people of the Netherlands. More important, Las Casas would have King Philip deny "these tyrants" [i.e., the colonists] the right to further conquests: "the Indies ought not to be giuen to the Spaniardes ... under any ... title whatsoeuer."[21] The many wrongs the Spanish have committed against the Indians include allowing the Indians to regard them as "Gods," which keeps the Indians from "Christendome"; possessing the Indians as "swine" and "very strange bondslaues," "yoking them together like beasts to make them carry their burdens"; sucking "the whole substaunce of their bodies," and loading them with "torments, beatings, and sorowings." None of these practices take account of what the Indians have: "reasonable soules" (O2, O3^v, O4^v). Las Casas warned the king of the danger attending such a policy: the Indians suppose that "because you doe both sende thither and keepe heere such euill subiectes ... your maiestie doth feed vpon humane flesh and blood" (O2^v). Here

nations principles. In effect they were imitating the English, although on a much vaster scale and in the context of a legal tradition that made their actions illicit. For a study of *The Tempest* in the context of fictions of empire, see Jeffrey Knapp, *Empires Nowhere: England, America, and the Literature from "Utopia" to "The Tempest"* (Berkeley: University of California Press, 1992).

[20]In effect, de Vitoria could be said to have tested Aristotle's assertion that those living in "distant regions" were inhuman and found that the evidence did not warrant such a conclusion. The theoretical status of the natural slave was not, however, generally accepted. Spanish jurists protested that the papal bull of 1493 giving the Spanish crown the right to enslave the people of the Antilles was illicit. In the course of these debates, the whole notion of a natural slave became paradoxical; Pagden, *Natural Man*, 28–30, 38–41, 49–55.

[21]Bartholome de Las Casas, *The Spanish Colonie* (London, 1583), O; STC 4739.

the charge so frequently leveled at Indians—cannibalism—is redirected at the monarch who is represented in figures reserved for the tyrant. Joseph [i.e., José de] Acosta's account of the "Indies"—*The Naturall and Morall Historie of the East and West Indies*, 1604, was written in the same spirit as Las Casas's *Spanish Colonie*. He denied the distinction between European civility and Indian barbarism fundamental to colonialism and insisted that the Indians were not "a grosse and brutish people": to use them "like bruite beastes" as the Spanish had was a "common and . . . dangerous . . . errour." In some ways the Indians resembled Europeans, in others they were even superior: "although they had many barbarous things and without ground, yet had they many others worthy of great admiration . . . , they did in some things passe many of our common-weales." Like Las Casas, Acosta framed his advice to colonists in self-reflexive terms. Ignorance of Indian laws, he declared, "besides the wrong which is doone vnto them, against reason . . . , is preiudiciall and hurtefull vnto ourselves; for thereby they take occasion to abhorre vs, as men both in good and in evill alwayes contrary vnto them."[22]

Directed at Spanish colonists, these critiques could also apply to English settlers.[23] The first letters patent gave no reason why a "vassal" of the English king—in this case, Sir John Cabot—could rightfully "subdue,

[22]Joseph Acosta, *The Natvrall and Morall Historie of the East and West Indies* (London, 1604), Ff, Ff2; STC 94. Cf. Montaigne's "Des cannibales" which offers a subtler critique of European colonialist practice. Montaigne condemns European disdain for the culture of the cannibalistic natives of Brazil because, when judged by a criterion that he terms "natural" and beholden to "natural law," it is less inhumane than European culture. In effect, however, his argument represents "nature" as no more than custom and hence the Indians as exponents of another kind of civic order, one arguably better than any in Europe but nevertheless not natural. Like de Vitoria, Montaigne might be thought to be testing Aristotle's hypothesis of the natural man. See David Quint, "A Reconsideration of Montaigne's *Des cannibales*," *Modern Language Quarterly* 51, 4 (1990): 459–89.

[23]The most comprehensive of justifications for English colonization—Richard Hakluyt's *A Discourse Concerning Western Planting written in the year 1584*—was not in print before 1877; how widely it was circulated in manuscript is unclear. In any case, Hakluyt did not consider the arguments of the Spanish Thomists. He rejected the Pope's right to make his "donation" on the grounds that his kingdom was spiritual not political. Hakluyt claimed English dominion (and possession) on the grounds of first discovery: the New World was originally settled not by Columbus and the Spaniards but a prince of North Wales, Madock op Owen Guyneth, in 1170. According to Hakluyt, proof of this is the fact that the language of "Newfoundland" "is said to agree with the Welshe in divers wordes and names of places, by experience of some of our nation that have bene in those partes." Richard Hakluyt, *A Discourse Concerning Western Planting*, ed. Charles Deane (Cambridge, Mass., 1877), 118–19.

occupy and possesse . . . such townes, cities, castles and isles . . . of the heathen and infidel . . . getting vnto vs the rule, title, and iurisdiction," as were found in the course of his voyages. Letters to Sir Walter Raleigh suggest that it was their ignorance of Christianity that made such people appropriate subjects for conquest.[24] The Indians so "possessed" were evidently not supposed to be a sovereign people or have property rights (although their chiefs were called kings), because they were "heathen" or not Christian[25] (although this was not a supposition made about the people of the Far East with whom Europeans traded), and often represented as outlandish. Martin Frobisher's "second voyage," 1600, typifies such accounts which tend to irony as well as hyperbole. The Indians, Frobisher declared, live in "dennes," are "Anthropophagi, or deuourers of mans flesh," and harbor devils or witches. They are "voyd of humanity; and ignorant what mercy meaneth, in extremities looke for no other then death; . . . perceiuing they should fall into our hands, thus miserably by drowning [they] rather [desire] death then otherwise to be saued by vs."[26] It proved easier to argue why Indian territory should be colonized than to justify the project in natural law or the law of nations.

[24]"Letters patent to John Cabot," in Richard Hakluyt, *The Third and Last Volume in the Voyages, 1600,* in *The Principal Navigations, Voyages, Traffiqves, And Discoveries of the English nation,* 2 vols. (London, 1594–1600), 2 (1600): A3; STC 126269. Queen Elizabeth gave Raleigh "free liberty . . . to discouer . . . such remote, heathen and barbarous lands . . . not actually possessed of any Christian prince, nor inhabited by Christian people, as to him . . . shall seeme good and the same to haue, holde, occupy & enioy to him . . . for euer, with all prerogatiues, commodities, iurisdictions, royalties, priuiledges, franchises, and preeminences"; V6, V6^v.

[25]"Heathen" often meant "barbarous" or "uncivil." English settlers in Ireland saw the Irish, who were Christian, in these terms; see Nicholas Canny, *The Elizabethan Conquest of Ireland: A Pattern Established, 1565–76* (New York: Barnes & Noble Books, 1976), esp. 117–36.

[26]"Frobisher's second voyage," in Hakluyt, *The Third and Last Volume,* D^v, C6. For more on such negative perceptions of Indians, see André Thevet on cannibals, *New found world,* ch. 61; George Best on the "dennes" and "beastly feeding" of "sauages," "A true Reporte of such things as hapned in the second voyage of Captayne Frobysher," [George Best], *A Trve Discovrse of the late voyages of discouerie for the finding of a passage to Cathaya* (London, 1578), C$_{ii}$, STC 1972; Jacques Cartier on Indian thievery, promiscuity, and polygamy, [Jacques Cartier], *A shorte and briefe narration of the two Navigations and Discoueries to the Northweast parts called Newe France* (London, 1580), E$_{iii}$, K$_{ii}$, STC 4699; and John Nicholl on cannibals, *An Houre Glasse of Indian Newes* (London, 1607), B3, D3^v, STC 18532. See also Richard Hakluyt, "Virginia richly valued, by the description of the main land of *Florida,* her next neighbour," 1609, on Indians as "the greatest traitors of the world," in *Tracts and Other Papers Relating Principally to the Origin, Settlement, and Progress of the Colonies in North America,* ed. Peter Force, 4 vols. (Washington, D.C.: 1836–46), 4: 6; and "Virginia Council: Instrucions,

From the first decades of the sixteenth century, English readers found accounts of the Americas that could be construed as encouragement to colonization. Two views predominated: Indians are tractable and easy to deceive, and they are degenerate forms of human life. Antonio Pigafetta's "A Brief declaration of the vyage or naavigation [*sic*] made abowte the worlde," 1526, depicted the natives of the cape of St. Marie as gigantic cannibals. One was "verye tractable and pleasaunt; he soonge and daunsed." When the expedition's captain wanted to capture two of these men, he "tooke them by a deceyte," giving them "knyues, sheares, lookynge glasses, belles, beades of crystall, and suche other tryfels: he so fylled theyr handes that they coulde hold no more."

> Then [he] caused two payre of shackels of iren to bee put on theyre legges . . . which they lyked very wel by cause they were made of bryght and shynynge metal. . . . When they felt the shakels faste abowte theyr legges, they begunne to doubte: but the Captayne dyd put them in comforte and badde them stande styll. In fine when they sawe how they were deceaued they rored lyke bulles and cryed vppon theyre greate deuyll Setebos to helpe them.[27]

Pigafetta's account is emblematic of the most generally recognized relations between Indians and European colonists. The Indian was perceived as physically anomalous and socially barbarous; he was characterized as intellectually naive rather than simply innocent; and

orders and constitucions to Sr. Thomas Gates" on Indian "tirrany" and bonding with the devil, *The Records of the Virginia Company of London*, ed. Susan Myra Kingsbury, 4 vols. (Washington, D.C.: United States Government Printing Office, 1906–35), 3 (1933): 14. Karen Kupperman instances numerous testimonies (especially by Thomas Hariot) to Indian civility, including descriptions of language, government, agriculture, town planning, and religion; this evidence does not seem to have made questionable English claims of possession; *Settling with the Indians*, esp. 45–63. For the "gentle" Indian, see below, and i.a., John Brereton, *A briefe and true relation of the discouerie of the north part of Virginia* (London, 1602), B^v, STC 3610; Acosta, *Natvrall and Morall Historie*, Ff; and [John] Smith, *A trve relation of such occurences and accidents of noate as hath hapned in Virginia since the first planting of that Collony* (London, 1608), B4, B4^v, STC 22795. Théodore de Bry's powerful images of the New World natives, beginning with the Indians of Virginia (first published in 1590 with Thomas Hariot's *Briefe and true report of the new found land of Virginia*) reveal how ambiguous were European impressions of these peoples; see *L'Amérique de Théodore de Bry*, ed. Michèle Duchet (Paris: Editions du Centre national de la recherche scientifique, 1987).
[27]In Eden, *The Decades of the newe worlde*, in *The First Three English Books on America*, ed. Arber, 251–52. Editors and critics have generally agreed that this text was one of Shakespeare's sources for *The Tempest*.

he was spiritually diabolical as well as heathenish. All these traits vindicated his enslavement for which no apology appeared necessary.

Gonzalo de Oviedo y Valdés' *The Hystorie of the Weste Indies*, 1526, also portrays the Indians as gullible. They have "familiaritie" with the devil, who is "so auncient an Astronomer" that he "knoweth the tymes of thynges":

> And [he, the devil] maketh theym beleue that they come so to passe by his ordynaunce, as though he were the lorde and mover of all that is and shalbe: And that he gyueth the day lyght and rayne: causeth tempest and ruleth the stations of the tymes.... By reason whereof, the Indians being deceaued of hym, and seing also such effectes to coome certeynely to passe as he hath tolde them before, beleue hym in all other thynges and honoure hym in many places. (In Eden, 215)

Similarly, the Indians of André Thevet's *The New found Worlde, or Antarctike*, 1568, beg to be protected from "wicked spirites," sent from the devil, as "the deuil studieth onely to seducte that creature that hath no knowledge of God": "you shal hear them make a pitiful cry, saying in their language, (if there be any christian by or neare,) seest thou not *Agnan* that beateth me, defend me if thou wilt that I shal serue thee, and cut thy wood."[28] Depicted by both Valdes and Thevet is the Indians' tendency to invest a human (and apparently priestly) figure with divinity and to see him managing cosmic forces. The image suggests how easily the European or English colonist could seize power and acquire authority were he to be seen as divine.

Assumptions of the kind registered in this varied literature were given a real reference in pragmatic accounts of colonial ventures, particularly of the Virginia Company, furnished to encourage prospective colonists and their backers from the 1580s onward. Representations of the Indians as gullible as well as "devilish" were embellished by references to a providence guiding their colonization. English colonists were repeatedly impressed with their sanctified mission. Hakluyt's letter to Sir Philip Sidney noted that if they had taken "a more godly course" than they

---

[28]"Of visions, dreames and illusions," in André Thevet, *The New found worlde, or Antarctike* (London, 1568), Ch. 35, H$_{iiii}$; STC 23950.

had done, owing to a "preposterous desire of seeking rather gaine then Gods glorie," God would have nevertheless rewarded them and turned "euen their couetousnes to serue him." "Godlinesse is great riches" of a spiritual kind, but it also leads to material wealth.[29] English colonists often described Indian territory and its wealth as God-given, the price and prize of their missionary efforts. Such inferences were coupled with the observation that the English could find it advantageous to be taken for gods themselves. Thomas Hariot's famous claim that the Indians "could not tel whether to think vs [English] gods or men" because they died from disease while the English did not, was reasserted as the basis for later "Instructions for government" issued by James to the Council of the Virginia colony in 1606: "Do not advertize the killing of any of your men . . . if [the Indians] perceive that they are but common men . . . they will make many adventures upon you."[30] Apologies for English possession of Indian territory were frequently framed by a commitment to spread the gospel, as if providence could not intend that a territory so like Eden remain unchristian. By 1609 preachers such as William Crashaw, Robert Gray, Robert Johnson, Daniel Price, William Symonds, and Robert Tylney were representing the territory of Virginia as England's special destiny, a Canaan for the new Israelites, the English (Kupperman, *Settling with the Indians*, 169–88).

Arguments for possession were usually preceded by advertisements of great wealth and sometimes included directives implying de facto possession.[31] George Peckham's apology for English trade moves

[29][Richard Hakluyt], "To the right worshipfull and *most vertuous Gentleman master* Phillip Sydney, Esq.," in Richard Hakluyt, *Divers voyages touching the discoverie of America* (London, 1582), ¶2ᵛ; STC 12624.

[30]Thomas Hariot, *Briefe and true report of the new found land of Virginia* (Frankfort, 1590), d; "Instructions for government," in *The Genesis of the United States*, ed. Alexander Brown, 2 vols. (London, 1890), 1: 83. For further comment on Indian perceptions of the English as "Demy-Gods," see Kupperman, *Settling with the Indians*, 111.

[31]The anonymous "Gentleman" who framed "Notes . . . to be giuen one that prepared for a discouerie and went not," emphasized Indian wealth: "Nothing is more to be indeuoured with the Inland people then familiaritie. For so may you best discouer al the naturall commodities of their countrey," which might include "the Grape as good as that at Burdeus," or the "Olif tree" like that of "Spaine or Barbarie"; Hakluyt, *Divers voyages*, K2. René Landonnière urged that because the Indians were of "a good and amiable nature, which willingly will obay: yea be content to serue those that shall with gentlenes and humanitie goe about to allure them," colonists should proceed in the same manner, "to the ende they may aske and learne of them [the Indians] where they take their gold, copper, and turquesses,

from praise for missionary activities to a defense of military action. "Planting" the faith, he declared, needs no excuse. Trade is guaranteed by the law of nations; to get the "sauages" to entertain both conversion and trade "some kindes of our pettie marchandizes and trifles" can serve as persuasion. Finally, he asserted, "by their [the Indians'] franke consents"

> [we] shall easily enioy such a competent quantity of Land, as euery way shall be correspondent to the Christians expectation and contentation, considering the great abundance that they haue of Land, and how small account they make thereof, taking no other fruites thereby then such as the ground of its selfe doeth naturally yeelde.

If the Indians fail to "consent" to English appropriation of their land and consequently resort to "violence," Peckham warned, the English could "pursue reuenge with force."[32] This was a conclusion of critical importance in that it implied both English dominion and possession. The "force" in question was not that authorized by an Indian court (which would have had jurisdiction in the case of English dominion), but rather of an entity which had at best the status of a foreign landowner and was certainly not entitled to wage war. English possession of Indian "Land" could only be legitimized by a version of squatter's rights. Some argued that the Indians did not really own any property, and thus it was not possible to dispossess them. Robert Gray had declared that "these savages have no particular propertie in any part or parcell of that Countrey but only a general recidence there, as wild beasts have in the forest . . . there is no meum and teum [*sic*] amongst them: so that if the whole lands should be taken from them, there is

and other thinges yet unknowen vnto vs." Theirs is a "countrie . . . of such fruitfulnes as cannot with tongue be expressed, and where in short time great and precious commodities might bee found . . . . And to be short, there lacketh nothing"; "*The true and last discouerie of Florida* made by Captaine Iohn Ribault in the yeere *1562*," in Hakluyt, *Divers voyages*, F4^v, G^v. Cf. Arthur Barlowe on Virginia: "I thinke in all the world the like abundance is not to be found . . . The soile is the most plentifull, sweete, fruitfull and wholsome of all the worlde"; "The first voyage made to the coasts of *America*," in Hakluyt, *The Third and Last Volume*, X^v, X2^v.

[32] George Peckham, "A true Report of the late discoveries, and possession taken in the right of the Crowne of *England* of the *Newfound Lands*, by that valiant and worthy Gentlemen, Sir *Humfrey Gilbert*, Knight," in Hakluyt, *The Third and Last Volume*, O4^v, O5, O5^v.

not a man can complaine of any particular wrong done to him."[33] But the simple fact that for nearly a century the English had traded with the Indians made such an assumption untenable. And in any case, English possession was suspect in natural law.

The textual evidence connecting Shakespeare's Caliban to figurations of the New World native is as inferential as that which associates him with the political slave of absolute monarchy. I think to the Jacobean playgoer, and perhaps especially one who saw his interests reflected by the Commons, the plight of Caliban as the New World native who had been subjected to a tyrant might have appeared structurally comparable to his own condition. Were he of the party resisting impositions in 1610, he might have seen himself as threatened with "slavery," dispossessed like the New World native, and in a sense represented by Caliban. At the same time, there were countervailing reasons why this playgoer might have wished to see Caliban as fundamentally alien from any figure who could be identified as English or European. Many Members of the House of Commons, and those whom they represented, maintained connections with the Virginia Company and therefore saw themselves as masters of colonial enterprise. To justify their activities would have been natural; it was also difficult, at least in the abstract. An image of the Indian as prepolitical would have had obvious ideological appeal, but philosophy suggested that such an entity was a fiction, and in general, colonial experience testified to the civility of New World peoples. Insofar as Caliban was judged to be a civil man or as capable of civility, he had to be seen as dispossessed and as the victim of a tyrant. He could not be used as a figure to argue for the justice of dispossession. In short, to have made a judgment about who or what Caliban represented was to invite speculation, if not criticism. One point, however, is clear: if tyranny was to be resisted at home, and if no man was naturally bestial, servile, or deserving of uncivil treatment or rule, then tyranny could not be exported abroad. To sympathize with the political slave who had been dispossessed of his property was also to reject the violence proposed by such colonists as George Peckham.

[33] *A Good Speed to Virginia* (London 1609), ed. Wesley F. Craven (New York: Scholars' Facsimiles and Reprints, 1937), 2. On Indian liberty, see Pagden, pp. 55–56.

This enigma made attractive if not imperative the identification of a model colonial government and a model governor. Both could be illustrated, to a degree, by the histories of Sir Thomas Gates's colony at Jamestown. Gates was able to command his men to work, to be productive, and to establish a social order. His was an "absolute" rule—no assembly intervened to question his will. But it was not distinguished by kind. Reports from Jamestown state that Gates worked with his men and was not set apart from them by pretending to a godlike office; these reports raise the threat of tyranny, apparently in order to dismiss it.

A Model Governor

Strachey's account of the wreck of Sir Thomas Gates's pinnace, the only one of eight ships not to reach their destination in Virginia, represented Gates's safe landing in the Bermudas as his "redemption" by a providential God. The island, "hideous," "hated," "called commonly the Devil's Islands," and inhabited only by animals, especially tortoises—"a kind of meat as a man can neither absolutely call fish nor flesh"—was yet "the place of our safety and means of our deliverance" (*Reportory*, 16, 33). Relying on "his own performance" not his "authority," Gates governed his men not as "the tortoise" is drawn by "enchantment" but by "example"—"what was so mean whereto he would not himself set his hand?" Strachey asked (39, 40).[34] Having arrived in Virginia, Gates descried and deplored idleness of the colony. Recognizing that without his governorship it was a "headless

[34]Gates was exemplary in his dealing with two separate conspiracies: he pardoned Stephen Hopkins, who had preached that "the authority [of the governor] ceased when the wreck was committed and [that] they were all then freed from the government of any man" (*Reportory*, 44), after Hopkins expressed penitence. And although Gates ordered Henry Paine shot for having tried to murder him, he urged that Paine's followers be persuaded to be penitent by the promise of pardon: if they "would at length survey their own errors . . . he [Gates] would be as ready upon their rendering and coming in to pardon, as he did now pity them"—"whatsoever they had sinisterly committed or practiced hitherto against the laws of duty and honesty should not in any sort be imputed against them"; 52, 53. These accounts are summarized by D. G. James, *The Dream of Prospero* (Oxford: Clarendon Press, 1967), 72ff. On the obligation of a "Generall" to be "always couragious in dangers and forwarde in labours, [for] no lawes, nor precepts can doe herein more then the generals example"; see Matthew Sutcliffe, *The Practice, Proceedings, and Lawes of Arms* (London, 1593), H4ᵛ, STC 23468.

multitude," he commanded his subjects to work. A second history of Gates's colony, *A True and Sincere declaration of the purpose and ends of the Plantation begun in Virginia*, 1610, asserted that Gates brought order to a colony of a "headless and unbridled multitude" given to "disorder and riot."[35] His stable rule was made more attractive by the lure of wealth: this was promoted by instancing "Commodities" found "in great abundance" in Indian storehouses. Such positive signs were to be taken as "certainties and truths"; before "every equal and resolved heart," the "accidental misadventures and errors" of the past "would vanish and become smoke and air" (349).

A third history was more expansively apologetic. Like Strachey, the anonymous author of *A Trve Declaration of the estate of the Colonie in Virginia*, 1610, celebrated providence: "they [Gates and his men] were forced to runne their Ship on shoare, which through Gods prouidence fell betwixt two rockes that caused her to stande firme and not immediately to be broken," and everyone escaped to land. They had landed on the Bermudas which, despite common belief, were not enchanted or a "desert inhabitation for Diuels": "all the Fairies of the rocks were but flocks of birds, and all the Diuels that haunted the woods were but heards of swine." "What is there," the writer asks, "in all this tragicall Comaedie that should discourage vs with impossibilitie of the enterprise? . . . in the gulfe of Despair [their ship] was so graciously preserued. *Quae videtur paena est medicina*, that which we accompt a punishment of euill is but a medicine against euill."[36] The ships that avoided the tempest and went on to Virginia encountered yet another and greater "shipwrack" caused by the "tempest of dissention," but this too was rectified. The colony was in a state of anarchy:

> euery man ouerualuing his own worth, would be Commander: euery man vnderprising an others value, denied to be commanded. The emulation of *Caesar* and *Pompey* watered the plains of *Pharsaly* with bloud, and distracted the sinewes of the Romane *Monarchy* . . . . *Omnis inordinatus animus sibi ipsi fit paena*, euery inordinate soule becomes his owne punishment. (14, 15)

[35] *A True and Sincere declaration of the purpose and ends of the Plantation begun in Virginia of the degrees which it hath received; and means by which it hath beene advanced, 1609,* in Brown, *The Genesis of the United States*, 1: 347.
[36] *A Trve declaration of the estate of the Colonie in Virginia*, in Force, *Tracts*, 3: 10, 11.

Gates ordered all to work, even "Gentlemen," and thereby cured the "restie diseases of a diuided multitude. . . , euery man endeauouring to outstrip each other in diligence" (20). The writer's emphasis on work appears intended to counter expectations of limitless plenty. "It is but a golden slumber that dreameth of any human felicity which is not sauced with some continent miserie. *Dolor & volputas, inuicem cedunt,* Griefe and pleasure are the crosse sailes of the worlds euer-turning-windmill," he concludes (24).[37]

The principal points of consonance between the Virginia histories and *The Tempest* reveal the extent to which Shakespeare fashioned Prospero to the measure of a model governor. Like Gates, Prospero is the object of providential care. But unlike Gates, who never pretended to exercise divine powers, Prospero's history reveals his exploitation of art to promote an image of his own divinity. In this respect he resembles the "Astronomer" mentioned by Valdés whom the Indians credited with cosmic power. Again unlike Gates, Prospero does not work, unless by exercising his charming powers of illusion, but gets others to work for him. By abjuring his art at the moment he regains Milan, therefore, he signals a turn to the model governorship that Gates had already illustrated in the Virginia histories.

[37]Yet the *Trve Declaration* also left in conceptual limbo the legal status of the Jamestown colony. Evidently sensitive to the possibility that the colony might be stealing Indian property, its author asserts: "Wee should not make shipwracke of our intentions concerning Virginia . . . [it is not] unlawful"; 4, 5. Critical of the Spanish example—"Let the diuines of *Salamanca* discusse . . . how the possessor of the west Indies first destroied and then instructed"— the *Trve Declaration* insisted that the English could legally "possess part of [the Indians] land and dwell with them, and defend ourselues from them. . . . [T]here is no other moderate and mixt course to bring them to conuersion but by dailie conuersation . . . , there is no trust to the fidelitie of humane beasts, except a man will make a league with Lions, Beares, and Crocodiles"—a statement suggesting that the Indians are natural slaves and hence without civility or rights of possession. The spirit of this claim is later contradicted when the *Trve Declaration* describes under what auspices the colonists purchased Indian land: "*Paspehay*, one of the Kings, sold vnto vs for copper, land to inherite and inhabite. *Powhatan*, their chiefe King, receiued voluntarilie a crown and a scepter, with a full acknowledgement of dutie and submission" (i.e., he is acknowledged as a monarch and a vassal of James I; *Trve Declaration*, 6). The ceremony described in the *Trve Declaration* represented the English as tenants in fee simple of Paspehay, who was a vassal of Powhatan, who was a subject and vassal of James I. Of the histories of the plantation published in 1610, the author of the *Trve Declaration* was alone in recognizing that there was a difference between English ownership of Indian property and English dominion in the New World. D. G. James notes that in 1609 the London Council for the Virginia Company had made Powhatan a tributary of the English crown; *The Dream of Prospero*, 87.

The terms of Prospero's reformation are clarified by Shakespeare's references to Carthage that recall passages in the histories of Gates's colony. Together they bring into a single perspective the subjects of magic and work. Antonio had mocked Gonzalo for confusing Carthage with Tunis and comparing Claribel to the "widow Dido" (2.1.73). By referring to Gonzalo's "word" as the "miraculous harp" of Amphitrion which built the walls of Thebes (because Gonzalo described a Carthage which did not exist [80–84]), Antonio also reminded the audience that the legendary Dido did in fact raise the walls and houses of Carthage by encouraging her people to work and that this was witnessed by Aeneas in a special moment of poignancy. To Aeneas, Carthage signified both the fallen walls of Troy and the future walls of Rome; it told him of the labor of empire.[38] *A True and Sincere declaration* had noted that prior to the establishment of Gates's colony, "three supplies" of colonists, in 1606, 1607, and 1608, had failed to prosper (342). Gates's government of 1610 was expected to do better, a hope that subsequent reports confirmed. The colony flourished because he and his subjects worked—the fort he ordered constructed was said to have the dimensions of Dido's Carthage (*Reportory*, 78, 79), and, like its prototype, to have entailed "some continent miserie" and hard labor. It was not built in a "golden slumber" or by art and magic (*A Trve Declaration*, 24). The Vergilian reference affects the topicality of the Shakespearean text by giving it a relation to history. *The Tempest*'s Carthage figures a *translatio imperii* that takes place in time and also, by virtue of its continuous repetition, throughout time. To Prospero, who by his art can create a kind of reality in the wink of an eye, the idea of constructing a Carthage may seem tedious. Hence he can indulge in a certain rather cynical detachment—the "globe" and all that it inherit are a "dream"— entirely inappropriate to a ruler. Ferdinand, closer to the Vergilian hero and with a future as a monarch to look forward to, does not (and must not) share this vision.[39] Even so, Prospero's view of history as itself illusion

[38]The most popular contemporary history of Africa, Joannis Leo Africanus's *A Geographical Historie of Africa* (London, 1600), STC 15481, suggests a sameness and a difference: Carthage, once great, is now in ruins and its townsmen are "greevously oppressed with the king daily exactions" (Y3ᵛ); neighboring Tunis, by contrast, increased as Carthage decayed, but it too suffers from the king's taxes: "he is marvellous cunning to procure money out of his subjects purses" (Y6).

[39]Among the characters who work for Prospero, Ferdinand most resembles an ideal Virginia colonist modeled on Gates. Ferdinand gains Miranda for the reason Caliban lost her;

is not easily dismissed: while it is no excuse for his illusionistic art, it conveys the fact that *sub specie aeternitatis* temporal government of any kind is ephemeral. The tension between the commitment of a ruler to a present that his subjects and the commonwealth share, and the detachment of an artist that allows him a long and luxurious view of *translatio imperii*, is registered at the conclusion of Prospero's wedding masque.

Designed to please Ferdinand and Miranda, the masque is cut off when Prospero remembers that "the minute" of Caliban's "foul conspiracy" is at hand (4.1.139–41). Mindful of time, he likens the "insubstantial pageant" he has just produced to an endless dream, as outside time and, therefore, insofar as he must use his art to rule, as an instance of his intemperance. His "vex'd" state of mind reflects how difficult it is to harmonize the two kinds of sensibility he has just experienced (148–60). For if the times require action, but action is only dream from the perspective of all who inherit the globe, then to attend to the times by taking action is to contend with a sense of futility and even despair. In part, it is Prospero's "old brain" that conjures up this *contemptus mundi*. His comments are at one with his remark on what Miranda sees as a "brave new world"—" 'tis new to thee" (5.1.183–84) he answers—and contrast with Ferdinand's impressions of a quickening. In part, too, it is a vestige of Prospero's bookish self that registers frustration at the limits of a kind of art—celebratory, diverting, a "revel"—that no ruler can afford to practice too much or too often. His masque, undertaken ostensibly to celebrate Miranda's nuptials, is not only illusionistic, it is also pure *ars*.[40] As such it cannot be experienced for long without a reminder of the world to be governed. Prospero must leave timelessness for time, and *ars* for *prudentia*. His vexation at this prospect momentarily defies the (Vergilian) spirit of resolution recommended by the Vir-

temperance and self-restraint achieve what desire, paradoxically, loses. Las Casas had claimed that the Spanish behaved toward the Indians as a rapist does toward his victim. "To put the Indians into the Spaniardes hands is . . . as a man shoulde commit a faire young virgin to the guiding of a young man snared, transported, and doting in her loue, whereby shee shoulde be spoiled and deflowred, vnlesse shee were miraculously preserued" (*Spanish Colonie*, O4ᵛ). Inasmuch as *The Tempest* alludes to colonial experience, Ferdinand both repeats and avoids the behavior of the Spanish colonist.

[40] As an instance of Prospero's art, it is virtually self-commenting; as John Gillies notes, Prospero's masque draws on the Virginia histories for its themes of temperance and fruitfulness; John Gillies, "Shakespeare's Virginian Masque," *ELH* 53, 4 (1986), 673–707, esp. 686–90, 699–702.

ginia histories which consistently stress the need for timely work. Both
Declarations consider the place of dream in active (as opposed to contemplative) life. The colonists are warned against a "golden slumber"
which does not accept that a "continent miserie" is the sauce of "human
felicity." They are also promised that before a "resolved heart," the colony's "misadventures and errors" "will vanish and become smoke and
air"; this will "not only keep upright but raise our spirits and affections,
and reconcile our reasons to our desires" (*A True and Sincere declaration*,
349). The threat of Caliban's conspiracy is also a timely warning. As
the image of the body, both the flesh which needs nourishment and the
people who need nurture, Caliban provokes Prospero to forgo a creation of his art that obscures what is immediate, temporal, and political,
and to resume a temperate and prudential activity.

He Who Binds Is Unbound

PROSPERO: Now does my project gather to a head:
My charms crack not; my spirits obey; and time
Goes upright with his carriage. How's the Day?

ARIEL: On the sixth hour; at which time, my lord,
You said our work should cease.

PROSPERO: I did say so,
When first I rais'd the tempest.

(5.1.1–6)

It would seem that Prospero's special powers have been perfectly
deployed. The work that remains to him—to confront the conspirators
and take the last steps to establish political order in the Dukedom of
Milan and the Kingdom of Naples—is not, apparently, the kind to be
effected by magic. His charms have imprisoned Caliban, Stephano, and
Trinculo in a "line-grove," and brought the court party to a state of sor-
rowful distraction. But from now on, his "tender affections," an attribute
he acquires after prompting from Ariel, will determine how he con-
fronts those in his power (5.1.18–19). Ariel's task will also change.

Rather than bind Prospero's enemies with his master's charms, he is now charged with action to "restore their senses" (31), with releasing first the court party (30) and then the clowns (252)—tasks which are punctuated with promises of his own freedom (87, 241) and conclude finally with his release: "Be free, and fare thou well," Prospero tells him (318). Ariel, advising clemency for the court party, functions no longer merely as an instrument of coercion through the devices of art, but rather as a counselor who speaks the wisdom of temperate rule.

Prospero dismisses his art in terms that convey its suspect nature. Casting himself in the role of Medea, popularly held to be a witch, he domesticates the supernatural powers he commands by naming them "elves of hills," "demi-puppets" that work by moonshine, and makers of "midnight mushrooms." At the same time he demonizes them. He states that by their

<blockquote>
aid—
Weak masters though ye be—I have bedimm'd
The noontide sun, call'd forth the mutinous winds,
And 'twixt the green sea and the azur'd vault
Set roaring war: to the dread rattling thunder
Have I given fire, and rifted Jove's stout oak
With his own bolt.
</blockquote>

(5.1.40–46)

Having claimed *Jove*'s power as his own, he will now dismiss even the most divine of its functions: the resurrection of the dead, the defiance of mortality.[41] When he states that "graves at [his] command/Have wak'd their sleepers, op'd, and let 'em forth" (48–49) he recalls other instances in which characters in the romances *seemed* to be resurrecting the dead (Cerimon, Paulina).

As I have suggested, the ambiguity of Prospero's art has a basis in theology. Augustine had rejected neo-Platonic claims that a spirit world could be controlled by mortals for their own spiritual health. James's *Daemonologie*, 1597, both contains and condemns the practice

---

[41]John Pitcher notes that ll. 44–46 is Shakespeare's own addition and that they recall *Aeneid*, 6, 585–86, a passage in which Salmoneus, in the underworld, is paying the penalty for counterfeiting Jove's own fires; John Pitcher, "A Theatre of the Future: *The Aeneid* and *The Tempest*," *Essays in Criticism* 34, 3 (1984): 193–213.

of various kinds of magic in terms that are consistent with an Augustinian view of salvation history: the devil exists as "Gods hang-man," and although he intends to destroy soul and body, "God by the contrarie drawes euer out of that euill glorie to himselfe, either by the wracke of the wicked in his justice, or by the tryall of the patient, and amendment of the faithfull, being wakened vp with that rod of correction."[42] The devil's power gets strength from the passions to which men are subject: "Curiosity in great ingines, thrist [*sic*] of revenge for some tortes deeply apprehended, [and] greedie appetite of geare, caused through great pouerty" (5). Most obviously pertinent to Prospero's case are revenge, the refuge of the deeply wronged; and curiosity, a particular fault of "Astrologers" who "are at last entised, that where lawfull artes or sciences failes [*sic*], to satisfie their restles mindes, even to seeke to that black and vnlawfull science of *Magie*" (7). Curiosity is obviously at issue. As long as magic is informative or diverting, James sees the effects of "Magie" as insubstantial: the spirits of the devil can "carrie . . . newes from anie parte of the worlde" and reveal "the secretes of anie persons, so being they bee once spoken"; they can also produce "faire banquets," "faire armies of horse-men and foote-men . . . castles and fortes which all are but impressiones in the aire . . . thinges but deluding of the senses, and no waies true in substance" (15) Such is Prospero's banquet and his masque; such, too, is the prescience that tells him to raise the tempest that begins the play. Revenge is the more important motive. In *Daemonologie*, it finds expression in the magic of "witches": "[t]hey can make men or women to loue or hate other . . . rayse stormes and tempestes in the aire . . . in such a particular place . . . as God will permitte them so to trouble. They can make folkes to becom phrenticque or Maniacque" (31, 32). Prospero's tempest separates Ferdinand from the court party and unites him with Miranda and thus with Prospero; the words of his Harpy, Ariel, drive the court party to distraction; his magic wardrobe catches the commoners, Stephano and Trinculo, who are driven by "appetite of geare."[43] As no more than necessary evils, however, the

---

[42]James VI and I, "Preface," *Daemonologie*, in *Minor Prose Works*, ed. James Craigie (Edinburgh: Scottish Text Society, 1982), xx.

[43]See Barbara A. Mowat on Prosper's "Streetcorner" magic; "Prospero, Agrippa, and Hocus Pocus," *English Literary Renaissance* 11, 3 (1981): 281–303, see 297–98.

devil's operations serve either as a means to reform sinners or as sins to be reformed by the virtuous. James argues that the devil's power to harm is never decisive: he "*goeth about like a roaring Lyon* . . . but the limites of his power were set down before the foundations of the world were laid, which he hath not power in the least jote to transgresse" (21). He can "cure" some "diseases" "for a shorte time," although finally a cure of this kind "will doubtleslie tend to the vtter perdition of the patient, both in bodie and soule" (34). Measured against James's criteria, Prospero's art would appear to be both diabolical and, because of divine powers of redemption, also salutary.44 At the conclusion of *The Tempest*, Prospero's magical art disdains revenge and works providentially.

In his *Basilicon Doron*, James recommended self-discipline and clemency toward those who offend:"Embrace trew magnanimitie, not in being vindictiue . . . but by the contrarie, in thinking your offendour not worthie of your wrath, empyring ouer your owne passion and triumphing in the commaunding your selfe to forgive." He also endorsed "reuenge taking" upon "oppressours" within the kingdom and "iust warres vpon forraine enemies":"where ye finde a notable iniurie, spare not to give course to the torrents of your wrath. *The wrath of a King is like to the roaring of a Lyon.*"45 Prospero betters the prescription, however; he forgives Alonso, Sebastian, and Antonio even before he can determine that they have repented, as he instructed them to through

---

44Cf. the limited use Justus Lipsius assigns deceit in government in his *Politicorum sive civilis doctrinae libri sex*, 1589:"The Philosopher doth note, *that kingdomes are subuerted by subtiltie and guile.* Doest thou say it is not lawfull to conserue them by the same meanes? and that the Prince may not some times *hauing to deale with a foxe, play the foxe*, especially if the good and publike profit, which is alwayes conioyed *to the benefit and profit of the Prince, doe require it?* . . . [But] that he should wholie decline from that which is honest, there is no force that can force me to persuade it"; Justus Lipsius, *Sixe bookes of politickes or ciuil doctrine* (London, 1594), Q; STC 15701. Bacon's essay on "Daedalus" the "mechanic" in his *De sapientia veterum*, 1609, makes a different and subtler point; he promotes the notion that the arts, fundamentally "ambiguous" (*ambigui*) and illustrated by activities that are both rational and abstract as well as mysterious and illusionistic, play a part in policy but must be used without "ostentation." He cites Tacitus who states that mathematicians and fortune tellers are "a class of men which in our state will always be retained and always prohibited" (*genus hominum quod in civitate nostra semper et retinebitur et vetabitur*). Their "arts" are condemned by law but actually "perish" (*pereunt*) because of their "very ostentationess" (*ipsa ostentatione*). *De Sapientia Veterum*, in *Works*, 13: 29–30.

45James VI and I, *Basilicon Doron*, in *Political Writings*, 47.

Ariel. When neither Sebastian nor Antonio ask for pardon, as Alonso does, Prospero manifests pure statecraft. He claims that he will continue to control them by recourse to their common liege lord, the King of Naples, and to the law the King administers. Threatening to "justify" them as traitors before the King, he declares he will "require" his duke-dom of Antonio, which he knows Antonio must restore "perforce," that is, because Alonso will order him to do so (5.1.125–34). His mercy to these traitors is foreshadowed by his gratitude to Gonzalo, whom he calls his "true preserver" and a "loyal sir" to his master, Alonso (69–70), an acknowledgment that he, Prospero, must accept blame for his own deposition. Gonzalo has behaved as a virtually perfect courtier, obey-ing his monarch yet mitigating as far as humanly possible the direst consequences of a harsh order. At the same time, Gonzalo is no more than a courtier and without the interventions of Ariel is incapable of dealing with court treachery; by complimenting him, Prospero is show-ing him another form of the mercy he shows to all his enemies.[46] He forgoes punishment, not only because he has been at fault but also because he can get what he wants without it.[47] The alignment of authority and power at the play's conclusion reconstitutes the politi-cal hierarchy Prospero's bookishness destroyed and his art won back.

In the last moments of the play, nothing is clearer than that Pros-pero is mortal. The marriage of Miranda and Ferdinand not only secures the future of his dukedom as a part of Naples, it marks his own rule and generation as one that is passing. After their marriage, he states that he will "retire me to my Milan, where/Every third thought shall be my grave" (5.1.310–11). He is left with Caliban, a "demi-devil" and

[46]Paul Yachnin argues that Gonzalo's role is definitive in establishing Shakespeare's belief in the paramount virtue of obedience in political settings; in particular, Gonzalo plays to an audience that would not have "valued individual rights over the interests of the state" especially in 1611 when Englishmen were fearful of Catholic treachery in the aftermath of the assassination of Henry IV; "Shakespeare and the Idea of Obedience: Gonzalo in *The Tempest*," *Mosaic* 24, 2 (1991): 1–18; 10. This account of Gonzalo overstates the value Shake-speare gives obedience; it is even possible to see in Prospero's praise of the old man a hint of irony.

[47]Prospero has always wanted reformation rather than revenge. Given the illusionistic nature of Prospero's magic, he could not, as John S. Mebane suggests, "easily have annihilated his enemies in the initial storm scene"; John S. Mebane, *Renaissance Magic and the Return of the Golden Age: The Occult Tradition and Marlowe, Jonson, and Shakespeare* (Lincoln: Univer-sity of Nebraska Press, 1989), 183. But he could have allowed them to annihilate themselves.

"thing of darkness," whom he acknowledges as his own and who, in turn, accepts his master's government as a subject who seeks not rights but grace: to get Prospero's pardon he will be "wise hereafter,/And seek for grace," not only as his food (i.e., grease) but also to signal the fallenness of flesh (294–95).

As Prospero's political subject, however, Caliban has another and contradictory reference: knowing no more than to "seek for grace," his subjection is lamentable. He is an index of the failure of absolute rule to produce a subject worth ruling. Prospero's claim that Caliban is his is therefore both a cause for shame and a warning. Caliban reveals Prospero's political sin: like La Boétie's abject subject, Caliban can only lose his monstrosity when he stops being servile. He also exposes what some considered the colonists' error. Commenting on the impact of European civilization on the peoples of the New World a half-century after de Victoria and others had appealed to the Spanish crown, Michel de Montaigne had noted the negative effects of colonization and condemned it generally: "by our contagion, we shall directly have furthered his [the native's] declination . . . we shall too dearely have sold him our opinions, our new-fangles and our Arts. It was an unpolluted harmelesse infant world; yet have we not whipped and submitted the same unto our disciplines, or schooled him by the advantage of our valour or naturall forces, nor have wee instructed him by our justice and integrity; nor subdued by our magnanimity."[48] Whether Caliban can transform his servility into civility is uncertain. There is a sense in which he appears too degenerate ever to be able to demand the rights of a subject under the ordinary powers of the monarchy. If Prospero cannot see a brave new world, his subject may be doomed to a perpetual servitude. In that case, the audience must

---

[48]Montaigne, "Of coaches," in *The Essayes of Michael Lord of Montaigne, Translated by John Florio*, 3 vols. (Toronto: J. M. Dent, 1928), 3: 142. Shakespeare's notion of Prospero's art is, I think, more precise than Montaigne's in that it refers not to generalities ("opinions" or "new-fangles" which impair a natural human purity) but rather to practices that can constitute an abusive political power. I assume that Caliban as Prospero's "earth" will remain with him as the externalization of the bodily impulses requiring domination; as his political subject, he will live wherever Prospero governs and assume a character that corresponds to Prospero's rule. Philip Edwards insists that Caliban remains on the island; Philip Edwards, *Threshold of a Nation: A Study in English and Irish Drama* (Cambridge: Cambridge University Press, 1979), 109.

look to the government of Ferdinand and Miranda for a different kind of subject.[49]

The concluding action is the audience's; it is given the power formerly Prospero's:

> Let me not,
> Since I have my dukedom got,
> And pardon'd the deceiver, dwell
> In this bare island by your spell;
> But release me from my bands
> With the help of your good hands.

(Epilogue, 5–10)

In early modern usage, "bands" define the terms restricting any kind of liberty, particularly of the servant but also of the criminal. Prospero's unbinding is a reciprocal and self-reflexive act of grace. He has unbound his subjects; he now wishes to be unbound by them. He is in possession of his dukedom and his fleshly desires; he has exhibited self-restraint, temperance, and a "magnanimitie" that pardons criminals and invokes the law. By giving the audience the power to enchant him to a continued isolation or to set him free in the country he returns to govern (if only for a time), he acknowledges their power as similar to that which he just exercised. Here, at the conclusion of the most imposing and enigmatic of his last plays, Shakespeare dramatizes the constitutionalist paradox: a ruler is most free when his subjects—rejecting the status of a Caliban—enjoy their liberties; his servitude is most onerous when they are enslaved.

---

[49]Critics differ on whether or not Prospero returns to Milan to rule or whether he effectively abdicates in favor of the joint rule of Miranda and Ferdinand. I have understood him to return to government, albeit mindful of death. But it may be that his future—like that of Caliban—is left ambiguous.

Afterword

I HAVE ARGUED THAT SHAKESPEARE'S ROMANCES CAN BE UNDERSTOOD AS
political drama. Depicting conflict in royal households, kingdoms, and
finally within the expansive terms of empire, these plays are informed by
contemporary ideas of government at all levels of society and under the
laws of nations and nature. Whether they endorse a political position with
respect to alternative systems of rule is, however, problematic.

Certain gross distinctions help to define the political dimensions
of drama and they are essential to a discussion of the romances. The
representation of agency is of paramount importance. A character
whose actions determine his or her fate irrespective of divine justice
illustrates what might be termed the humanist imaginary. Its ethos is
brilliantly registered throughout Machiavelli's treatise on despotic rule,
Il Principe, first published in 1532 and disseminated throughout Europe,
often in accounts wildly critical of its author's assumptions and the
practices they authorized. Comparable to schemes for self-advancement
promoted by the so-called civic humanism of the early Renaissance in
Italy, Machiavelli's politics took to a logical end the proposition that
societies were shaped by the *virtù* of talented and fearless men. Trou-
bling in persons of little authority and power, the endorsement of doc-
trines promoting the temporizing calculations of a ruler—monarch or

magistrate—over the customary judgments of a people was simply fearful. Absolutism elevated such calculations to a level at which they could
appear as policy inspired by godlike knowledge; hence, too, it made
appeal to a constitution of some kind even more critical.

What enthusiasm there was for a politics of expedience could be
checked by established habits of thought that celebrated history as
providential. But such habits were increasingly susceptible to doubt.
Resistance to the idea that a government might submit to determination by a self-fashioned ruler was made ambiguous by a fear that
God did not—after all—write the course of history. His providence
was not always in evidence. The recorded triumphs of Christian (nom-
inal, at least) despots whose arraignment and trial under God had to
be supposed as taking place only on the Day of Judgement seemed to
indicate divine indifference to human misery. They suggested, moreover, that the doctrine of a Christian rule, rooted in the conviction
that all government was "from God" or, in the words of Thomas
Aquinas, *a deo descendit*, could quite easily be set aside, that it had no
considerable claim on the consciences of those who were called to
political office. Were this the case, the future of the body politic was
bleak. It was small consolation that a tyrant, an abuser of the public
trust, one who wreaked havoc with custom and positive law, would
eventually roast in hell fire. Nor was the prospect of revolution, in
which the people inevitably suffered all kinds of hardship, in any sense
attractive, however much revolution might be justified. What was
needed was a ruler who from his own love of justice governed as if he
were, indeed, a minister "from God."

Needed certainly but forthcoming only infrequently. Represented
in Plato's *Politicus*, government by a monarch or single man was recognized as notoriously susceptible to corruption. The "Apology" of the
Commons in 1604 had put the case directly: were the king infallible,
the Commons would not need to represent the people. As he was not
infallible, they should not relinquish their rights. Plato had lamented
that a constitutional monarchy, a government by a monarch under
written or positive law rather than absolute, was no better than second
best. To the extent that it followed such written law, it tended to be
arbitrary and even, at times, inequitable. But from a practical point of
view, it was the government of choice.

In the romances, tyranny does not prevail. The rule that they celebrate is less easy to identify. Shakespeare shows that a ruler who cannot acknowledge that his immense power comes from the people and is in some sense their power does not prosper. But Shakespeare does no more than hint at the constitutionalism that usually follows references to such popular power. His tyrants ostensibly reform because they accept the divine law of mortality and the natural law of generation. Implied in scenes dramatizing the contributions of the people to the commonweath is, however, a rationale for a constitution. If a ruler is mortal, then he can hope for an eternity only through generation; if he is generative, then he must agree that the people, his "co-workers," share in the work of production and reproduction—in short, they have property and thus also rights. Such a polity establishes the generativity of the body politic. By contrast, a ruler committed to absolutism (always in danger of becoming a tyrant), indifferent to evidence that God loves his people, and ignoring his obligation to do the same, risks inflicting a terrible sterility upon the commonwealth. Without "heirs," a testimony to its generativity, the body politic lacks "airs"—the breath of life. This theme is broadly registered throughout all the plays.

Their plot structure at its simplest is consistent. A figure representing a rule that has the marks of a tyranny loses the means to govern. These means, both material and ideological, are provided by the body of the body politic. Without that body, the ruler remains only a severed head; his state is therefore a headless body. The work of restoration is not, however, entirely his although it depends on his good will, his conscience, and his willingness to acknowledge what he has refused to consider earlier: the special status of the figures who represent generativity, his wife and her daughter who appear to be protected by providence. The reunion of parts comprised in the body politic that testifies to the just relations between head and body, husband and wife, father and child is effected by loyal servants and by a strange confluence of circumstances represented as fortunate, but recognized finally as owing to divine will. Chance is generally confusing; characters remain mystified and profess faith in providence. At critical moments, divine will is more than revelatory; through its manifestations, characters become conscientious. Its expression is often in an art that is conscientiously human, that does not pretend to miracles, but remains rooted in nature and determined by temporality. Time is restorative in that its passage provides moments in which art can do its revolutionary work.

Women characters are central to these developments as both vehicles of power and agents determining the reform and return of rulers to their offices. Initially a victim of tyranny, Pericles takes on its principal attributes: he abdicates responsibility for the people and their future. Cymbeline also abdicates; he is ruled by his Queen. Leontes succumbs to "Affection," and Prospero, deposed as a result of his neglect of office, recovers his just rule by a practice—rough magic—that is finally inimical to justice. None of these rulers is educated in the proper art of government in the absence of female kin. Marina is the agent who heals her prince (and father), and she will be the body that preserves his dynasty and hence his state. Thaisa and Hermione are vehicular bodies; like the body politic, their eclipse is transient, and they are Phoenix-like in their restoration. Imogen and Perdita are each exponents of equitable generation and a natural fecundity. Imogen learns the virtue in natural man, and Perdita defies rank in favor of a common humanity. Miranda is the least prominent of these women. An obvious factor in the project of dynastic integrity, she becomes an object of art briefly as Prospero draws aside a curtain to show her playing at chess.

The virtue of women is also dramatized by what appears to be its aberration. The demonization of the Daughter and Dionyza in *Pericles*, the Queen in *Cymbeline*, and the absent Sycorax in *The Tempest*, is not, I think, to be regarded as illustrating the nature of woman as Shakespeare understood it. The vice in question is actually of the subordinate. As a matter of doctrine and custom, the female in relation to the male stands for whoever answers to a superior. She is the archetype of the subordinate and may represent a male in service as well as a woman in relation to her male kin. The tyranny of Dionyza and women like her indicates not that the nature of the female is corrupt, but rather that a subordinate who moves out of his (or her) proper place is dangerous. In this case, the superior is also at fault: she (or he) has failed to rule according to the requirements of office, whether by being tyrannical or by permitting anarchy. The diabolical wit of the abused or abusive subordinate signals the madness of his (or her) superior who is always structurally masculine—as the head of state is a prince—whether actually male or female.

The fact that some women characters suffer terrible privation does not indicate Shakespeare's uncritical endorsement of a cultural consensus on the status of women, although it does allude to such opinion. It points to the errors responsible for this privation. The action of these plays does not show that woman is silenced, neglected, or forced into a social eclipse tantamount to a living death as a matter of social order. It reveals that the authority and power of a tyrant, having had such effects, are reformed to achieve just rule when tyranny is recognized and renounced, when characters structurally gendered as feminine speak, give counsel and have a presence in political economy. To dramatize the abuse of whatever is gendered as feminine by the illness of the body politic, and, conversely, the restoration of the one as the health of the other, evokes an image of reciprocal rule and a generative body politic. It is to imply that persons in the category of subordinate—both males and females—are owed a degree of instrumentality sufficient to thwart the exercise of absolute authority and power.

The romances insist on distinctions of office, especially of ruler and people. Such distinctions are emphasized in conflicts between characters who stand in analogical relations to the ruler and his subjects as individuals and a collective: husbands and wives, fathers and children, masters and servants. Character is generally shaped by office; a character is meant to be judged by criteria appropriate to his or her office. What those criteria are is often disputed; Paulina, for example, understands her service differently than does Leontes. Her actions typify the loyal integrity required of a servant; they recall those of others in subordinate roles: Helicanus, Cornelius, Pisanio, Belarius, Camillo, Antigonus, Gonzalo, and Ariel. They also draw attention to the jeopardy in which subordinates routinely find themselves. Every office, even of the most subordinate, owes a duty to divine law—a law that in effect equalizes all offices. This doctrinal fact receives scriptural authorization in *The Winter's Tale* when Perdita refers to the sun that shines on all alike. It is registered in the performance of equitable judgments, like those of the sun, that efface distinctions of place in light of interests shared among a few or held in common.

Acts of grace always recognize equity; they suspend what gender, rank, class, region, or the particular terms of a contract require in favor of relations mutually beneficial. In the romances, marriage epitomizes relations of grace because it unites persons occupying two offices.

Hermione's suffering comes about because she believes in the equity in marriage. Conversely, Leontes' "Affection" reveals a disbelief that is also a disgrace. Gracefulness returns to rulers who have insisted on an absolute rule after they participate in rituals that effectively suspend distinctions of office: Pericles who states that he is begotten by his daughter, Marina; Cymbeline who takes his prerogative from his son-in-law, Posthumus; Leontes who comes to love his wife, Hermione; and Prospero who is counselled to show mercy by his servant, Ariel.

But equitable government is not only a matter of a moral and Christian politics, supported by a theory of corruptible power as expressed in Plato's *Politicus* and by a doctrine of divinely bestowed benefits as in Matthew. It is also prudent. What guarantees the authority of Shakespeare's rulers in romance is the power of the people. The body politic consolidates all ranks by making superiors depend on subordinates. Registered as material and morale, the power of the people defends the kingdom in *Pericles* and *Cymbeline*, turns dearth (a desert) into plenty in *The Winter's Tale*, and sails the ship of state in *The Tempest*. It is a power that can revolt: in *Pericles*, the Tharsians depose Dionyza and Cleon; and in *Cymbeline*, the vassal Britons defeat their lords, the Romans. More often, it supports authority. Masked by (and masqued in) the festivities of sheep-shearing in *The Winter's Tale* and of betrothal in *The Tempest*, the energies of common folk are represented as benign. The Clown's social ambition is accommodated by a comic legal fiction; Caliban's rebellion is easily aborted. The people as a political entity are not, however, clearly distinguished. Although characters representing workers express grievances, especially in *Pericles*, they have no official voice of their own; they must count on the voices of their superiors.

Claims against rulers take shape around developing concepts of the liberties or rights of the subject. As concepts featured in contemporary discourse on forms of government, they were not yet well defined; they hardly constitute explicit principles. And when they do achieve a specificity and a function, they are directed at securing the interests of the propertied classes. But for all their partiality, they remain important to the politics of the plays: "a principle is not necessarily vitiated because its practical bearing is limited."[1]

---

[1] C. V. Wedgwood, *Oliver Cromwell* (New York: Macmillan, 1956), 31.

Like the virtue of a wife, the liberties of the subject are expressed by omission and inversion: the property a superior confiscates or gives away, the speech he silences, the trust he betrays, and the law he flouts identify him as a tyrant. His restored self—as represented in Pericles, Cymbeline, and Leontes—respects property, honors speech, confirms trust, and would seem ready to obey positive law. Prospero's is a somewhat different case. The continuing presence of an abject and servile Caliban, who lacks rights and can only sue for grace, points to a certain ambivalence in the character of Duke's rule. Inasmuch as Caliban figures his master's natural man (or natal subject), his unqualified obedience is a matter of moral and Christian doctrine and a guarantee against the bestialization of rule. The fact that this Caliban is ruled absolutely suggests that Prospero as Duke of Milan will never resume his tyranny. But inasmuch as Caliban also represents a servant whose work profits his master (his political subject), his inability to secure his liberties points to the weakness in theories of absolutism. Given that rulers are not divine, it is never long before their absolute rule degenerates into a tyranny. Hence the political subject must insist on his liberties; to fail to do so is to become complicit with the tyrant, to join him in bestiality. Debased beyond a point of reform and deprived of his property, Prospero's "slave" will remain incapable of revolution. He will survive as merely indispensable, serving in "offices/That profit" his superiors, Prospero and Miranda.

Such, I think, are the principal political elements of the romances. They reveal that Shakespeare was aware of absolutist theory, that he did not dismiss it out of hand, but rather showed its relation to tyranny. The absolute ruler of the romances, who governs only by his own inspired art, obeying divine and natural law at least in theory, is not entirely the fantastic creature Plato had sketched centuries earlier. But his status is constantly tested by temptations to misrule. His abuses point to the merits of a constitutional government: by a variety of symbolic action the romances evoke a Fortescuean form of monarchy in which all but the prerogative powers of the monarch remains within the confines of positive law. His rule was to be a kind of servitude to expressions of what was understood as the people's will manifest in history; at the same time, this servitude was a kind of freedom. Without the support of his people, a ruler was incapable of action, could not exercise his will, and in that sense remained unfree. The enigma was a familiar one in Jacobean debate, and it had extensive representation in treatises on the monarchy that drew the outlines of government from idealized models of medieval feudalism. Its brilliantly allusive representation in Shakespeare's romances gives them a kind of topicality that reflects very little of court life, but has much to do with issues that made that life appear creditable or, conversely, worth criticizing. As a feature of discourse on the Englishness of a mixed monarchy, the topos of servitude as freedom could not be attacked as new-fangled, however much it seemed to promote reform. More important for the playwright who was a member of an acting company that played before the king, the topos as enigma could remain essentially non-prescriptive, a profound reflection on the best form of government, and a matter for continuous debate, if not an incitement to immediate action.

Index